understanding s

understanding
stuart hall

Helen Davis

SAGE Publications
London • Thousand Oaks • New Delhi

First published 2004

Apart from any fair dealing for the purposes of research or
private study, or criticism or review, as permitted under the
Copyright, Designs and Patents Act, 1988, this publication
may be reproduced, stored or transmitted in any form, or by
any means, only with the prior permission in writing of the
publishers, or in the case of reprographic reproduction, in
accordance with the terms of licences issued by the
Copyright Licensing Agency. Enquiries concerning
reproduction outside those terms should be sent to
the publishers.

SAGE Publications Ltd
1 Oliver's Yard
55 City Road
London EC1Y 1SP

SAGE Publications Inc.
2455 Teller Road
Thousand Oaks, California 91320

SAGE Publications India Pvt Ltd
B-42, Panchsheel Enclave
Post Box 4109
New Delhi 100 017

British Library Cataloguing in Publication data

A catalogue record for this book is available from the British
Library

ISBN 0 7619 4714 0
ISBN 0 7619 4715 9 (pbk)

Library of Congress Control Number: 2003103981

Typeset by C&M Digitals (P) Ltd., Chennai, India
Printed in Great Britain by TJ International Ltd, Padstow, Cornwall

contents

Acknowledgements   ix

Introduction   1

1   Encountering the mother country   5
    Introduction   5
    Negotiating class and colour   6
    The New Left   8
    A sense of classlessness   11
    The popular arts   18
    The critique of popular culture   21
    Conclusion   24
    Further reading   25

2   A deadly serious matter   26
    Introduction   26
    Early days at the centre for contemporary
        cultural studies   26
    A sense of purpose   29
    Class and the political climate   31
    Class and the mass media   34
    The summer of love   37
    Conclusion   39
    Further reading   40

3 **The media in question**   **41**
   Introduction   41
   Manufacturing consent   42
   A world at one with itself   43
   The determination of news photographs   44
   Gramsci and the concept of hegemony   46
   Althusser's theory of ideological and
       repressive state apparatuses   47
   Television and its relationship to British culture   49
   Television aesthetics   51
   The limits of broadcasting   54
   Deviancy, politics and the media   55
   The move towards the audience   59
   Encoding/Decoding   60
   Implications for media studies   66
   Conclusion   67
   Further reading   68

4 **Wrestling with the angels**   **69**
   Introduction   69
   A decade of discontent   70
   A complex Marxism   73
   Althusser and the problem of interpreting history   74
   Settling accounts with Althusser   76
   The role of theory   77
   Culture, the media and the ideological effect   79
   Capitalism, class and the market   80
   The function of common sense   81
   The practice of dominant ideology   82
   The function of the state   84
   The functions of the mass media   87
   The case of football hooliganism   90
   The status and functions of sport within the press   92
   Mediating violence   92
   Investigating hooliganism   94
   Official responses to hooliganism   95
   Conclusion   96
   Further reading   97

5 The politics of representation **98**
Introduction 98
Young, black and British 99
The 'problem' of race 100
The failure of liberalism 102
Policing the crisis 104
Hegemony in crisis 105
Moral panics and the threat from America 107
Capitalism in crisis 110
The signification spiral 112
Policing the black community 113
The enemy within 115
Race, capitalism and employment 116
A Marxist theory of crime? 118
The function of the black working class 121
Black resistance 123
Reproducing inequality 125
The impact of feminism 126
Women take issue 127
Conclusion 130
Further reading 130

6 Taking the risk of living dangerously **132**
Introduction 132
Problems with the left 134
The failure of labourism 135
The swing to the right 137
Gramsci and the 'historic bloc' thesis 138
Thatcher's appeal to the working classes 140
The limitations of 'authoritarian populism' 142
The limitations of ideology theory 144
Accusations and recriminations 146
Against false consciousness 149
The critique of ideology 151
Problems with interpellation 152
Hall's definition of ideology 153
New Times 155
Strategies of difference 156

New labour, new problems   157
Conclusion   159
Further reading   159

7   **In the belly of the beast**   **160**
    Introduction   160
    Hall and postmodern approaches to identity   161
    The cultural turn   163
    Implications for the analysis of race   166
    Reclaiming the personal   167
    Understanding racism   170
    'Englishness' and the 'Tebbit test'   171
    Gramsci's relevance for Marxism   173
    Gramsci's relevance for Hall   175
    Understanding hegemony and resistance   177
    Hall and ethnicity   179
    New ethnicities   182
    The production of identity   184
    Imagining 'home'   185
    Policing black identity   186
    British identity in a multicultural society   188
    The Parekh Report   188
    Further reading   191

8   **'Fragmented and concrete', in conversation
    with Stuart Hall**   **193**

Endnotes   **206**

Selected Bibliography   **211**

Index   **218**

acknowledgements

I am extremely grateful to Willie Thompson for lending me his vintage copies of *Universities and New Left Review*, and for helping me to understand some of the contexts of British communism in the post-war era. Any misunderstandings are mine alone. I am indebted to Anthony Purvis and Elaine Jones for their insightful comments on the early chapters, and to Bob Ferguson and Martin Conboy for not laughing (out loud) at the idea in the first place.

Grateful thanks go to the University of Sunderland for granting me research leave in which to write the book, and to colleagues, family and friends who provided much-valued support and encouragement whenever necessary. I am indebted to Julia Hall at Sage for her critical understanding and lightness of touch, and to Chris Fanthome for her encouragement and wisdom. I want to say a special thank you to all those people who had faith in what I was trying to do, and to doff my cap to the nay-sayers who *also* helped by drawing attention to the problems and pitfalls.

I am particularly grateful to Stuart Hall for consenting to be interviewed for this book. His candid responses and good humour helped to make this a most enjoyable project. Special thanks go to Ceri for her understanding, to Keith for helping me to see the bigger picture, and to Max for keeping it all in perspective.

introduction

Stuart Hall's name has become synonymous with cultural studies, but his contribution to public life has been more than academic. He is a scholar and an intellectual, a critic and a teacher. But this still does not bring us any closer to understanding the full scale of his involvement with British culture over the last 50 years.

The historian Eric Hobsbawm recalls meeting Hall in the early 1950s and being rather impressed by the young Oxford radical. Martin Jacques once described Hall as 'one of the finest orators on the left, or anywhere, a cross between Jesse Jackson and the best academic you ever heard.' (Jacques, 1997: 26) Outspoken, controversial and fiercely independent, Hall has been celebrated and vilified by critics at both ends of the political spectrum, yet few would deny the enormous influence his work has had on Britain's political landscape of the last 30 years.

Since his retirement, Hall's public appearances are less frequent and ill-health has made travelling very difficult. Despite this, Hall continues to show enormous spirit and energy, intervening at critical moments in public debates and championing the work of younger artists and scholars. His insistence on ideology as a material practice has drawn attention to the lack of fit between what people in authority say and what they really mean and do. Though he has never claimed to speak for anyone else, he has, through his actions, given voice to many marginalised groups who have otherwise been excluded from the modern public sphere.

To his students he has been an exciting, encouraging and well-loved teacher. To his peers he is an enervating, challenging thinker and an articulate speaker. He has written extensively on politics, even coining the term 'Thatcherism', though he is not a politician and has never shown any interest in the electoral machine. He has instead chosen to stand outside of the party political structure and take his arguments out to the public domain. For some, this has been a point of fierce criticism, yet Hall makes no apology for adopting his own brand of 'independent socialism'. He believes in the politics of difference and the potentiality of achieving democratic socialism through a solidarity that unites different groups and individuals while valuing diversity. The problem for Hall however, is how best to negotiate that difficult terrain, in order to achieve 'a common horizon' (Hall, 2000: 237) that gives 'greater recognition of difference and greater equality and justice for all'.

Born in Jamaica, Hall has lived his entire adult life in Britain, 'in the shadow of the black diaspora – "in the belly of the beast"' (Baker et al., 1996: 211). His experience of coming to England in the 1950s and his constant negotiations with British culture have afforded him important insights which have been fundamental to his recognition of the importance of ethnicity and subjectivity in the context of modernity and the new era of globalisation. His challenge to government in recent years has been the consideration of 'the multi-cultural question' in which he poses the very real problem of how Britain can achieve cultural integration of its many ethnic and racial classes without subjugating the same to an essentialist idea of Englishness. 'Britishness as a national identity', he argues, 'is in a transitional state, beset by problems and up for extensive renovation and renegotiation' (Hall, 2000: 237). It is time to rethink what we understand by the term 'British' in order to avoid the endless proliferations of racial and ethnic inequalities that inscribe public policy and lend legitimacy to acts of violence and exclusion.

Though Hall's main arena has been Britain, his ideas have travelled well. His analyses of multiculturalism and ethnicity have been highly influential in the field of cultural and postcolonial studies, opening up new avenues of thinking in relation to cultural hybridity in the Caribbean, Australia and the United States of America.

He is ever alert to the dangers of liberalism and the threat to individuals' liberty from the practice of Enlightenment discourses regarding culture, civilisation and the supposed neutrality of the western

2

liberal democratic state. There is, he argues, a dark side to the Enlightenment project and it is the cultures that 'lost' the power-game with western liberalism that have suffered ever since. The concept of 'universal citizenship' and 'human rights' have never been on offer to the colonised peoples of the world.

But Hall did not begin his work with considerations of ethnicity and race. His has been a long journey of (self) discovery in which he has cut across the grain of established custom and practice. Notably, he was instrumental in advocating new ways of analysing the mass media and has been a keen advocate for reading the work of European intellectuals – the names of which now grace every humanities' undergraduate reading list. His most enduring legacy to British academic life has been the establishment of cultural studies, a field that has grown and developed in ways that still astonish Hall and confound many sceptics. With characteristic modesty, he has always dismissed any notion that he 'invented' cultural studies, or that his work within the field constituted a grand scheme or project. 'We were making it up as we went along', he insists.

People often create histories in order to shore up a fragile sense of identity. It is also often the case that in trying to narrate a history, one tends to look for continuities rather than disjunctures, progressions rather than problems. Though it is very tempting to seek out origins and certainties it is not the purpose of this book to rehearse a definitive account of Hall's life and work. Nor is this book a history of cultural studies. This introduction offers a discussion of Hall's work that tries to give some context to the debates and, in so doing, attempts to locate and identify the different emergent and developing strands of Hall's ideas and arguments over a sustained period of intellectual labour. The aim of this book is to encourage you to read Hall's work and judge for yourself. Hall may not have all the answers, but he knows better than most how important it is to keep asking questions.

a note about references and recommended reading

Many of Hall's writings appear in different volumes and have been re-issued in collections and readers. I have tried to reference

3

wherever possible the edition that is most readily available as well as supplying the original reference. I have recommended some texts at the end of each chapter in case you wish to follow up a particular area of interest. The selected bibliography at the end of the book includes all the material used to write this book. References and notes for each chapter are contained in the endnotes.

reading the text

This book is organised chronologically rather than thematically, and is designed to trace the development of Hall's interventions over many years. However, it is possible to read this book in sections in order to explore a specific problematic or area of research within a given chapter. For example Chapter 7 is largely concerned with Hall's most recent work around ethnicity while Chapter 3 focuses on Hall's work concerning television and media studies. I encourage you to choose how you organise your reading according to your own particular interests. However, I should stress one key point: the primary aim of this book is to encourage you to read and engage with Hall's ideas directly, and it should be used as a supplemental text not as a substitute! This book is only an introduction to Stuart Hall's work and is not designed to bring down the curtain on the lifetime of a significant intellectual.

Meeting Stuart Hall has been a great privilege and I believe that discussions with him helped to make this a better book. He was very open and encouraging and made no attempt to influence my approach or comment on my interpretations of his work. Any mistakes or misunderstandings are down to me.

Writing this book has been a great challenge and a real pleasure. It has allowed me the time and space to immerse myself in ideas that I believe to be of critical importance. I hope that in reading this book, you are stimulated to ask more questions and to challenge established orthodoxies. It is my hope that in due course you will become eager to adopt your own 'war of position'.

Helen Davis
Sunderland

4

1

encountering the
mother country

The story in my family which was always told as a joke, was that when I was born, my sister, who was much fairer than I, looked into the crib and she said, 'where did you get this coolie baby from?' (Hall, quoted in Morley and Chen, 1996: 485)

introduction

Stuart Hall was born in 1932 into a middle-class family living in the suburbs of Kingston, Jamaica. The youngest of three children he was noticeably 'blacker' than his siblings. This marker of difference within the family was an early signal for Hall that his family was not a straightforward homogenous entity. As with many families of Hall's generation it was not unusual for members of the same family to have different skin tones. The marriage of different classes resulted in an intermixing of plantation-colonial and Jamaican blood. The idea of pure Jamaican ancestry however is a misnomer since the lower middle-class origins of his father described by Hall were distilled from many ethnic backgrounds such as Portuguese, Indian, African and Jewish. Race and class are not therefore encountered by Hall as foundational or distinct categories for identification. Hall instead experienced Jamaica as a hybrid culture that was highly race and class conscious. The tensions between the local, largely black and impoverished population and the middle-classes did not necessarily broker an understanding of their shared colonised situation, particularly as the middle-class families tended to identify with the colonising powers. Hall describes his growing-up in Kingston as a series of continuing negotiations of these different cultural spaces.

negotiating class and colour

As a young adult, Hall had no wish to kowtow to the colonial establishment. This provoked arguments with his father who was keen for his son to benefit from mixing with the expatriate community. 'My father wanted me to play sport ... He was negotiating his way into this world. He was accepted on sufferance by the English. I could see the way they patronised him' (Morley and Chen, 1996: 485). Committed to the politics of an independent Jamaica, Hall's choice of friends did not please his parents but they were at least agreed on him making the journey to England in 1951 to study at Oxford. In the fifties, a Jamaican student had to travel to Britain or the United States to gain a university education. Hall was a bright student. The scholarship to Merton College was an enormous privilege. For his mother in particular this move away was a kind of home-coming since she always harboured deep feelings for England as the 'mother-country'. Hall's experience of Oxford, however, confirmed in him a sense of familiar disjunction. Though English culture was well known to him, Hall understood he was not, and never could be, English. This experience is what he has termed 'diasporic', suggesting a continual negotiation between the situation of exile/loss and arrival/acceptance. Hall's experience of Merton College confirmed his sense of unease with the dominant culture of the university.

Hall took refuge in the society of friends and colleagues whose interests lay beyond the scope of college life. His first three years were devoted to studies of literature and the pursuit of Caribbean politics. Yet rather than return home, he chose to remain, becoming increasingly involved in the origins of a movement in British politics that would have profound effects on the evolution of radical and left-wing politics in general. This movement became known as the New Left. Hall's close circle of friendships with fellow black students intent on reform and Caribbean independence was further enlarged by his contact with fellow Rhodes scholars, the Labour Club, and people within the Communist Party. Though never a member himself, Hall met to debate interpretations of Marxism with Communist members, while continuing to oppose imperialism and Stalinism. It was during this time that Hall met, among others, Raymond Williams, Raphael Samuel, Richard Hoggart and Charles Taylor. Williams encouraged Hall to get involved in the adult education movement in Oxford and as a result Hall taught extra-mural classes for many years. These friendships were intensely formative for Stuart Hall and provided him with a strong supportive community beyond the scope of college life. Many years later, on the occasion of Raphael Samuel's untimely death, Hall wrote movingly of his friend's passionate intellect and political activism. Hall describes spending 'many long hours together reading proofs and arguing in the kitchen' (1997: 122) in the house in Jericho he shared with Samuel, and attributes many of the early New Left initiatives to his friend. Their student house became the nerve centre of the first New Left. With art students from Ruskin lodged in the attic and a jazz band in the basement, this was an alternative space far removed from the formalities of high table and official college activities.

Having won a second scholarship that would enable him to undertake postgraduate work, Hall was soon to be shaken by the world political events that were unfolding. In the summer of 1956, Russia invaded Hungary. Later the same year, an Anglo-French force was despatched to Egypt to regain control of the Suez canal. Hall had travelled down to Cornwall with some friends for the summer. Williams had given him a couple of chapters of *Culture and Society* to read as Hall was planning to write a book with Alan Hall about the changing face of British culture. All that changed however when news broke of events in Hungary. The enormity of the situation could not go unacknowledged. It now became imperative for Hall and his peers to find a way of mounting an oppositional stance. 'The world turned. That was the formation, the moment of the New Left' (Morley and Chen, 1996: 493). British Communists were confronted by the appalling truth that Russia was in fact realising its own imperial aims in the most bloody and overt manner. The Suez crisis provoked international outrage and condemnation. Britain was forced to withdraw and renounce its claims to Egyptian territory. It was a blow to the Empire. It was also the moment when the New Left was born.

the new left

The New Left was formed as a response to the deepening crisis facing socialists, communists and other leftwing activists. When Khruschev addressed the twentieth Congress of the Communist Party of the Soviet Union in 1956, he spoke of the Stalinist purges that had been an integral feature of communist rule. The shock was profound, though for many communists it did not come entirely as a surprise. The system, which had appeared to offer Eastern Europeans a radical alternative to Capitalism, had instead been an instrument of repression and terror. This realisation, coupled with Russia's territorial claim on Hungary, led to a deep political and moral crisis for Communists everywhere. Hall had never been a member of the Communist Party and was therefore spared much of the disillusionment and confusion that beset many of his friends and colleagues at the time. But he was profoundly sensitive to their predicament and the political ramifications of these events.

When Britain and France tried to reclaim the Suez Canal from the newly independent Egypt, the United States joined with the rest of the world in condemning this imperial act of aggression. These world events engendered in Hall, Thompson, Williams and others, a radical reappraisal of the realities of the post-war settlement. How could socialism function in the modern world? What new subject positions were emerging as a result of national and international politics? What was the role and function of the British Labour Party in the midst of such upheaval? How could socialism best serve the interests of so many disparate and newly enfranchised groups within society? Though their primary focus was Britain, the New Left were also internationalists, drawing their ideas, theories and examples from a broad range of perspectives.

Encouraged by Raphael Samuel,[1] Hall, Samuel, Taylor, and Pearson set up the journal *Universities and Left Review*, one of the precursors to *New Left Review*. The publication was energetic and eclectic, pulling together both new and established writers and commentators. Hall introduced Raymond Williams to Richard Hoggart, thereby initiating an important debate concerning the post-war conditions of working-class education and leisure.[2] *ULR* emerged under the watchful eye of the other New Left journal, the *New Reasoner*. Edward Thompson, the editor of the *New Reasoner*, was suspicious of *ULR*'s approach and content. Unlike the *New Reasoner*, the editors and writers of *ULR* were more concerned to adopt and adapt new and existing models in order to explore socialism's relationship to contemporary culture. Having broken with Stalinist Communism, Thompson was intent on reconstructing a socialism which was both historically materialist and ethical. There is no doubt that the ethical intentions of both journals constituted a consensual approach across the New Left. However, it was the theoretical differences between the two journals that would provoke debate and uncertainty.

By 1957 Hall had given up his thesis on Henry James and left Oxford to teach in south London. On their removal to London, the over-subscribed meetings of the *Universities and Left Review* club inspired the Club's committee to create links up and down the country. Hall's memories of some of Raphael's initiatives give a vivid insight to the New Left counter-culture which started to evolve at that time.

> The idea of calling a meeting of journal readers in London to hear [Issac] Deutscher speak – the beginning of the New Left Club movement – was also his [Samuel], as was the layout of the room we hired for the occasion in a Bloomsbury hotel: casually arranged for informal political exchange around tables for about sixty people, in a style, he assured us, somewhere between the Parisian Left Bank café and the inter-war Berlin cabaret scene. When we returned from a leisurely Indian meal, 700 people were standing impatiently in a queue outside. (Hall, 1997: 121)

In the face of such overwhelming demand, Hall and his colleagues committed themselves to the establishment of regional centres, which would help to recruit new readers and organise local groups. The journal sought to unite political activism with popular culture by hosting and advertising music and dance events. Thus the journal's editors envisaged leftwing activism as firmly embedded within ordinary social and cultural practice. In addition, they thought it was

9

imperative to maintain a critical intellectual outlook. The editors were young and eschewed any sense of hierarchy. The number of activities organised and promoted by the journal escalated as the New Left gained increasing momentum. At one stage they even started up a 'post-espresso left-wing coffee house' in Carlisle Street as a means of financing Soho premises for the journal. Raphael was in charge of the food; 'Old-fashioned pea soup ... Borscht ... Irish peasant stew ... Baked Yorkshire ham with sauce Cumberland. ... Boiled Surrey Fowl with parsley sauce and Patna rice [ ] Apple dumplings with hot lemon sauce ... Whitechapel cheese-cake and pastries ... Vienna coffee. ... café filtre ... Russian tea.' (Hall, 1997: 122).

During this time Hall travelled all over Britain attending New Left club events, sleeping on friends' sofas and talking politics till the early hours. His friendship with Edward and Dorothy Thompson resulted in many visits to their house in Halifax, en route to meetings up and down the country. Hall even joined the Labour Party, attending regular meetings of the Clapham Branch. However he found canvassing extremely difficult. 'I couldn't say "we". I couldn't speak from inside the experience'.[3] As a middle-class Jamaican, Hall was struck by the absurdity of his situation. He had no desire to return to the middle-class role awaiting him in Jamaica.[4] Nor could he in all conscience try and re-invent himself as a member of the British working class. His vision of socialism was much more broad and inclusive than that being proffered by Labour at that time and he was frustrated by the absence of genuine analytical debate within the Party. By contrast, the New Left engendered debate and controversy that impacted on Labour Party policies, yet was mercifully free from the bureaucracy of electioneering. Hall allowed his membership to lapse in 1964 on his move to Birmingham.

Meanwhile the editors of *The New Reasoner* had concerns for the future of their journal. Edward Thompson and John Saville were suffering from chronic overload. Thompson felt that *ULR* ignored many of the centrally important issues concerning the re-articulation of a core Socialist philosophy governed by Marxist theory. It seemed to him that the eclectic and broadly Socialist agenda of *ULR* seemed to undermine that endeavour. The *Universities and New Left Review* was also facing an economic crisis of its own. Over the next two years, the editorial boards of both journals debated the prospect of a new journal which would satisfy the needs and vision of all concerned. Amid much prevarication

10

and mutual suspicion, the *New Left Review* was launched in December 1959 with Hall as editor.

Within an increasingly fractious and divisive environment, Hall edited the journal virtually single-handed from 1959 to 1960, cycling from school into Soho of an evening. He also commuted to Tunbridge Wells every Friday night to teach evening classes in literature. Within six months of his appointment, Hall was looking to quit his role as editor. Subjected to increasing criticisms from certain members of the editorial board and some vocal representatives from the regional clubs, Hall found himself in an impossible situation. Frustration gave way to exhaustion and exasperation. From the beginning, Thompson expressed disappointment in the content and style of the journal. Following a debacle at the journal's joint conference in 1961, Hall set about trying to design a new structure to suit everybody. However, at the next editorial meeting, Saville resigned from the board. Hall resigned and an emergency 'caretaker' team comprising Raphael Samuel, Dennis Butt and Perry Anderson took on editorial responsibility. Anderson would subsequently go on to edit the journal for many years, taking it into a wholly different terrain, bitterly contested by Thompson. By 1962 however, Hall was immersed in teaching at Chelsea Arts College. He also continued to work within adult education during this period, commuting to Maidstone in Kent on a weekly basis.

a sense of classlessness

Though Hall's early work from these years is less well known than his later analyses, it does warrant close examination. Given the contemporary nature of Cultural Studies, it can be tempting sometimes to eschew events and issues that have become part of the historical backdrop. To adopt such a position may result from two inter-related assumptions. First that the modern reader is totally familiar with the background, and second that the issues or events are already so well rehearsed, that further analytic excavation is completely unnecessary. I agree with Kenny however, who argues that in the case of Stuart Hall, Edward Thompson and Raymond Williams, 'this period in their intellectual careers has generally been underplayed' (1995: 2). Kenny (1995) offers an extremely readable and incisive history of the New Left's formation as well as its impact and the legacies of New Left thinking in British politics. Central to Kenny's analysis is the importance of the New Left in re-orienting British Labour politics away from its more traditional Communist and Labourist roots towards a more inclusive leftwing politics.

> In particular, scant attention has been paid to the possibility that the movement prefigured the shift to a more diverse and counterpolitical politics akin to the radical currents which emerged in British political life, such as feminism, environmentalism and anti-racism, in the 1970s and 1980s. (Kenny, 1995: 14)

Given the diversity of views and allegiances within the movement, it comes as no surprise that the early articles and papers were the setting for many hotly contested debates. The New Left was concerned to challenge Labour Party and Communist Party orthodoxies in its search for a practical and meaningful socialism. This necessarily caused some disquiet and argument between members of the movement. Hall's piece, 'A sense of classlessness', published in 1958 is just such an attack. It demonstrates Hall's keen engagement with what he identifies as the post-war shifts and accommodations in spending and consumerism in relation to high levels of unemployment. He takes as his main thesis the uneven patterns of progress, change and stability within the physical environment of working-class Londoners. Work, leisure and consumption cannot be easily separated. He yokes together Marx's theory of alienation and the consuming habits of the urban working class. The increasingly managerial style of labour relations in the late fifties is identified as contingent upon a form of false consciousness where 'the rhetoric of scientific management' meets 'the ideology of consumer capitalism' (Hall, 1958: 28). It represents a decisive break by Hall from the traditional received wisdom about working-class formations.

Whereas Williams espouses a notion of neighbourhood that he sees as synonymous with class solidarity, Hall is quick to point out the problems of the finely-tuned class distinctions heralded and exacerbated by modern practices of consumption. Hall does not agree that there can be any innate correlation between working-class communities and their working or leisure pursuits. For example gardening, he argues, is not an innate community skill but rather a subtle means of signalling an individualism that whittles away at the idea of a class identity. Class action thus becomes thwarted by patterns of consumption and new lifestyle practices: 'Self improvement and self-advancement are now parts of the same process. That is the message of the capitalism of the proletariat. That is the tragic conflict within the working class which has freed itself only for new and more subtle forms of enslavement.' (Hall, 1958: 31) Hall concludes somewhat pessimistically that although technologically the conditions are 'ripe' for liberation, the structures of human relationships contradict that possibility and therefore nullify it. What is striking about this early piece aside from the vigour and confidence of the writing, is the extent to which Hall's arguments appear relevant today.

As soon as the working class embraces the idea of self-advancement up the bourgeois ladder of consumption, it becomes impossible to think in terms of class or community prosperity. Instead we begin to see conspicuous consumption in the guise of one-upmanship – 'a Smith against a Jones'. This is because, as Hall rightly points out, in the world of the social ladder, 'a class *as a class* cannot advance by means of it. We each must go it alone.' (Hall, 1958: 29) Hall is taking issue with what he sees as the empty promises of government and politicians. Affordable television sets and motor cars will not lead to a dismantling of the social and economic conditions that keep working-class men and women in their subordinated places. It just makes social injustice a bit more comfortable.

Hall's concern in 'A sense of classlessness' focuses on what he sees as the gulf between the socialism constructed within British politics and what he believes socialism *should be*. First, in his view, a socialism worth fighting for does not begin once the 'revolution' has occurred. His vision of socialism is that it should be rooted in the imperfect *present* not an idealised *future*. This distinguishes Hall from many other intellectuals and over the years has earned him the reputation of being somewhat pessimistic. Pessimistic or not, Hall argues that we must first look at the conditions of the here-and-now even if to do so means admitting our own weaknesses, failures and prejudices. Second, Marxism as it is so often understood by scholars and intellectuals, does not refer to a 'sealed house of theory', but a 'body of analytical concepts' that are usually only partially read, and frequently misunderstood. Hall goes even further when he quotes Engels in the final footnote of the article:

According to the materialist conception of history, the *ultimately* determining element in history is the production and reproduction of life. More than this neither Marx and I have ever asserted. Hence if somebody twists this into saying that the economic element is the *only* determining one, he transforms that proposition into a meaningless, abstract, senseless phrase. … We make our history ourselves, but in the first place, under very definite assumptions and conditions. [ ] Unfortunately, however, it happens only too often that people think they have fully understood a new theory and can apply it without more ado from the moment they have mastered its main principles, and even those not correctly. And I cannot exempt many of the more recent 'Marxists' from this reproach, for the most amazing rubbish has been produced in this quarter too. (Hall, 1958: 32 quoting from Engels *Selected Works*, vol 2 pp. 443–4)

This is a long extract but I think a very important one. It indicates a number of Hall's concerns at this point. Principally it is a warning to all that we should beware of enslaving ourselves to a new or modish way of thinking without sufficient independence of reason and thought. In addition, Hall is returning the reader to the source, Engels himself, who worked closely with Marx and co-authored *The German Ideology* in 1848. We are being urged here to read the primary texts and not to rely on the glosses of others who may inadvertently misinterpret the work in trying to meet their own agendas. Hall is making the case for understanding *before* action. Understanding is one of the core values at the heart of Hall's work. It is the key to Hall's reasoning. Without sufficient understanding – i.e., the application of time and thought – we cannot address real situations and seek real solutions. Theory and hypothesis are not enough. Understanding demands empathy and reason, not just logic.

Perhaps the most interesting aspect of this lengthy footnote is the elusive concept of 'real life'. Engels is emphasising the point that economics does *not* determine everything in life. Rather, he suggests that a form of agency is at work here which, though often originating within given economic structures and situations, *still* requires that men be active in the production of their own lives. Hall understands this distinction though at this moment in time, he is unable to articulate it except in terms of an ethical choice. In the late 1950s, Hall is grappling with an idea of 'conscious moral decisions', which he knows 'we cannot slip or slide over by means of some convenient theory of economic inevitability.'

(Hall, 1958: 32) This article from 1958 clearly pre-dates the English translation of Gramsci's writings, but nevertheless, this work to some extent prefigures Hall's engagement with Gramsci's term 'hegemony'.

In Chapter 4 we will see how Hall is able to progress his ideas through his rethinking of Althusser's work and his embrace of Gramsci. For now, Hall recognises the dangers of an interpretation of Marxism that denies human agency and free will. He is partly influenced here by Thompson's writing on working-class culture. Hall is already casting wider than the more typical interpretations of Marxism advocated by Williams, in his search for an understanding of *culture* and the social means by which society produces and reproduces itself at both the micro and the macro level. That is to say, Hall is just as concerned with how the *individual* feels and functions as he is with society in general. Colin Sparks (Morley and Chen, 1996) has argued that this article expresses Hall's view that the base and superstructure model had become obsolete. Sparks suggests that Hall is dismissive of the model and consequently that 'Hall identified Marxism as an obsolete and reductivist system of thought' (1996: 78). I think there is more subtlety at work here.

Hall's major criticisms are launched at what he terms, 'vulgar-Marxist interpretations' (1958: 27). He suggests that some of the problems of interpretation are created because Marx himself used the base/superstructure model in different ways at different periods of his life *as well as* the fact that a number of Marx's earlier writings are still unavailable in translation. He does not reject Marxism. Rather he insists that (as before in the Engels's quotation), there is more to this question. Alienation and superstructure are complex concepts which reward further thinking. He rejects a 'simplistic economic- determinist reading of the formula' whilst acknowledging that there is some 'organic relationship' to be understood between cultural life and economic conditions of living. Hall is able to use Engels (himself a revisionist of Marx) in order to fully justify a revision of Marxism, but this does not equate with a rejection of Marxism. That would be akin to throwing the baby out with the bath water.

What is also becoming clear is that just as Hall is concerned with the role of the Left in British Politics, the main arena in which he chooses to site his arguments are those of popular culture and, increasingly from 1960 onwards, the mass media. I agree with Sparks' insightful point that

15

Hall's own origins made it possible for him to engage directly with contemporary British culture in a new way:

> Unlike Hoggart and Williams, for example, Hall could not look back, with a measure of sentimentality, on a provincial British childhood within which the positive values of working- class culture were embodied in concrete human behaviour. (Morley and Chen, 1996: 78)

Thus we can see how Hall was in a unique position to move the debate around culture onward to embrace modern and popular consumption. This did not however sit well with Thompson and Samuel who responded critically to Hall's arguments. 'A sense of classlessness' (1958) is important because it shows up the internal theoretical conflicts within the New Left, by asking some very pertinent questions. Hall is looking directly at post-war culture and situating his analysis on the edge of contemporary Marxist theory. In short Hall is looking to a revision and reconstruction of a contemporary socialism fit for the present, rather than trying to resurrect a more benign version of communism. Furthermore, he sees the contemporary spheres of cultural and social practice as fundamental spaces for the employment of socialist principles in sharp contrast to Thompson, who is suspicious of any analysis that does not prioritise the historical materialist conditions for modern culture. In other words, where Hall wishes to discuss the contemporary phenomenon of 'classlessness' as a modern feature of post-war capitalism, Thompson prefers a reading of 'class' as an endemic structural function of capitalism. What is clear throughout Hall's work is the extent to which he sees the world as a complex, uncomfortable and worrying place. Therefore any attempt to assuage such a view through the importation of a theoretical position which does *not* recognise that truth, simply will not satisfy him. Hall argues that if one does not at least acknowledge the widespread articulation and function of 'classlessness', how can political language ever hope to permeate and make sense of the *cultural* sphere in which 'classlessness' has become so broadly adopted?

Early *New Left Review* editorials by Hall reveal a great deal of frustration with the political scene – a lot of which is aimed at Labour and Conservative politicians alike. Anthony Crosland's[5] optimism regarding the breaking down of class boundaries through the new consumerism

16

comes in for tough and sustained criticism by Hall. The Labour Party, founded in 1900 to represent the working man, far from offering up effective opposition to the Conservative push for more spending and increased manufacture of luxury goods, appears totally complicit with a mythology of post-war British society as prosperous and classless. Hall warns that the road to Bourgeois individualism comes at the cost of working-class community but crucially Hall never romanticises working-class experience. Neither does he deny the need for change. Rather he argues that we risk moving away from class altogether towards the division of status groups that are predicated on wealth and opportunity. Any core values are swept away, creating, 'a crisis in the psychology of the working class itself, and therefore, by extension of that, a crisis in the Labour Movement' (Hall, 1960a: 93).

The Left in Britain was facing a crisis hitherto unknown. After the Labour landslide victory of 1945, which enabled the government to push forward the enormous state reforms that generated the Welfare State, the Labour Party suffered three consecutive election defeats between 1951 and 1964, each by a larger majority than the time before. The Party was thus desperate to connect with the electorate.

Labour's endorsement of the new consumer culture comes in for sharp criticism from Hall. He quotes Hugh Gaitskell's[6] Blackpool conference speech of 1959:

> In short, the changing character of labour, full employment, new housing, the new way of life based on the telly, the *frig[de]*, the car and the glossy magazine – all have their effect on our political strength
>
> The *way of life* based on the telly and the glossy magazine? Life? Has the Labour Movement come through the fire and brimstone of the last fifty years to lie down and die before the glossy magazine? (Hall, 1960a: 95–96)

Hall's frustration is almost tangible. We can also see here the beginnings of a fascination for media production as evidence of false consciousness. If politicians can point to the media as indices of cultural prosperity, what precisely is the role of the media in constructing such images and ideas for society at large? Hall is asking two major questions.

What is the function of the Labour Party, and what exactly is the political role of the mass media? The first question continues to exercise Hall still today. The second question would begin to generate some complex, far-reaching and influential research that would help to kick-start academic interest in culture and the media around the world. Within the New Left, Hall's position created a stir. He was not only urging an analysis of contemporary culture, but simultaneously calling into question the Left's traditional Marxist approach.

the popular arts

Hall continued to stay in touch with Hoggart and Williams while he taught film and mass media at Chelsea College, from 1961–64. At the same time Hall worked in Film Studies at the British Film Institute (BFI) with Paddy Whannel. Further work for SEFT[7] and *Screen* culminated in an important volume of work, *The Popular Arts* in 1964. The National Union of Teachers' Annual Conference of 1960 had passed an important resolution that, congruent with educational debates of the time, stated a need for media producers to join with teachers in order to 'counteract the debasement of standards which result from the misuse of press, radio, cinema and television; the deliberate exploitation of violence and sex; and the calculated appeal to self-interest.' The popular view of the 1960s is that of a swinging permissive decade that celebrated sex, dugs and rock n' roll. Bill Wyman, base guitarist for *The Rolling Stones* once famously remarked 'If you can remember the sixties, you weren't really there.' But for the vast majority of people, such excesses were associated with a vulgarised culture that threatened the sensibilities of young people.

The mood of the conference evoked a siege mentality with regard to the rising tide of media consumption. To many, commercial culture seemed poised to engulf and sweep away the treasured culture of the past. Len Masterman, who was present at the conference, recalls how Stuart Hall and fellow teacher Tony Higgins made more optimistic representations about the value of teaching discrimination and the pleasures that this might engender for children and young adults. 'It was the move towards more cautious discriminations within the media that were to provide the most immediate growth points from the conference' (1985: 52).

The media was coming under attack from many different quarters including the influential Crowther Report[8] which warned against the effects of the mass media on young people. Three years later, the 1962 Pilkington Report was savaged by the tabloids and the broadsheets of the British press. The Report focussed on television's need to identify and cater for all the different tastes of the viewing public. However, this was misinterpreted by many as a direct attack on the popular programmes of the day.

> How dare you prefer watching commercial television to looking at what Auntie BBC so kindly provides for you? Twice as many watch ITV as BBC. Disgraceful say the Pilkingtonians. Why? Because the BBC programmes are good and uplifting, put out by very worthy ladies and gentlemen. The ITV programmes are 'naughty' and 'bad' for you. They are produced by ordinary men and women who like the same things as you do. Pilkington is out to stop all this rot about you being allowed to enjoy yourselves. (*Sunday Pictorial* 1st July 1962)

Against the backdrop of this debate, *The Popular Arts* (1964) was well-received by the Sunday papers, probably on the grounds that it resisted what many journalists saw as a government crackdown on popular media[9]. Hall and Whannel are quick to identify the common position being established that situates mass and popular culture in opposition to good authentic and traditional culture. *The Popular Arts* is premised on the idea that mass media is not necessarily a conduit for the transmission of traditional cultural forms, but argues that it can be an object of study *in its own right* and *on its own terms*. Despite this argument, the authors are not prepared to endorse popular culture as intrinsically valuable.

In the case of television, the medium is barely touched upon by Hall and Whannel, except in relation to the media effects debate. The aesthetic and cultural properties of television as an art form are dismissed by the authors in favour of a chapter on the Pilkington Report and concerns around the depiction of violence on television.

> If television is an 'art', those who make this claim for it must take responsibility for what they do with it, along with the compensating excitement of working in a new medium (1964: 115)

19

There is an implicit series of assumptions at work in this attitude to television. Hall and Whannel are clearly not persuaded that television is an art form, particularly in comparison with film or music. The only chapter of the book dealing explicitly with television concentrates mostly on the transition of literary texts to the small screen. Where television programmes created *for* the medium are discussed, the greatest compliment paid is that they can, on occasion, compare very 'favourably with films' (ibid.: 127).

In addition to this apparent handicap, those who work within the medium are judged to be in need of some rather paternal advice; television producers and directors must not let the racy appeal of this exciting new medium overshadow their incumbent responsibilities. Hall and Whannel do not extend the argument to include either film makers or even music producers. Commercial television was licensed in 1954. At that point the BBC not only lost its broadcasting monopoly but also faced repeated reviews of the licence fee. There is perhaps a slight suggestion in the authors' comment that television is very much in its adolescence and that commercial television in particular is something of a teen rebel. From our position some 40 years later, this might seem odd given the tendency of many producers and critics to describe this as the golden era of television production. Yet in the days before television franchising and independent production companies, this period in British broadcasting is remembered chiefly for its institutional power-base. Strong institutions not only secured future talent by nurturing writers and producers, but also embodied the fourth estate. Hall would later review many of his ideas and concerns regarding television and its importance within the common culture. In particular he would look at institutional power and the functions of broadcasting. Questions concerning the ideological function of media production would dominate much of Hall's writing in the 1970s and lead him to question the nature and purpose of public service broadcasting and its paternalistic agenda.

The Popular Arts was intended as a book for teachers and lay readers with an interest in the broadly educational value of popular and media culture. The influence of Hoggart and Williams is clearly acknowledged by the authors in their introduction. Hall and Whannel also make direct engagement with FR Leavis and Denys Thompson, whose book *Culture and Environment* had more or less shaped the entire debate around the value and uses of mass-produced culture from the 1930s onwards. The legacy of the NUT conference was a renewed sense on the part of Hall and Whannel that popular culture and the mass media should not be discriminated against on the basis that they were abandoning and devaluing the common culture. According to the authors, popular culture *can* be an enlightened and affective space, but only in the hands of responsible media producers. Though Marx is never mentioned in *The Popular Arts* we can see the traces of that earlier argument; the 'real life' that men and women create comes out of their historical and economic circumstances: 'The old culture has gone because the way of life that produced it has gone' (1964: 39). To go back and recapture a culture that may be passing from us would necessitate a return to the older forms of production and labour that produced it; instead of lamenting an imaginary golden past, we should be engaging with the culture as it is emerging in the present. Hall and Whannel are adamant that such an engagement is necessarily critical. Theirs is, by no means, a wholesale endorsement of popular culture.

the critique of popular culture

In their determination to show the value of the good within popular culture, Hall and Whannel offered some excellent analyses of selected films, popular songs and advertising. However, it is one of the most common criticisms made against *The Popular Arts* that Hall and Whannel were unable to escape the strictures of Leavisite thinking (Storey 2001; Turner 2000): 'The book is limited by the lack of more appropriate analytical tools than those provided by Leavisite literary analysis' (Turner, 2000: 68). However, there was, at that time, no language of cultural analysis other than that derived from English Literature, principally in the work of Leavis and his sister Queenie at Cambridge. Barthes' *Elements of Semiology* was not translated into English until 1964. Saussure's posthumous collection of lecture notes *Course in General Linguistics* did not appear in translation until 1966. The continental influences of post-structuralism would not begin to be felt until nearly ten years later. Leavis's influence on Hall and Whannel therefore needs to be understood within this context. In their analysis of advertising we can see an absence of formal terms yet the meaning is clear, and the analytical principles of style, tone and meaning are well-applied.

21

But the image or picture is, most frequently, the real point of sale, carrying the burden of the 'message'. The language or copy reinforces the appeal of the photograph, extends the mood of the picture in words, and rivets the name or brand of the product in the mind. (Hall and Whannel, 1964: 321)

Their description of the function of text in relation to image even appears to anticipate Barthes' seminal term 'anchorage'. But the failure to invent a new mode of analysis is not their only fault. Masterman (1985) draws attention to the other main channel of criticism. David Holbrook writing in the journal *The Use of English* had this to say: 'Hall and Whannel simply have no perception of the sincere and beautiful, nor sufficient anger with the mean and false. Yet their book is quite useful – as useful as sociology without a sense of values and relevance can ever be' (1985: 57).

It would be more accurate to say that Hall and Whannel clearly did not share Holbrook's sense of values. Or did they? Both Masterman (1985) and Storey (2001) have argued that it is not so much the method that is problematic as the view of culture shaping it. In making the case of discrimination *within* popular culture, Hall and Whannel nevertheless seem to fall into the trap of condemning that which is 'mass' culture, largely commercial and undistinguished. By inventing a new term, the 'popular arts', the authors attempt to reclaim elements of popular mass culture, but the value judgements made are still derived from the standards of high culture and high artistic form. This is precisely the point that Hall and Whannel sought to advance – a new kind of critique – one that recognised the limits, forms and aims of different media without producing crude comparisons. However, as I have shown in the case of television and as Storey rightly points out in relation to popular music, the argument folds back on itself. Once Hall and Whannel start to distinguish between good and bad popular culture, they are required to formalise their distinctions. Certain genres, such as situation comedy and the crime drama, are condemned on the grounds that they are formulaic, stereotypical, repetitive and as such emotionally worthless. Yet pleasure, familiarity and identification with the text have been shown to be highly commensurate with meaningful relationships between the television audience and the text (Radway, 1984; Geraghty, 1991; Fiske, 1995). There is also much to be said of the serial appeal of the soap opera (Brunsdon 1990). This failure to really confront some of the dominant 'unacknowledged class-based notions of aesthetic taste' (Masterman, 1985: 54) was a stumbling-block.

Yet there are many useful things to be said about *The Popular Arts* and its effect on the development of media education in Britain throughout the 1970s and 1980s. Hall and Whannel were the first to articulate a serious educational engagement with contemporary mass culture – the popular arts movement – that developed, sought and eventually conferred legitimacy on an area of study hitherto deemed unworthy of serious reflection. The philosophy behind this teaching was, however, to be a largely defensive one. Hall and Whannel made very important claims for the integrity of performance and the necessary respect for the audience. The book stressed a need to break with the dominant American behaviourist models of mass communications research and went some way towards analysing the lack of fit between audience interpretation and media producers' intended meanings. The authors are particularly attentive to the social mores, attitudes and behaviours of teenagers who reflect and assemble their own identity in relation to the popular entertainment of music, magazines and dance. Many of the questions raised in the chapters concerning youth culture would re-surface later at the Birmingham Centre for Contemporary Cultural Studies as research projects and investigations.

Thus *The Popular Arts* stands as a significant station in Hall's development. It marked his public entry into the educational field and provided the spur for the future development of his research within the academy. It brought a good deal of attention to the school experience of teaching children in the modern era, contributing to a series of debates about the value of popular culture and kick-starting questions about media education in Britain. *The Popular Arts* was also notable as a project that elided the traditional disciplinary boundaries in favour of an eclectic and multidisciplinary approach. Part Sociology, English Literature, and History, this was a method of working that was bound to cause some disquiet among the practitioners of the more traditional and established subject areas. It was perhaps unsurprising that Richard Hoggart approached Hall in 1964 and offered him a Research Fellowship in the emergent and controversial Centre for Contemporary Cultural Studies.

He thought that, with my combination of interests in television, film and popular literature, my knowledge of the Leavis debate and my interest in cultural politics, I would be a good person. I went to Birmingham in 1964 and got married to Catherine – who transferred to Birmingham from Sussex – the same year. (Morley and Chen, 1996: 498)

Hoggart had negociated an impressive deal with Birmingham. The University had secured Hoggart as Professor of English but Hoggart wanted to continue some of the graduate work with which he had started at Leicester – work that emanated from his *Uses of Literacy* focus. Four years earlier Hoggart had appeared for Penguin in the *Lady Chatterley's Lover* trial when the publisher had been accused of obscenity. As a return favour, Hoggart subsequently approached Sir Allen Lane, head of Penguin Books, and negotiated annual funding to support the creation of a new research centre. The Centre for Contemporary Cultural Studies was thus born out of one of the most infamous legal-literary cases to hit the British Statute books with Birmingham's English and Sociology departments looking on. Its genesis did not go unremarked. Some felt distinctly threatened. Hall describes how the opening of the Centre 'triggered a blistering attack specifically from Sociology' with two sociologists threatening 'reprisals' if the Centre overstepped the mark (1980: 21). Stuart Hall undertook the running of the Centre while Hoggart continued as Professor of English. Hall was 32 years old.

conclusion

As a result of Suez and Hungary, Hall's academic ambitions were thrown into stark relief by what he saw as more immediate and urgent concerns. His decision to give up his thesis and make a direct intervention into the political debate at a national level was one of the founding initiatives of the New Left. The inclusive left wing politics generated through the New Left movement constituted an important arena for political debate that was neither circumscribed by party loyalties nor predicated on achieving electoral power.

Hall's political formation during the 1950s and early 1960s not only confirmed his commitment to the analysis of the *British* political scene, but would also have an impact on his methods of working. Hall's pursuit of a more independent socialism coupled with the collaborative mode of Hall's early activism would become a feature of his work as a teacher and cultural critic. Out of his enthusiasm for intellectual debate, and his readiness to engage with oppositional views, would come many influential and productive partnerships. These would, in time, generate some of the most provocative and prescient analyses of British social, political and cultural formations.

further reading

Kenny, M. (1995) *The First New Left*. Lawrence and Wishart: London.
Masterman, L. (1991) rep. *Teaching About Television*. Macmillan: London.
Masterman, L. (1992) rep. *Teaching the Media*. Routledge: London.
Turner, G. (2000) rep. *British Cultural Studies*. Routledge: London.
Williams, R. (1969) *Mayday Manifesto 1968*. Penguin: London.

a deadly serious matter

I come back to the deadly seriousness of intellectual work (Hall, quoted in Morley and Chen, 1996: 274)

introduction

In this chapter we will look at Hall's early experiences at the Centre for Contemporary Cultural Studies in Birmingham. In particular, we will focus on the innovative studies of culture undertaken by Hall and his colleagues at this time, and consider the significance of their approach to European philosophers and theorists. This marked a particular break from established theories of mass communication, and paved the way forward for an eclectic and productive engagement with ideas around culture, politics and society.

early days at the centre for contemporary cultural studies

The three years from 1964 to 1967 were hectic and productive. Though it was never meant to become a centre for research, work gathered pace as increasing numbers of graduate students were recruited, although the number of teaching staff never rose above three at any one time. The

Centre was a decidedly small affair, located in a temporary hut on the green lawn opposite the University's Great Hall. But what it lacked in size was amply compensated for in terms of industry. Hall described the nature of the Centre and its work as 'a collective, exploratory, self-educating one, in which individual work is related to a set of common concerns and problems' (Hall, 1967a: 154). The key term to note here is 'self-educating' since cultural studies as we understand it today was in the process of its own making. The majority of the teaching was under-taken through individual tutorials and via weekly seminars, where staff and students gathered to discuss common features of research and review each other's work-in-progress. The Centre was able to attract out-side speakers because of Hoggart's profile, and was starting to develop a reputation for innovation and iconoclasm. While Hoggart's vision was clearly the driving force behind the Centre, as student research projects began taking off in different directions, so the scope and emphasis of the original manifesto began to shift. In addition to the English debates around literature and culture, students were encouraged to engage with European writers on culture and society – Weber, Durkheim, Marx, and later Barthes, Eco, Althusser and Gramsci. The problem of method was foregrounded and the close analysis of texts and practices became an essential component of cultural study: 'And this lead us to the need for greater familiarity with some of the tools and concepts, the methods and approaches, of disciplines other than those of literary criticism' (ibid.: 155). Integration was the core wisdom of the enterprise. Not only as a means of evincing a working method from the disparate disciplines of Sociology, History, English and Philosophy, but also in the practice of analysis itself.

> We believe that for the purposes of a cultural analysis, both kinds of work have to be done – no rough division of labour will suffice. Such a broken-backed procedure only leads to further fragmentation: close studies of texts and events here – 'social background', 'history of ideas' or 'conditions of production' there. Useful work has been done in this way before, but it is our intention to try to develop a different, more integrated style of work. (Hall, 1967a: 155)

Such work could not be value-free, as any kind of cultural judgement operates from a synthesis of core values. It was therefore essential that as analysers of contemporary culture, students should also be self-aware. Hall addressed the problem of the subjective experience by emphasising the desirability of just such a tension. The way forward could no longer be accomplished through the kind of moral criticism advanced by Leavis, no matter how encompassing his vision of culture, nor could mass communications theory accommodate those subtleties of cultural experience which were demonstrably unquantifiable. For Hall, Weber's concept of interpretation went some considerable way towards reconciling the problem. Rather than making a value-laden judgement concerning a particular aspect of high culture, it might be possible to look at culture in its broadest sense (Leavis' vision of 'man, society and civilization') by examining and understanding the *relationship* between that culture and a particular artefact, text or practice.

> Beginning with the work or the event, our purpose must be to find the best means at our disposal for 'reading' its cultural significance, for reaching an 'interpretation' in Weber's sense. The term culture must embrace 'significant social behaviour' which, in so far as it has meaning at all, must be a *cultural* event. [ ] But it includes such meanings and values as they are embodied in and structured by institutions, as they are carried in the encounters and actions of men, or expressed through language, gesture, custom and art. These are all bearers of meaning in and between men in society. (Hall, 1967a: 157)

These 'cultural studies', as the Centre began to develop them, emanated from concerns over the articulation of class and race. As feminism gathered momentum, gender issues became increasingly pertinent and many students started to question the very assumptions under which the Centre had been operating.[1] The questions and concerns at the Centre were very much as Hall later described them, 'within shouting distance of Marx', but that did not mean that cultural studies was operating out of a classic Marxist framework at all. 1956 had proved to be a decisive point when the New Left had started to re-orient its vision of the globe. Hall (1958) had called for a necessary and urgent revision of Marx's work. The work of the Centre was not formulated at this point around an adoption of Marxist principles or theories, precisely because of what Hall termed, 'its [Marxism's] orthodoxy, its doctrinal character, its determinism, its reductionism, its immutable law of history, its status as a meta-narrative' (Hall, quoted in Morley and Chen, 1996: 265). However this did not mean that Marxist concepts were without value.

a sense of purpose

The analyses that Hall generated in the mid-to-late 1960s reflect this situation. Yet Hall was also concerned to push forward the debate about what socialism as a lived experience might be, and the real purpose and possibilities of political action. Ultimately, however, we need to ask the questions; Given the established strength and solidity of the other disciplines within the academy at that time, what was the real *purpose* of the Centre? How was it making a difference? What, if any, were its political objectives? Unusually, within a university environment, the Centre emphasised the generation of new and challenging analysis specifically embedded within actual contemporary cultural practices outside of the academy. The focus on collaborative projects and the quest for intellectual rigour were two important elements that generated within individuals strong commitments to social and cultural change. In an important retrospective piece, Hall answers this question of 'purpose' with reference to the work of Antonio Gramsci, an Italian Marxist intellectual who would come to have an enormous impact on Hall's entire philosophy:

> On the one hand we had to be at the very forefront of the intellectual theoretical work because, as Gramsci says, it is the job of the organic intellectual to know more than the traditional intellectuals do: really know, not just pretend to know, not just to have the facility of knowledge, but to know deeply and profoundly. [ ] But the second aspect is just as crucial: that the organic intellectual cannot absolve himself or herself from the responsibility of transmitting those ideas, that knowledge, through the intellectual function, to those who do not belong, professionally, in the intellectual class. And unless those two fronts are operating at the same time, or at least unless those two ambitions are part of the project of cultural studies, you can get enormous theoretical advance without any engagement at the level of the political project. (Hall, quoted in Morley and Chen, 1996: 268)

Hall stresses the wider political strategies at work within education, with the idea of 'two fronts'. He is not content to disseminate in the traditional manner of the university, of a body of knowledge conferred to a cohort of students. The making of that knowledge requires involvement, participation and collaboration on the part of students and academics. It also requires that each is firmly working within the cultural world, and not at a discreet (and therefore élite) distance from it. More importantly, culture can no longer be envisaged as an homogenous entity. We are speaking now of cultures – dominant, subordinate, alternative, underground, mainstream and diasporic – that individuals and groups create, negotiate and participate within. A person teaching cultural studies must be someone who is active within these cultures, otherwise it is not cultural studies anymore, but anthropology or history.

The 'organic intellectual' is self-created from the conditions and practices of his or her own culture. S/he is intellectually *and politically* alert to the meanings and constructions of different cultural practices within his or her own time. At the same time as pursuing the understanding and analysis of culture, the organic intellectual should be communicating and exchanging ideas with the broad range of classes and groups within the society. In other words, the knowledge must be open, accessible and subject to debate at all levels. Organic intellectuals are not often made within the university. In Gramsci's case, the organic intellectual arose from the serial ranks of the workers rather than from academic institutions. Whatever is generated within the academic enclosure of the university must be expanded beyond its parameters so that 'knowledge' does not become the preserve of a privileged minority. But what is the value of this knowledge? What is it for? Hall employs a sense of urgency and importance to communicate what he sees as 'a deadly serious matter'.

> I come back to the deadly seriousness of intellectual work. It is a deadly serious matter. I come back to the critical distinctions between intellectual work and academic work: they overlap, they abut with one another, they feed off one another, the one provides you with the means to do the other. But they are not the same thing. I come back to the difficulty of instituting a genuine cultural and critical practice, which is intended to produce some kind of organic intellectual political work, which does not try to inscribe itself in an overarching metanarrative of achieved knowledges, within the institutions. (Hall, quoted in Morley and Chen, 1996: 274)

The work to be done here does not rest at the level of producing research, publishing papers or acquiring MAs, though the Centre was engaged in all of these activities to a greater or lesser extent. Rather, the vision that Hall describes is one where such activity can make an intervention in the world. Clearly this is with a view to making a difference; Hall's focus is always directed at intervention. Can the analysis of culture work in the service of that culture? Might it be possible to read culture in order to question it, inflect it or change it? Could education be infused with a socialist imperative to work towards the democratised production and articulation of culture – one that served the needs of an evolving socialist society? Although Hall never claimed that the Centre had ever succeeded in creating an organic intellectual, what is very clear is the sense of purpose and drive that infused both him and his colleagues. He was 'prepared to imagine or model or simulate such a relationship in its absence: "pessimism of the intellect, optimism of the will"' (Hall, quoted in Morley and Chen, 1996: 267).

The powerhouse of activity of the Centre from the mid 1960s onwards resulted in an investigation of the nature of modern society through a succession of studies of contemporary and popular phenomena. These ranged from Scouting to the hippy movement, from housewives' consumption of radio to advertising and magazines. During the 1960s, the Centre did not orchestrate its research in terms of a specific theory of mass society or communication. However, the early 1970s saw a gradual and difficult turn towards Marxism via Althusser and Gramsci. This formalising of theory within the Centre would have important repercussions both in terms of Hall's own journey and the way in which the Centre was perceived and acknowledged by a burgeoning community of cultural studies scholars elsewhere.

class and the political climate

Hall's energies were directed into his political writing as well as his academic research. A chapter from *The Committed Church,* published in 1966, expresses many of those concerns alluded to above. The question that most vexed Hall was the nature of political consciousness in modern society.

The overall tone of the piece is one of frustration. As Hall sees it, the rising interest in political behaviour by sociologists, students and others within academic fields relating to human action fails to grasp the meaning of political action. By failing to take account of the subjective experience of political activity, the categories of explanation are subsumed into objective accounts that Hall dismisses as 'bogus pseudo-scientism' (1966: 6). Equally, Hall rejects the trend towards psephology[2] on the basis that articulating a new party image (what today might be referred to as 'spin') tells us nothing about the real activity of making political decisions based on human needs and core values. Hall argues that the intellectual climate is indeed 'hostile to politics' and that there appears to be a certain logic of inevitability at work whereby political parties are persuaded, by the latest techniques of electoral sampling, that people are less politically aware or motivated than in previous decades. Thus the 'praxis' of politics is lamented as a lost feature of the nineteenth century.

Hall's earlier work (1958; 1960) identified the rising consumerism of the post-war period as prejudicial to working-class values. In this piece he pursues the logic of such consumption and asks why it is that the tensions between working-class expectations and middle-class consuming habits have not led to the formation of a radical politics.

> And there must be factors at work in the formation of political consciousness which have so *shaped* the issues that they fail to take the configuration of a radical consciousness. What we have instead is the false consciousness of a transitional period, and the political conditions which have helped to make that consciousness so far prevail. (1966: 11)

Hall goes on, 'Thus Britain is neither a class society in the old sense, nor is it a classless society: paradoxically, it is closer to say that Britain is a society which, while remaining rigidly class-bound, gives the distinct impression that it is growing more classless' (1966: 12). The 'false consciousness' to which he alludes is made out of the particular historical and social conditions of the time. The latter half of the decade is one in which discourses of value-for-money and productivity prevail. Hall links these discourses directly to the influence of successive Tory governments, which have highlighted the desirability of affluent consumption and individualism. In his example of the National Health Service, we can see how Hall's argument strips away the rhetoric to look at the dominant perception of health provision as a private and individualised service. Hence public confidence in the health service is whittled away by constant griping, rather than by addressing the needs of communities. Hall sees the reduction in class identity as having a direct influence on how we view public services. It is difficult sometimes to remember that Hall is not talking about Thatcherism, or the present day New Labour discourses of public-private partnership financing, but about the political landscape of the late 1960s. 'Among the public, the stories of inefficiency multiply. In the [Health] service, discontent with conditions of work increases' (1966: 15).

As Hall sees it, the big mistake is for the Labour Party to accede to the dominant discourses rather than to challenge them. By failing to address the false consciousness generated under the Tories, Labour colludes with the same and therefore surrenders the opportunity to establish a genuine socialist position. The Party is too concerned with power. The desire on the part of Labour politicians to seize power prevents them from articulating a socialist consciousness:

> The commitment of the socialist in this period is to the making of socialist consciousness, rather than the accession to political power. [ ] To take office in the name of structural change and reform without an accompanying consciousness and a popular mandate is to become the prisoner of the system (1966: 21).

Despite Harold Wilson's election success in 1964, the Labour Party in power does not give Hall any great cause for celebration since the government failed, in his view, to offer any radical socialist policies. The only commitment appears to have been one based on modernisation and the application of new technology. Wilson famously spoke of forging a new Britain in 'the white heat of technology'. Education was to be modernised and the curriculum had to reflect this so that a generation of school leavers could face the new technological demands of manufacturing and engineering. But such a drive to modernisation lacked a necessary accompanying political vision; exactly how this generation of school-leavers could be emancipated rather than enslaved by the new technology was never considered, let alone addressed.

The other example that Hall mentions as a footnote is that of Labour's failure to challenge and expose the racist discourses fermenting in the political arena. During the 1964 general election, the Conservative candidate for Smethwick in the Midlands ran his campaign under the banner, 'If you want a nigger for a neighbour, vote Labour'. Smethwick had been a Labour stronghold that fell to the Conservatives. Hall argues that the result in Smethwick and the success of the slogan, which had seemingly convinced the electorate, sent shockwaves through Labour. The absence of Labour migration policies in the ten years running up to their election victory left them exposed and vulnerable at the point of winning power. The new government now found itself caught up in a discourse of race and immigration that it had not challenged and could not resist. The result was that the government published a white paper that set an arbitrary and harsh cap on immigration numbers.

class and the mass media

At this stage, Hall wants to identify the route towards a genuinely inclusive socialism. 'The enormous problem facing Labour politics is whether they can create their own "forms, structures, and relationships" which represent real alternatives to those which belong, typically, to the dominant social system' (1966: 24). Hall pursues this concept of a radical politics again in 'Class and the mass media', published in 1967 as part of a collection of essays. If Hall's earlier essay asked the question 'who shapes public perceptions of class and political action?' then this essay begins to answer it directly. The myth of a classless society is once again unpicked in favour of an analysis describing the dissolution from older class formations into contemporary consumption-oriented classes. He articulates a relationship between the, largely commercialised, mass media and the class structure in Britain in three ways. First, he argues that since the media is comprised largely of commercial and private enterprises, then the media is itself operating according to certain class perceptions. Second, audiences and readerships are demarcated according to their habits and tastes, which reflect the class structure to a certain extent. Third, and perhaps most significantly, the media reflect and mediate class notions to their audiences because so much of their material is filtered through social assumptions, and because so much of their content, whatever its manifest social purpose, consists of the circulation of latent social images and stereotypes. Class, that is to say, is also a language and a tactic. (1967b: 95)

Such a relationship requires a more formal analytical model if it is to demonstrate the truth of such a statement. Hall looks to the press for his evidence, drawing primarily on the major national daily newspapers. Different newspapers perform different roles and focus on different kinds of stories. Hall uses a hypothetical example of a 'Scunthorpe grammar-school boy' trying to make sense of a story that takes him to 'the sacred portholes of the Foreign Office' (1967b: 96). Class origins and social background must play some part in the recruitment and training of journalists, no matter how relatively open the profession might be in comparison with television or radio. Advertising revenue demands that newspapers target successfully the optimum quotient of readers. The readership of a specific paper is thus identified by social class groupings. Circulation is also important to the commercial success of the newspaper and, in trying to maintain a solid financial base, the newspaper must often peg itself to a particular class formation in order to deliver consistently to advertisers and sponsors. We can argue that the newspaper is itself a textual phenomenon as it creates identities and subject positions in order to generate discourses about the world. Hall identifies advertising as the principal means whereby new and revised class relationships are created and communicated to the readers: 'The style of advertising carried in a newspaper or a magazine is a running commentary in the margin of the production as to the social universe which the newspaper and its readers inhabit or aspire to' (1967b: 98). This is however only one aspect of the relationship between the newspaper and its selected readership. The entire paper is oriented around a set of assumptions concerning the reader – myths that sustain media production and act reciprocally so that both the journalist and the reader meet through a common set of core values and interests. It is therefore in the tone, the editorial inflection, the shared attitudes and the mode of reporting that newspapers create a loyal readership. But how do we test such a theory in relation to class structures in general?

Hall continues, 'we can tell more about a paper by testing its assumed *stance* towards authority than by which political party it supports – though the two are not unrelated, just as, in the population as a whole, voting is still to a large extent related to social class' (1967b: 101). Hall argues that *The Times* can be understood in terms of its close proximity to power and the Establishment. Governments may come and go but *The Times* continues, traditional and steady in its own authority. The house style of a particular paper is something that exists beyond the scope of the individual journalist. The *Mirror,* by contrast, speaks to its readership in terms of how it can exert influence from *outside* the Establishment. The paper's tone is far more closely aligned to a view of public opinion as mutable, persuadable and subjective. So far then, the categories of class readership can be seen to be relatively stable. The 'social educator' function (1967b: 105) of the press also plays a large part in the transmission of values and aspirations. Hall cites in particular the rise of fashion magazines *Honey* and *Nova*, which challenge conventional class identities by focusing on the consuming power of women. But this is not to say that class has disappeared. Rather, Hall is arguing that class is being reconfigured because of the great changes in consumption, aspiration and individual spending power. The liberation of women, envisioned by magazines like *Nova*, is only possible by them becoming 'the most clued-up, switched-on consumption objects of all' (1967b: 109).

The latter part of the chapter looks at the differences between BBC and ITV. Hall identifies the ways in which the BBC has surrendered much of its paternalistic tone, in order to compete with ITV to win younger and broader audiences. However, as with *The Popular Arts,* television fares less well as an object worthy of sustained criticism. Hall points to the success of *That Was the Week That Was* in capturing such a huge audience share, and suggests that, for once, the BBC was able to draw its audience from across the class spectrum. His concluding comments suggest that he is unconvinced by media claims that society is moving into a period of greater freedom and openness. It seems to Hall that the media have a tendency to close down and simplify social shifts and changes in attitude. He warns us against the media and their evasion of the *real* questions of class identity and class power.

What is worth noting about this piece is how far removed it is from any discussion of the Marxist problematic. Class is the focus and the media are targeted as the agencies of false consciousness, yet Hall withdraws from any direct reference to Marxist principles of alienation or base/superstructure. Marxism is not a straightforward conduit for Hall's thinking at this time, though it is a strong influence, and his disillusionment concerning the political scene is quite evident. He is pondering whether it is in fact possible to create a sense of political consciousness *outside* of the party political system. Is it possible to defy the system?

the summer of love

In 1967, British audiences were enthralled by a daring TV drama series called *The Forsythe Saga*. It was the year of *The Graduate*, and *Bonnie and Clyde*. *The Beatles* were cutting their *Sergeant Pepper* album. In April Paul McCartney flew out to see the crowds gathering in the Haight Ashbury district of San Fransisco. It was the Summer of Love and young people were making pilgrimages to the west coast city, turning on, tuning in and dropping out. In the heartland of western capitalism, a counter-culture was emerging. It challenged the US involvement in the Vietnam war, held protests and demonstrations against fascism, racism and nuclear defence strategies. It was the time and the place for free festivals, free food and free love. The Hippie movement represented a new social phenomenon in US culture. It was the most visible example of the many emerging counter-cultural groups and associations of the period. It was just the kind of phenomenon to attract the attention of those working at the Centre. Hall published his paper on the Hippies in 1968. It was subsequently published as a chapter *in Student Power* (1969).

This is an early example of the cultural studies writing from the Centre and is marked by its energy, engagement and fluidity. The piece draws upon the vibrant and contemporary scene in American culture and addresses the linguistic and metaphoric power of hippiedom and its significance as a counter- cultural movement. Hall recognises the political and class implications of this youth movement and takes it seriously – as an object worthy of analysis. However, it is important not just to describe Hippies, but to 'situate Hippies as a social formation within this set of structures' (1969: 193). While Hall acknowledges the habitual tendency to place Hippies as the peace-loving reaction to the more militant elements of the counter-culture, he observes that the 'meaning' of the Hippies extends far beyond that, into a wider spirit of political defiance of the system. They have effectively and 'without much conscious intention' evolved 'a set of *counter-values* to those of straight society. Despite their apparently patternless eclecticism, the latent value-system of Hippie society can be seen as a direct dialectical contraposing of alternative values to the sacred values of the middle class' (ibid.: 195). Where straight society is knowing, orderly and consumed with power, Hippie society offers naivety, spontaneity and love.

Hippies are engaged in a 'tactical withdrawal', which actively contests the dominant logic of affluent middle-class society by living out an alternative lifestyle. Simultaneously, Hall argues, the Hippies emerge as 'second or third wave partisans in a new kind of guerrilla warfare' that constitutes 'an attempt to *prefigure* a new kind of subjectivity' (Ibid.: 196). The Hippie movement is however unable to sustain a revolution because it is experienced at the personal and fragmented level of the individual against the system or the state. 'They are doomed to disappear' because they exist in a dialectical rather than transcendent relationship to the civic society they inhabit. They play out the negative scenario in which it is necessary, or may become necessary to 'drop out' of society. Thus the Hippies, according to Hall, offer a fleeting utopian glimpse of how the future could be. If we learn anything from the Hippie movement, it is the necessity of redefining and reorganising society so that the needs of individuals will be placed above the needs of capital;

> Men may not have to assert their right to 'do their own thing' – but that will be because society will have been made responsive to the authentic and spontaneous sources of the creative self. Men may not then want to deny society – but it will be because society is seen to be, and becomes, the transparent enactment of human freedom, rather than the prison-house of reification. (1969: 202)

The spirited conclusion to this article – that in their 'moment' Hippies began to anticipate and sketch in the revolutionary dream of a new society free from the tyranny of civil and political society – brings together the two important strategies in Hall's work. One must analyse from 'within' the culture, seeking to describe and interpret the phenomenal forms and practices. At the same time there is a political imperative at work. The point of analysis is not merely the construction and dissemination of knowledge, but the articulation of knowledge for change, be it social, cultural or political.

conclusion

Hall's writing in the late 1950s moves from indignation through pessimism to a more optimistic stance in the 1960s that coincides and is doubtless influenced by the wider social and political student movements of 1967 and 1968. As Hall's work starts to evolve on two fronts, the political and the academic, we see, in the activity of the Centre, a negotiation of both. There is no doubt that Hall's experiences within the New Left movement engendered a deep respect and enthusiasm for collaborative theoretical and political work. As the Centre becomes a hive of industry under Hall's leadership, he continues to argue the urgent need for a socialist political consciousness/agenda, which he sees as lacking in left wing politics of the period. But how is a radical politics to be achieved? As work at the Centre for Contemporary Cultural Studies begins to focus on the analysis of cultural phenomenal forms and questions concerning class, politics and the methods of interpretation, Hall becomes increasingly engaged in revising Marxism in order to look again at the base/superstructure model.

In Chapter 3, we will see how Hall's concentration on mass media forms and the function of television in particular, is driven forward by his anxieties around politics and the representation of social behaviours.

further reading

Mabey, R. (1967) (ed.) *Class: A Symposium*. Anthony Blond: London.
Nagel, J. (1969) (ed.) *Student Power*. Merlin Press: London.
Grossberg, L., Nelson, C. and Treichler, P. (eds) (1992) *Cultural Studies*. Routledge: New York.

3
_____

the media in question

But of course the real world is not outside of discourse; it's not outside of signification. It's practice and discourse like everything else. (Hall, quoted in Cruz and Lewis, 1994: 261)

introduction

In this chapter we will examine Hall's interpretations of Gramsci and Althusser, in order to explore his developing arguments concerning the ideological functions of the mass media. By examining his analyses of the mass media and their contexts, I intend to trace the development of Hall's argument concerning media activity and the political landscape. From the warnings given in *The Popular Arts* we can see how Hall's original concerns begin to find more cogent and sustained expression, particularly through his focus on television and the press.

As we saw in Chapter 1, Hall's primary areas of investigation focused on the post-war political climate, class identity, popular manifestations of political action beyond the electoral system and the role of the mass media. Although the Centre is probably best know for its ethnographic output, Hall's contribution in the 1970s is less specifically concerned with researching the emergence of subcultures and more inclined towards the productivity and function of the mass media, in particular the press and television.

manufacturing consent

The radical political climate of 1968 that briefly threatened the complacent institutional structures of western capitalism left its mark on education too. In the introduction to their edited to volume *The Manufacture of News* (1973) Stanley Cohen and Jock Young refer to the slogans daubed on the walls of Paris as counterparts to those found daily in the British national press. The comparison suggests that the institutionalised mass media boasts no more legitimacy as a signifying network of ideas and commonly held beliefs about the world, than does the graffiti on Parisian street corners. Though diametrically opposed, both media 'systems' of communication are engaged in the same activity; both seek to represent a particular reality through the production and representation of an image of society. This represents, perhaps, an early example of 'encoding' at work. The mass media 'provide the guiding myths which shape our perception of the world and serve as important instruments as social control'. Stuart Hall contributed three chapters to this edited volume, first published in 1973. His contributions date from 1970 to 1972 and demonstrate both a focused examination of the media and its relationship to dominance and deviance, and a more formalised method of analysis: 'The ideological concepts embodied in photos and texts in a newspaper, then, do not produce new knowledge about the world. They produce recognitions of the world as we have already learned to appropriate it' (Hall, 1970a: 154).

What does Hall mean by 'recognitions'? In order to recognise something, we must have encountered the object or relation in a previous encounter. Recognition, therefore, depends upon a subject position that is both relatively fixed and relatively stable. The difficulty with this relationship of the seer to the seen is that there is a tendency on the part of the seer to always try to fit the seen object or relation within an existing cognitive framework or map. Otherwise, we cannot make sense of it. The smaller the range of legitimised positions, the narrower the frame of reference for interpreting objects, relations or events. The shift in Hall's approach to the analysis of media forms tells us a lot about the influences on his thinking during the early 1970s. In contrast to his work on advertising with Paddy Whannel (1964), news media is analysed here in terms of its approximation to the dominant cultural and political status quo. However, the difference here doesn't lie in the choice of media forms or texts, it is instead Hall's interpretation that has undergone profound revision as a result of reading Barthes, Althusser and Gramsci. The analysis of news media does not proceed in natural succession from advertising, television or popular music. Hall's attention is drawn to news media as a direct consequence of his continuing examination of the political landscape of British society.

a world at one with itself

Hall critiques what he identifies as the inherent ideological properties of media practices from the 'journalistic folklore' (1970a: 147) imbibed by the copyeditor or journalist, to the 'inferred assumptions about society' (1970a: 148), which shape the manufacture of news itself. He is already working within a framework that references the Frankfurt School and, in particular, the work of Theodore Adorno. The problem as Hall sees it lies in the tendency of the mass media to align itself with the dominant consensual political culture. Those radical or disaffiliated sections of society seeking to challenge the status quo are routinely marginalised by the media as renegade and deviant groups engaged in meaningless activities. The concepts of bias or objectivity, so favoured by mass communications researchers in the United States, are of no particular relevance to this enquiry since the production of news does not rely on the good auspices of one or two individuals. Indeed, the objectivity of a particular newscaster or editor is no defence against the machinery of news production. It is rather the 'institutionalised ethos of the news media as source of hidden consensus', which Hall identifies as the central issue at stake.

> Areas of *consensus* cover the central issues of politics and power, the fundamental sanctions of society and the sacred British values. To this area belong the accredited witnesses – politicians of both parties, local councillors, experts, institutional spokesmen. (1970a: 150)

Given this relationship – between the media and the 'gatekeepers' on whom they depend for their stories and interviews – it is not difficult to see how those outside of this relationship are disenfranchised and misrepresented.

43

we are now at the crunch. For the groups and events upon which, increasingly, the media are required to comment and report, are the groups in conflict with this consensual style of politics. *But* these are precisely the forms of political and civil action which the media, by virtue of their submission to the consensus, are consistently unable to deal with, comprehend or interpret. (Hall, 1970a: 152)

Hall is astonishingly alert to what we might term the textual nature of reality. He sees the direct impact and consequences of an increasingly mediated world where the meaning of events becomes synonymous with their representation. Hall concludes with an example of the reporting of riots in Trinidad in 1969. The accredited witnesses or 'experts' on BBC radio were unable to explain the riots as anything other than an issue of law and order, and violence on the part of marauding youths, simply because they lacked the necessary context for the real political situation in the Caribbean:

> When faced with this sudden eruption of yet another incidence of political violence, the explanatory concepts of 'neo-colonialism' and 'native bourgeoisie' were not available – nor anything which could do duty for them – in the world of radio. (1970a: 152)

As with newspaper publishing, radio and increasingly television are media that depend upon immediacy of the event. However, without appropriate framework or context, the actuality of the here-and-now results in an ideologically distorted representation of events as they happen. This analysis of the news media's predilection for interpreting events according to the dominant consensual political landscape, is further developed in a seminal paper by Hall first published as a stencilled paper in 1972.

the determination of news photographs

At the conclusion of their chapter on advertising, Hall and Whannel state:

> The continual manipulation of language, and the manipulation which this implies of one group in society by another is an unhealthy and

44

dangerous trend. A free society means inevitably, a society in which people are encouraged to search for the truth, without mystification, substitution or distortion. (1964: 337)

Whereas many might contest such an argument on the basis that it undermines an audience's credibility by assuming an inability to determine truth from fantasy, it also suggests that there are no legitimate pleasures to be had from the consumption of advertising. Perhaps even more significant, is the prevailing assumption that the practice of advertising to manipulate language and create false scenarios is a *trend*. This suggests that there could indeed be other trends, depending upon social and cultural changes to the composition and management of society. If we compare this idea with Hall's argument in *The Determination of News Photographs*, we see another theoretical proposition emerging. Hall writes that 'the rhetoric of connotation saturates the world of events with ideological meanings. At the same time, it disguises or displaces this connection.' (1973a: 241)

Hall draws on Barthes' seminal terms of analysis, *denotation* and *connotation* in order to make the point that far from being a trend, the mode of representational strategies on the behalf of the news media is endemic within the mass media as a social structure. In other words, these are not trends, subject to minor inflections of taste or fashion. Rather, the practice of representation within the media is systematic, institutionalised, specific and ideological. Media practices thus reflect the internalised logic of a consensual approach to representation. The *structures* of the mass media and their close proximity to the institutions of power – government and industry – create the conditions for, and parameters within which, representation takes place. This shift in interpretation strengthens Hall's argument for the analysis of not just advertising, but news and by extension , all and any media production. Hall starts to grapple with the fundamentals of mediated representation itself. These moves toward a more Structuralist[1] account of media production owe much to the writings of Roland Barthes and increasingly also the work of Louis Althusser and Antonio Gramsci. This interest in the philosophical work of foreign' continental writers had a major impact on the direction of cultural studies at the Centre and further marked the break between British cultural studies as practised at Birmingham, and US mass communications sociology.

45

gramsci and the concept of hegemony

Gramsci's influence on Hall is enormous, not just in terms of his work on media, but also later in his reflections on political formations, particularly Conservative politics of the 1980s and the function of consensus. Gramsci died in prison in April 1937 but his work was not published in English until the late 1960s. Like Althusser, Gramsci[2] engaged in a reworking of Marxism in relation to contemporary politics. He was not the first to use the term 'hegemony' but this is the concept with which he is now readily identified. Whereas Lenin had adopted the term in order to describe a strategy for the peasant overthrow of the Tsar and his class, Gramsci proposed a new articulation of the term: he used hegemony to describe the very idea of leadership and its relationship between different classes. Hegemony thus describes the winning of consent in order to gain and maintain power. Consent, however, is not a fixed goal. It is a moment of power which is always contestible and that has to be constantly re-won. It is often assumed that hegemony relates to a position of stability but this is not true. Where there is hegemony, there must also be resistance. This distinguishes hegemonic power from coercion. Hegemony contains within itself the necessity of resistance. Ideological control may be achieved but it is not secure. Another advance on the idea of ideological power is derived from Gramsci's argument that while it is capitalism that is the dominant driving force within Western society, this need not always be so. Through the generation of 'organic intellectuals' (Gramsci, 1971: 15) it should be possible for a class to advance to a position of power and influence. Hegemony is not therefore the property of any one particular class formation, but a way of understanding the relations of domination and subordination *between* classes. Hegemony is a lived reality, not a utopian theory for working class emancipation. A successful class will have to broker compromises in order to achieve and maintain power. It must take into account the needs and interests of other classes if it is to succeed. In Chapter 6 we will examine how Hall used Gramsci's work to excavate the foundations of what Hall termed 'Thatcherism'. Though beset by criticism from many sections on the Left, it is that analysis for which Hall is most widely known.

Hegemony, then, rests on an idea of negotiated power whereby members of a class are able to persuade other classes that they share the same class interests. Crucially though, such consent is not won by the creation of false consciousness. There is a knowing aspect of hegemony that points to the subordinated class's willingness to collude and negotiate with the dominant power block. Hall's use of Gramsci's concept of hegemony in the early 1970s denotes a continued interest in the marshalling of power by class interests and the maintenance of the values of a capitalist system. Hence, Hall argues that there are real class issues at stake in the way that the media systematically reinforces a dominant world view of society and its dissenters. It is a dialectical relationship enabling those in power to maintain power while apparently giving the people exactly what they want.

The second key theorist influencing Hall was Louis Althusser. Although at first glance Althusser seems to be at odds with Gramsci, he similarly posed a relationship between people that took account of the material practices of people's lives. The challenge for Hall was how to reconcile the structural aspects of Althusser's theory with Gramsci's of idea of resistance.

althusser's theory of ideological and repressive state appartuses

Louis Althusser's important contribution to the development of theories of ideology is overshadowed within British cultural studies by Gramsci, whose work he drew upon. Althusser's focus on the superstructural institutions of the church, family, school, and the media (among others) tried to identify the material connections between ideas and relationships between people, and their daily structures. Like Gramsci, Althusser is interested in the composition of civil society. However, ideology, according to Althusser, promotes false consciousness and recruits people by a process of 'interpellation', or 'hailing'. We are, according to Althusser, 'always already subjects' who are *called into a relationship* with an ideological viewpoint. This suggests that although Althusser's vision of social formations is one based on structure, repression and pessimism, one might be capable of resisting the call. However, Althusser regrets that those who fight or teach against the system, are nevertheless crushed by it, and may even end

47

up colluding with the very practices they seek to resist. Ferguson (1998) makes the point that Althusser's major contribution to ideology theory lies in his suggestion that 'Ideology is not a pre-existent body of beliefs which are somehow imposed upon, or merely inculcated, hammered in to an unsuspecting and innocent mass of people. It is, instead, a process and relationship of living' (1998: 31). Althusser's premise lies in an understanding of ideology as something that we internalise and rationalise.

In short, Althusser's notion of interpellation supposes that the subject resides in expectation of the ideological call: that the call is then recognised by the subject; that the ideological call has a specific effect on the subject; and that all potential subjects exist in a similar state of equilibrium, ready for the call. We are, accordingly, entirely social beings formed within society without any innate sense of 'self'. This approach to ideology has its detractors and critics. In terms of Hall's utilisation of Althusserian principles, we can see how fruitful this becomes in relation in Hall's analysis of media production as a structured and *naturalising* process of representing the status quo to the audience at large. The tendency toward the reproduction of a dominant and consensual view of the social order therefore, 'systematically produces visible news stories' (1973: 236) and in so doing, necessarily represses and labels as 'deviant', alternative and non-consensual stories, truths and testimonies. The inability to register that which is repressed, is one of the criticisms Hall makes of Galtang and Ruge's research into news values. A list of what constitutes news values does not constitute analysis; it is descriptive not analytical. It does not ask the question 'why?' Why, for example, are élite persons élite?

Hall's analysis of media structures is a means of understanding power and control. The effect of these analyses is draw attention to the areas or resistance that constantly nibble away at the consensus. Towards the late 1970s, Hall effectively substitutes a vision of working class interests are subordinated with their apparent *consent*. The ideological role and function of the mass media thus becomes the focus of media studies work within the Centre.

working with UNESCO

Hall was commissioned by UNESCO[3] to analyse the state of British television in relation to arts and culture. The published report, entitled

'Innovation and Decline in the Treatment of Culture on British Television' sounded appropriate, but what UNESCO received was not exactly what it had anticipated. Although the report, publised in November 1971, runs to a substantial length, it is the fourth and final part which is of most interest to us here. In this section Halll discusses the very nature of television discourse itself, and in so doing challenges the parameters of the UNESCO enquiry. The very title of the document suggests that there is indeed a crisis around the representation of traditional and mainstream culture on the small screen.

television and its relationship to british culture

Hall begins by reflecting on television's deficiencies in comparison to cinema. Despite pointing out television's technical limitations, he is keen to remind us that television is still in its infancy and, given the huge leaps in technology already achieved, it is likely that 'Its great and significant work, in terms of which an aesthetic might be convincingly elaborated, remains to be accomplished' (1971: 80). This question of a televisual aesthetic resurfaces throughout the argument. Its primary importance lies in its relationship to other cultural forms. As such, television in the early 1970s did not command respect as an art form. Fundamental questions were on the daily agenda. How could such a medium adequately contribute to the nation's sense of its own culture? Did the television of high cultural art forms or events effectively devalue such artistic endeavours? Today these questions might appear to be redundant. There is probably not a single kind of human experience not expressed through television at some point or other. Ballet, opera and the concert chamber have all been the subject of televised broadcasts. Birth, death, sex and nudity are all part of the weekly schedule. Royal weddings and funerals are routinely broadcast by both public service and independent commercial broadcasters. But before we dismiss the question of form determining the value of content, consider how the internet is, in the early twenty-first century, typically demonised as a medium for the promotion of pornograph and violence. The internet is thriving as growing numbers of the population gain access to its services. The content varies hugely, from the indecent to the innocuous. The quality of the image varies according to your processor, it is even possible to download films aimed at a cinema audience to your hard drive. What might be possible within five or ten years' time? Yet within academic publishing, e-journals and home-pages are only just beginning to acquire respectability. In terms of UK research, publication online is still not officially recognised as a legitimate means of disseminating your work.

Although it may be difficult to imagine now, there was a time, within living memory, when people objected to independent television broadcasting state occasions. To do so, it was felt, would commercialise the event itself and lower the prestige value of the occasion. The issue of form is one still pertinent today and continues to inform public debate about new media technologies.

However, rather than stick at the issue of form as a sole determinant meaning, Hall moves through a sustained attack on Marshal McCluhan's position[4] regarding television's technical form, and seeks to argue that use-value is actually more significant than the hardware associated with television production itself. Hall is asking questions about television's function – its use-value – as a communicative form within society. McCluhan's well-publicised treatise on television as a 'cool medium' does not, according to Hall, answer the very question of television's social use: 'A social aesthetic depends, ultimately, not on the level of the 'hardware' but on the *human use of the hardware:* that is, on the form of its social appropriation, embedded in the different levels of social praxis' [Hall's italics] (1971: 84).

The technical development of any medium is not simply shaped by the technology itself, but by the needs and requirements of the society in which it is created. Technological development is, according to Hall, socially and economically determined. Hall draws upon issues central to a concern with the social and political determinants of culture in its widest sense. This appears therefore to be a very deterministic reading of television and its relationship to culture. Hall however resists a narrow conflation of ideas around the technical form of the medium's output. Nevertheless it is striking how little attention Hall gives to the idea of the individual viewer. He does, however, acknowledge the importance of understanding the role and function of the television producer. But this is not developed within his argument. This work would come later in his important paper entitled *Encoding Decoding*

(1973b). He is more concerned here with establishing the nature of television discourse itself.

television aesthetics

The early television of the 1960s and 1970s lacked quality in terms of definition, colour, tone and sound. Colour was only introduced in 1968. Despite this, a certain set of aesthetic principles governed the use of television sound and image. Close-ups and mid-shots were favoured over lone shots. The small screen was not the ideal space for lingering panoramic shots or remote figures in a landscape. Television was, and still is, a medium largely for the close and personal. Soap opera has been such a successful genre because it has made excellent use of television's technical and aesthetic limitations. Indeed we could even argue that soap opera actually did much to establish the aesthetic conventions of television production. Even state occasions and royal weddings are deemed incomplete without the emotional closeup, which once would have been deemed intrusive and unpardonable breach of etiquette.

It appears from Hall's arguments so far that television is an evolving medium with an uncertain future. He points to the advent of colour technology as evidence of a way in which the promotion of a particular technology worked against the democratic potential of this mass medium. Rather than pursue the refinement of the black and white image, which might one day equate with the aesthetic excellence of monochrome film, television research invested in the production of colour. The introduction of colour television sets proved very lucrative for manufacturers. However, this economic harvest was at the expense of the 'great heterogeneity of the majority audience' who could not afford the expensive luxury set and continued to view in black and white. This, Hall argues, has had the effect of undermining the achievements of television producers in evolving a television aesthetic. Consequently 'such ground is irrecoverable' (1971: 86). Hall is not so naïve however as to presume that television is therefore a failure and doomed never to evolve. He is merely pointing to one of the many technical features of broadcasting that has been realised, though at the

51

expense of other possible technical achievements. The push to colour effectively marginalised black and white television production before it had really come into its own as an art form. This is all part and parcel of a much larger question regarding the function of television within culture.

the cultural function of television

According to Hall's argument, television operates at two levels within culture. It produces its own cultural forms and it transmits a televisual version of existing forms. Hall characterises this 'canabalising medium' as 'a dirty medium', which manipulates existing raw material into processed packaged forms to be consumed by the audience. Hall does not credit television at this stage with great artistic merits or achievements in its own right: 'Television's power to "capture reality" in visual terms, and transmit it into the living room is, at the present time, *its dominant feature*' (1971: 92) (Hall's emphasis). Television's innate naturalism is a very powerful and dominant feature of its communicative value. Hall further points to the distinctions endemic to television production at this time.

High-brow cultural forms are transmitted with little reference to the elements of the medium, while low-brow or popular productions are scripted for the medium. Thus, an opera transmitted live from Convent Garden retains its aura as a high cultural form. The soap opera, by comparison, though it may be finely acted, well-written and lavishly produced, is, by virtue of its being written *for* television, understood to be a lower cultural form. Any television aesthetic is therefore 'massively interpenetrated by social values and relations' (1971: 98). Whereas this could easily become an argument for the redundancy of television in any artistic terms, Hall begins to build an argument for the credibility of a medium that, by becoming 'a sort of cinema', is able to do what cinema cannot. If television is indeed the product of its culture, could it not also become the space within which the culture is produced? By identifying the television aesthetic as one predicated on the everyday, could not this translation of the symbolic into the cultural be effected through making life into an art form?

Hall agrees with Walter Benjamin[5] that the traditional relationship between art and the audience has been destroyed. But in its place, why could we not have another equally resonant relationship of audience to art? Television could yet fulfil its potential and become the truly democratic medium.

> What is so striking, then, about the existing uses of television in the domain of art and culture is *its rooted anachronisms:* its playing over again of old tunes, its attempt to restore modes of deference, of dutiful attention, in a period and a medium which is beginning, in however contradictory a manner, to transcend them. (1971: 112) (Hall's emphasis)

Rather than emulate traditional art forms, television could be forging its own. Hall argues that television's function as a communicative art could be fully realised by actually raising everyday life into a artistic communication (1971: 111). Television culture is not comfortable with 'high art'. Hall signals an important messages; that television is in the grip of institutional, technical, political and economic structures which re-enact the same patterns of social exclusion and class power that characterise British society in general.

> Nowhere is it so clearly the case as in the domain of art and culture that television is, at present, a powerful mobilising mass medium of a special, and specially democratic kind, which is currently defined and used in sophisticated élitist ways. The images of an unintelligent audience, a homogenous mass of anonymous viewers, linked to the medium only by their common ignorance, which sustain so much television production, and of the privileged professional minoirty in its midst, are ideological fictions of a powerful sort which now constitute the major breaks and constraints on the development of television, of its intrinsic social and political qualities. (1971: 113)

Whereas UNESCO might have expected an analysis of television's relationship to art, and possible solutions to ensure that the medium maintains a commitment to broadcasting high cultural forms and events, Hall instead proposes a more radical policy. Television should cast off its elitist pretensions and engage with the everydayness of life: 'Television invites us, not to serve up the traditional dishes of culture "more effectively", but to make real the utopian slogan which appeared, in May 1968, adorning the walls of the Sorbonne. "Art is dead. Let us create everyday life"'(1971: 113). This rallying cry with which Hall concludes the report appears dated. However, it evokes the spirit of the times, and makes a determined bid for television as a signifying medium far exceeding, in political terms, the artistic supremacy of cinema.

I do not think however, that Hall was envisioning the docu-soaps of the late 1990s, or reality tv programmes like *Big Brother*. Be they hugely popular, such programmes do not constitute an elevation of everyday life into art. That television does not appear to have risen to the challenges is of course no reflection on Stuart Hall. Through his long association with arts councils, educational authorities and independent co-operatives Hall has championed the work of Black and Asian artists and film-makers working in Britain. Hall's collaborations with Issac Julien and his involvement with InIVA[6] are only some of the many examples of Hall's interest in and commitment to successive generations of artists, and the development of innovation within broadcasting and the visual arts.

the limits of broadcasting

Hall picks up many of the themes from the UNESCO report in a broadcast for Radio 3, Published in *The Listener* in March 1972. Hall reiterates his concern with the broadcasting institutions that seem to him to be both unwieldy and inyielding in their service to power. The article is an edited version of a much longer paper given at the *Fourth Symposium on Broadcasting Policy* at the University of Manchester in February 1972: 'Though exercising a wide measure of editorial autonomy, broadcasting must operate within the mode of reality of the state, and its outlook can't, in the last instance, transcend the ideological perspectives of society's dominant institutions.' (Hall, 1972a: pp. 328). The Althusserian influence on Hall is indicative of his more general position regarding broadcasting as a significant and pervasive ideological state apparatus. As such, broadcasting is caught in a 'double bind', wherein its statutory commitment to reporting the situation at large is at present clearly at odds with the maintenance of the status quo. Whereas earlier Hall argued that the media were fundamentally unable to represent alternative positions, which exceeded the boundaries of consensual discourse, he now states that they do not least attempt to convey some of the conflict in play. This is another attempt on the part of Hall to get away from the idea of bias and objectivity. He is still very much concerned with institutional power and its forms.

deviancy, politics and the media

At the British Sociological Association Annual Conference in 1971, Hall gave a paper that attempted to look at the issue of media dominance from the other end of the telescope. From this point on, Hall is able to begin examining the modes of representation that are structurally dominant in the formation of legitimate and deviant social and political questions and organisations. The question of deviance arises out of a sustained engagement with the radical politics of different groups acorss the world as they pose an alternate relationship to capitalism and its globalising tendencies. The political upheavals of 1968, and the social and political turmoil which wad created in their wake, are of great interest to Hall. They represent more than just a wave of disaffected and disgruntled student anarchist groups. What Hall and his colleagues at the Centre were increasingly drawn to investigate was the variant ways in which such disaffiliation from consensual capitalist politics was represented within and by the mass media.

In *Deviancy, Politics and the Media*, Hall dismisses tradional sociological enquiries into the nature and formation of deviancy on the grounds that they do not, with some exceptions, take adequate account of the role of ideology and power. To reiterate an earlier point, it is not a question of bias or the occasional manipulation of the truth. Hall is arguing that the systematic and ideological functionings of media practice determine what is, and what is not, deviant. Categorisations of deviancy are thus legitimated and disseminated through the media. The apparent increases in deviant activity may in reality reflect the increasing tendency of the media to use this categorisation. As Hall sees it, within western societies there seems to be a steady move toward the politicisation of fragmentary groups and associations. Such groups are routinely marginalised and vilified by the dominant political systems of western democracy. Hall is less concerned to identify the difference between the dominant and marginalised use of campaigns, actions and demonstrations as evidence of political will. He is much more concerned by the ways in which *any* and *all* political activity beyond that of 'politics', in its narrowest hegemonic sense, is routinely subject to ideological media analysis. Such analysis determines to a large degree whether the political actions in question are deemed legitimate, though expressed by and on behalf of a minority, or deviant, and therefore extremist and lacking legitimate grievance.

It is perfectly possible for a minority group to enter the political fray with what are recognised by the state as 'genuine' concerns or grievances. Such groups are no threat to the hierarchy and may, with relative safety, articulate their concerns. However it is those counter-cultural groups who want to explicitly challenge the system who are disenfranchised.

> Typically, such groups do not seek to advance their cause via the traditional access to elite influence; they do not seek to enhance their position within the system of political bargaining. Instead they embrace militant, activist, 'extremist' political tactics, and explicitly challenge the system itself and its 'rules of the game'. Their technique of protest and dissent contravenes the norms of political legitimacy which institutionalises political conflict (1971: 13)

Such groups are stigmatised by the mass media.

> They are especially sensitive to the hidden mechanisms by which the dominant system wins and manipulates consent to its own hegemony – socialisation through the family and secondary institutions, the manipulative content and constraints of the education process, the creation of an environment of consensus in the mass media. That is, their position makes them acutely sensitive to the spheres of ideological domination and coercion (1971: 13)

Althusser's ideological state apparatus model underpins this argument and confers a strong sense in which such resistance is dangerous because it invites the state powers to use coercion in order to secure control. However, as Hall rightly points out, such control is never totally secured. Hall identifies capitalism as one of the root causes of such insurgence. 'Conflict politics' is directly counterposed against consensus politics. Though the very idea of 'consensus' sounds fair and democratic, it is really the continued exercise of power, over 'so-called pluralist' society, by an élite class (1971: 14). The role of the mass media within such a society is to shape the prevailing wisdom of the situation.

Such power – to control the meaning of situations as they evolve – leaves the viewer relatively powerless. The agents of hegemonic representation cut across the traditional party political boundaries. Politicians and trade unionists are equally complict with this strategy. Those who are in position of power and influence are in turn reliant on the agency of the mass media who largely control the 'means of signification' (1971: 19).

Hall's case studies focus on two student demonstrations orchestrated in 1968 and that were reported by the media in various interesting ways. The reporting of 'militant confrontations between students and university authorities at the LSE[7]', and a sit-in at the University of Birmingham, arise out of the use of the 'majority/minority paradigm'. The media is unable to account for the explosion in student activity during this period, and why it has developed in such a militant way. The media therefore seek to make explicable these phenomenal events within existing ideological terms, consistently labelling such actions as being due to particular, unrepresentative (minority) and dangerous factions who must be stopped.

> Thus, minorities become 'extremists', and, in the course of time, accrete a variety of other qualitative attributes: they are 'hooligans' ... 'a hooligan clique' ... 'wreckers' ... 'agitating adolescents' ... 'cabal' ... 'thugs' ... 'adolescent hooligans' ... 'mentally disturbed' ... 'a smash-now-and-think-later caucus' ... 'outside agitators' ... 'rowdies' ... 'plotters'. (Hall, 1972b: 26–7)

Through such accounts of systematic marginalisation, the forces of ideological power are able to appeal to the presumedly moderate majority: 'In almost all cases, the minority/ majority paradigm attempts to build a coalition between the moderates and the agencies of control' (ibid.: 27). By winning over the consent of the majority, the minority voices are disenfrachised even further. Hall argues persuasively that this mode of signification has become a deeply embedded structure (ibid.: 28). But such a rhetorical paradigm also has deeply disturbing and far-reaching consequences.

> Its use has certainly also been a common feature of the process of public signification associated with developments in Northern Ireland. With respect, especially to events in Ulster since the later

months of 1970, this paradigm has indeed attained the status of a 'self-fulfilling prophecy', with the emergence of the IRA[8] stigmatised, split off from and counterposed to the vast majority of 'good and reasonable folk' of both religious persuasions in Ulster, whose grievances are being exploited for the pursuance by a tiny minority of a 'holy war' against Stormont, Whitehall, the army and forces of moderation and reform. Indeed, the emergence of the IRA – a known, labelled, stigmatised, extremist group, committed to the polices of armed insurrection and physical force – has powerfully crystalised and simplified the complex problems of signifying the Ulster crisis to British public. (Hall, 1972b: 29–30)

Hall goes on to argue candidly that the fact of the IRA's existence has enabled the British government of the day and the other 'agencies of signification' such as the public relations personnel within the British army, and the media in general, to:

extract, isolate and stereotypify a small, organised band of 'foreign' insurgents, committed to violence against the state, from the complex structure of exploitation, disenfranchisement and oppression of the Ulster minorities, and behind that, from the interlocking complex of immediate class-rule at Stormont and distant colonial oppression in the continuing links between Britain and the Protestant ascendancy. (Hall, 1972b: 30)

Hall is arguing that understanding the conditions that led to events in Ulster, and tracing the development of dominant notions of rule and oppression, are beyond the scope of a media industry that is so ideologically bound to the power relations of the state and the maintenance of the status quo. 30 years on from the events of 'Bloody Sunday',[9] debate has continued in the wake of the latest UK government enquiry into the events that led to the British Army killing 13 civilians during a civil rights demonstration in Derry. These events were recently brought to public attention again by the screening of two drama-documentaries, *Sunday* and *Bloody Sunday* in January 2002 on British television.

The actions of the army have long been called into question. The massacre signalled the end to the civil rights movement in Northern Ireland. 'Bloody Sunday' is now credited as the beginning of a push toward sustained paramilitary action. The IRA recruited hundreds of young men to its cause as a result of the British Army's response to civil demonstrations.

Hall is not condoning violence. He is not condoning the actions of the IRA. What he is pointing to, is the systematic ideological processes of media signification which create and maintain structures of differences, and in so doing, *create those very conditions for* deviant behaviour. Hall's piece is, by anyone's standards, a very courageous analysis. It opens up new avenues for considering the cause and effects of deviance within a changing British political landscape. Hall stresses the need to look at contemporary society and its moments of historical significance. The mass media is engaged in great ideological 'labour' (ibid.: 42); sometimes the rhetoric lies dormant, awaiting events to unleash them. At other times, the media must manufacture new definitions in order to achieve the 'ideological bricolage' (ibid.: 42) that enables them to classify the political world in a meaningful way.

> In crisis moments, when the ad-hoc formulas which serve, 'for all intents and purposes', to classify the political world meaningfully and within the limits of legitimacy are rendered problematic, and new problems and new groupings emerge to threaten and challenge the ruling positions of power and their social hegemony, we are in a specially privileged position to observe the work of persuasive definition in the course of its formation. (Hall, 1972b: 43)

There is a sense of vigilance here. Hall communicates urgency, a necessary awareness and a commitment to exploration, all of which characterise his idea of research. It is also a vision of the academic life which invites, even demands, that the researcher make swift and timely interventions within public debates. Research is not for a small group of like-minded intellectuals, but food for debate within the wider world. The academic investigation of phenomena is but a focused forum for the exploration of public life. In tandem with his analyses of deviance, Hall would shortly make an even more important intervention into the debate around television and its structures, through his analysis of the audience's responses to it.

the move towards the audience

Hall describes the period of the early 1970s in the life of the Centre in terms of its 'break' from orthodox and established theories of mass communications research. He describes the energy and commitment of those working there who embraced, not un-problematically, new ideas in order to construct new theoretical approaches, drawing upon early semiotics, psychoanalysis, structuralism and discourse theory.

In addition to the new methods of semiotics applied to the analysis of texts, audience research was gathering pace. Through their ethnographic studies, members of the Centre had nominally been engaged in audience research for nearly ten years. This is a particularly contentious area within British cultural studies. While many studies (Morley, 1980; Winship, 1980; Buckingham, 1987) have been important, for some, the very idea of the audience as a constituted body has been challenged (Hartley, 1992). Hall's contribution to the research was to theorise what people actually do when they watch television. The resulting paper entitled *Encoding/Decoding* is one of his best known works. It has provoked a number of critical reactions over the years. Among them, McGuigan (1992) stands out as the most critical.

encoding/decoding

First published by the Centre as a stencilled paper in 1973, it has often been revised and is available in many different forms. The extract that appears in *Culture, Media, Language* (1980b) gives the main points of argument and attempts to discuss the relationship between the producer of the media text and the consumer. I refer to this version as it is more widely available than the original stencilled document. Hall begins characteristically with a criticism of the traditional mass communications concept of media communication as a linear form, traditional mass communications concept of media communication as a linear form, in which the targeted audience for the message is a passive recipient. However, given the influence of Gramsci and Althusser, Hall's response is to look for a more complex structure of relations, one that would more satisfactorily 'explain' the relationship between producer and receiver as one acknowledging the activity of both. Hall is searching for a 'complex structure of dominance'; one which, in parallel with his thinking on Marxism, will offer an insight into the use of specific forms enabling the flow of communication. We can see how

60

Hall's thinking around issues of hegemonic relationships pushes the notion of the audience to a more active role than previously characterised by American mass communications studies. It is nevertheless a structure that prioritises the notion of dominance.

Hall is interested in the different forms and moments of communication between the producer and the audience via the mediated text of the television programme itself. Essentially Hall is arguing that the process of communication consists of many different and related moments in which a 'passage of forms' takes place. His description of the 'codes/syntagmatic chain of discourse' (1980: 128), is an elaborated formula, which appears overly technical and abstract. The argument begins with the point that an audience encounters the text as a *discursive form*. Hall is arguing that the form created by the producers of the text is necessarily different from the form in which the text is enjoyed and consumed. This is due to the different circumstances and conditions of production from consumption.

If we think for example of an episode from a soap opera, the production of the text may depend upon or be constrained by technical factors, such as the availability of daylight, the choice of location for outside shooting, the budget for a particular episode involving specific props or sequences, choice of director and casting, among many others. Added to this are the conventions of professional practice and in-built assumptions and values, such as decisions over the choice of mid or close-up shot, pace of editing for particular sequences, and the standard ways of lighting the subject. A television director who wishes to convey intense emotion within a particular scene will, in conjunction with the lighting director and the actor, decide on the best way for the subject to be lit – in shadow, from above or below, inside or outside – in order to create the desired effect. The pace and use of conventional or unconventional patterns of editing will also effect the overall meaning of the scene and communicate to the audience the charged nature of the relationship on screen. Taken altogether the construction of a particular sequence of events on screen is complex and subject to an enormous number of different professional, practical and technical factors. We also need to consider the ideological aspects of production. How are women typically represented on screen compared to men? How many characters in this soap opera are from ethnic minority backgrounds by comparison to the actual demographics for the city being represented?

Once the text has been produced, its reception on the part of the audience will occur in different circumstances and will be subject to different criteria. An audience will not generally be looking at the production methods but the content. We may not be alert to the subtle variations in camera shots between close-ups and extreme close-ups because we are concerned with the emotional exchange itself and how it tells us more about the particular character. Equally, we are unlikely to pause to consider the acting style of an *actor*, when we are caught up in the dilemmas of his *character*. For the purposes of understanding the relationship between producer, audience and text, we therefore need to understand how a text exists in different forms at each moment of the communicative process. To give another example, a sports event happening in real time is not in the same identical form as that shown on television. The television *form* of the event enables us to see replays, show motions, inter-cutting shots of other players and close-ups of the manager's face. All this is part of the selectively re-packaged and mediated, textual version of a real sporting event.

It is common for people to assume that consumption is a passive act. We just sit in front of the television and consume without engagement or activity. However Hall is arguing that consumption is not a passive act because consumption requires the generation of meaning. Without meaning, there can be no consumption. Meaning, in turn, cannot be generated passively. We do not passively receive meaning – we have to create it ourselves. This activity is another moment in the chain of moments to which Hall is referring. At the point at which we see the mediated televisual text, we begin to process the signs, sounds and images as meaningful text. How a text is created does not necessarily guarantee the manner of its reception, because audiences can embrace or reject a text. No particular moment in the chain of events guarantees the next moment.

Despite the uncertainty of the audience's response, the structure of relations does inscribe the text with a measure of dominance. An episode of a soap opera does not occupy the same space within the schedule as the news, and our cultural privileging of the soap opera as a particular genre of entertainment determines to a large extent the way in which audiences engage with it. Hence the text itself has a privileged position in relation to the audience because it 'determines to a large extent the mode of its reception and the conditions of its articulation'

(1980: 129). We talk about soap operas differently than we do the news. We have different expectations regarding its content, appeal and mode of address. However, the audience is not obliged to interpret and understand the text exactly as it was intended. The margin for difference between the manner and mode of production and reception can be narrow, or in some cases, exceptionally wide. What some producers imagine to be serious and important may be readily construed by the audience as ironic, funny or even offensive. Nothing is guaranteed.

encoding the televisual discourse

Hall is interested in understanding television as a mode of production. The broadcasting institutions are engaged, as he sees it, in the production of meaningful discourses that are 'encoded' within the text. What Hall refers to as the 'technical' infrastructure, frameworks of knowledge and relations of production' all combine to effect the realisation of the text. An actor wants to communicate an emotion; a director wants to 'say' something about a social issue; the broadcaster wishes to fulfil a remit to supply programmes of an educational nature. These communicative acts rely on a shared understanding of language and culture. The text thus embodies the shared linguistic field of discourse between producer and audience. While it is true that a French-speaking audience might find some meaning in a British situation comedy, much of the humour and most of the nuances of meaning will be lost because of the linguistic and cultural differences between France and Britain. Thus the text makes an appeal to the audience as a 'meaningful discourse' (1980: 130). However, the 'meaning structures' within the text require the action of the audience: in isolation, without an audience, the text is meaningless.

decoding the televisual text

'Decoding' the text is also highly dependent upon the 'frameworks of knowledge, relations of production and technical infrastructure' of the audience. The process appears to be symmetrical. However the degrees of difference in the process of decoding often constitute 'a lack of fit' because of the 'structural difference of relation and position' between the broadcaster and the audience. This is in fact an in-built 'asymmetry between the codes of "source" and "receiver" at the moment of transformation into and out of the discursive form' (1980: 131). If we take the example of soap opera again, we can see how the audience's prior knowledge of the text can determine meaning. Knowledge of the previous episodes, relationships between characters and possibly what they have already read in the tabloid press or fanzines about this week's episode will all have a bearing on how the audience constructs meaning from the text and 'decodes' the messages within it. In some instances, audiences know storylines well in advance of transmission. Any surprise value intended by the producers may then be lost on the audience, and replaced instead by a knowingness and a different kind of expectation. More often in the case of other genres such as news or drama however, it is the text that is more knowing than the audience. These apparent 'distortions' of meaning that occur are the result of a 'lack of equivalences' between producer and audience. This is due to the different weighting given to the production of text as a source of its legitimacy and authority. The audience, however, has its own strategies for resistance.

Hall elaborates on his use of the term 'code – a term which is introduced into linguistic analysis by Roland Barthes – in order to distinguish between those moments when the message of the text is created by the producer, and interpreted by the audience. This enables Hall to identify a 'dominant cultural order', where as a society we share a range of understandings about the meaning of particular signs, terms, images and sounds. This shared sense of our culture enables us to communicate, but it also imposes an established dominant view of how things are, and by inference, how things should be. This point about dominance is crucial to Hall's argument:

> The different areas of social life appear to be mapped out into discursive domains, hierarchically organised into *dominant or preferred meanings*. New, problematic or troubling events, which breach our expectancies and run counter to our 'common-sense constructs', to our 'taken-for-granted' knowledge of social structures, must be assigned to their discursive domains before they can be said to 'make sense'. ([Hall's emphasis] 1980: 134)

Hall is undertaking a number of different tasks in this argument. He draws upon his experience and understanding of how the media function in relation to the strange and the new. His earlier papers discussed above, which explored the news media, have enabled him to see the problem in close-up. His readings of Gramsci and Althusser enable him to revisit the question of dominance within the context of media production and consumption, and to quiz the idea of a straightforward linear communication. The influence of Gramsci can be detected in his choice of phrase, 'common-sense'. It is Gramsci who posits the idea of hegemony as a kind of common-sense, whereby a governed people internalise the ideas of their leaders and come to understand them as shared concerns, rather then imposed ideas. The very mode of reception that Hall is promoting is one based on that Gramscian idea of common values between the dominant leaders of a society and those it seeks to rule. It is not a coercive relationship. Nor does it equate to a propagandist model. There must after all be a modicum of recognition on the part of the audience for any media message to be successfully decoded as it was intended. Propaganda works on the basis that is the *only* possible truth. Hall identifies media communication as one firmly rooted in hegemonic practice.

> In speaking of *dominant meanings*, then, we are not talking about a onesided process which governs how all events are signified. It consists of the 'work' required to enforce, win plausibility for and command as legitimate a *decoding* of the event within the limit of dominant definitions in which it has been connotatively signified ([Hall's emphasis] 1980: 135).

Hall is pains to point out that it is not just at the level of audience that a subjective position comes into play. Media production itself, though professionalised and institutionalised, also emanates from a subjective position in its interpretation of an event to be televised. The ideal position of the audience for the broadcaster therefore is the 'dominant-hegemonic position', whereby audiences share the same subject position as the producer. The communication of an event's meaning is therefore relatively seamless, and can appear natural, legitimate and common-sensical. When audiences 'mistakenly' comprehend a television programme's meaning, it is because they are not 'operating within the "dominant" or "preferred" code' (1980: 135). Such an audience might be operating within a 'negotiated code or position' or even 'oppositional code'. This does not mean that the

65

audience is mistaken. A struggle for meaning occurs when the audience's reading runs contrary to the dominant messages encoded within the text.

To give a contemporary example, a televised broadcast of a royal state occasion may be constructed within a dominant-hegemonic position that decrees such occasions to be traditional, solemn, in the national interest and worthy of national and international broadcast. A negotiated position would see the audience accept some parts of the equation, for instance the idea of tradition and respect for monarchy, but perhaps a rejection of the personalities of the royals themselves. An oppositional position hears 'respect for monarchy' and 'national interest' but may understand and interpret these from within an alternate framework that dismisses such ideas as 'class privilege'.

implications for media studies

The encoding/decoding thesis has had a long history within media studies and prompted numerous responses and counter-arguments (see Morley, 2002). This is not least because some have assumed that Hall was speaking in terms of a rigid sociological model for analysis. This goes against the grain of Hall's thinking.

> The encoding/decoding model wasn't a grand model. I had in my sights the Centre of Mass Communications Research – that was who I was trying to blow out of the water. I didn't think of it as generating a model which would last for the next twenty-five years for research. I don't think it has the theoretical rigour, the internal logic and conceptual consistency for that. If it's of any purchase, now and later, it's a model because of what it suggests. It suggests an approach; it opens up new questions. It maps the terrain. But it's a model which has to be worked with and developed and changed. (Hall, quoted in Cruz and Lewis, 1994: 255)

Despite Hall's cautious judgment on the limitations of the model, we can see in the publishing aftermath, that this was the moment when media studies went *textual*. Furthermore, Hall's work in 'Encoding Decoding' clearly brings together the previous arguments rehearsed in the UNESCO report, and other articles and papers from the early 1970s. The issue of deviancy, however, is another strand of Hall's thinking that would have a significant impact upon his own work and the work of many of his students. Analyses of deviancy provided the pivotal space for bringing together the practice of media studies and the sociological concerns of cultural studies.

conclusion

In this chapter we have seen how Hall's work through the early 1970s began to move toward an increasingly complex analysis of the functions of the mass media. At the same time Hall reviews and refines his articulation of ideology and dominance, through an engagement with the work of Gramsci and Althusser. He is influenced by the writings of Barthes and traces the semiological function of text through examples drawn from press and television. He is committed to a systematic analysis of television's functions and sees the necessity of developing an appropriate method for the analysis of both forms and the communicative process.

We can summarise Hall's position in the following ways. Hall renounces categorically the American behaviourist models of media research in favour of an approach which prioritises form *and* meaning. Hall thus investigates questions about how to 'do' media studies. Reading Gramsci and Althusser has a profound effect on his thinking and, consequently, Hall's work increasingly reflects on the function of the media as agents of ideological practice. While he is particularly anxious to explore the notion of hegemony, Hall is also engaged in a long term project concerning the notion of deviance as a category of political, and therefore ideological, importance. In the next chapter we will explore in greater depth the ways in which Hall engages with Althusserian and Gramscian concepts in relation to class, ideology and the mass media.

further reading

Althusser, L. (1971) *Lenin and Philosophy*. New Left books: London.

Cohen, S. and Young, J. (1973) (rep. in 1980) *The Manufacture of News.* Constable: London.

Cruz, J. and Lewis, J. (1994) *Viewing, Reading, Listening, Audiences and Cultural Reception*. Westview Press: Oxford.

Gramsci, A. (1971) *Selections from the Prison Notebooks*. Lawrence and Wishart: London.

Hall, S., Hobson, D., Lowe, A. and Willis, P. (eds) (1980) *Culture, Media, Language.* Hutchinson: London.

Simon, R. (1982) *Gramsci's Political Thought.* Lawrence and Wishart: London.

McGuigan, J. (1992) *Cultural Populism.* Routledge: London.

Morley, D. (2002) *Television, Audiences and Cultural Studies.* Routledge: London.

wrestling with the angels

But my own experience of theory – and Marxism is certainly a case in point – is of wrestling with the angels – a metaphor you can take as literally as you like. (Hall, 1992: 279)

introduction

Hall has stated clearly that his entry into cultural studies from the New Left was never synonymous with a straightforward Marxist position. This is precisely because the New Left 'regarded Marxism as a problem, as trouble, as danger, not as a solution' (1992: 278). He rejects absolutely the idea that British cultural studies and Marxism were an exact and inevitable 'fit'. Hall goes even further in his characterisation of his own theory:

> I remember wrestling with Althusser. I remember looking at the idea of 'theoretical practice' in *Reading Capital* and thinking 'I've gone as far in this book as it is proper to go.' I felt, I will not give an inch to this profound misreading, this super-structuralist mistranslation, of classical Marxism, unless he beats me down, unless he defeats me in spirit. He'll have to march over me to convince me. I warred with him to the death. (Hall, 1992: 280)

This chapter will focus on the intellectual and theoretical problems that Hall faced as he sought to develop what he later termed 'a complex Marxism'.

a decade of discontent

The post-war settlement was tested to its limits during the 1970s. Soaring world oil prices were accompanied by rising unemployment, higher interest rates and increasing government debt. Capitalism was in crisis worldwide. The resistance movements of the 1960s had craved revolution and freedom. The 1970s brought neither. Britain faced one economic crisis after another. The Tory government elected under Heath in 1970 was no more enlightened than the Wilson administration concerning a solution. The world recession instigated by the oil crisis of 1973[1], had a major impact on manufacturing industries. Britain was already losing its share of the world trade market and insufficient levels of fuel led to the introduction of the three-day working week. The trade unions launched campaigns for new pay claims. There was an upsurge in civil disturbance.

The tensions around black immigration, which had been apparent in the late 1950s, now became a matter of extreme concern. In the 1950s black Commonwealth citizens were actively encouraged to come to Britain and take up work. All members of the Commonwealth were entitled to emigrate to the 'mother country'. However, one of the consequences of the race riots in Britain in 1958 was the introduction, in 1962, of legislation removing this right of residency. This marked a profound shift in thinking regarding Commonwealth citizens, who were now placed in the same category as other migrant workers. In 1968, it was no longer legal for Black UK passport holders to enter Britain unless they had parents or grandparents already in residence there. In 1971 the government passed a further Immigration Act identifying all Commonwealth citizens as alien immigrants. They would only be allowed entry on a permit for a specific job. At the same time, racial discrimination was targeted by successive governments over the 1960s and 1970s with the introduction of the Race Relations Board, and anti-discrimination legislation in 1965 and 1968. The 1968 Race Relations Bill was resisted by many. Chief among them was the Conservative MP for Wolverhampton SW, Enoch Powell. Powell was committed to a policy of repatriation for non-whites. In an infamous speech to the West Midlands Conservative Political Centre in Birmingham, he spoke of the dangers of black immigration, and called for an immediate cessation of immigration. His vision of Britain's future was both alarmist and racist: 'As I look ahead, I am filled with foreboding; Like the Roman, I seem to see "the River Tiber foaming with much blood"'[2]. The response was immediate. The Prime Minister, Edward Heath declared that the speech was 'racialist in tone and liable to exacerbate racial tensions' and sacked Powell from the Cabinet. He was not, however, expelled from the Conservative Party. Public opinion was divided over Powell's words. Some minor protests were staged in support of Powell, and many Black and Asian families were subjected to increased violence and verbal abuse. Despite its liberal intentions, the idea of anti-racial discrimination legislation does not address the fundamental political, economic and social inequalities of black workers. Such efforts run the risk of ascribing all the problems of the black community to racial prejudice. This then ignores the need to look at the structural and endemic causes of black disadvantage within society.

The Women's Liberation Movement was gaining in strength and significance. The distinction between sex and gender offered up new ways of thinking about gender discrimination and the place and function of women within western society. The Equal Pay Act (1970) and the Sex Discrimination Act (1975) went some considerable way towards addressing the issues of women in the workforce, though important exclusions concerning tax, pension rights and unemployment benefits mitigated against some of the apparent concessions already won.

The number of unemployed school leavers rose from 7.1 per cent in 1970 to 30.4 per cent in 1971. Attempts to revive the economy by increased public spending proved to be only temporary. The Keynesian economic policies of the post-war consensus had reached crisis point. The bitter and protracted miners' strike of 1974 brought down the Heath government and the large industrial and manufacturing unions were viewed by many on the political Right as too powerful and beyond government control. By 1976, Britain had to suffer the indignity and humiliation of applying to the International Monetary Fund for a loan.

Hall recalls this era in terms of the collapse of post-war consensus politics:

I think there is more direct confrontation in the 1970s. There is more of a politics of confrontation in all these areas – race, gender. The basic case for women's equality has been made. But now you get organised Feminism confronting the institutions which don't want to be changed. You get the police defending communities against young blacks – there is a sharpening of the contradictions. It was the last gasp of the old politics with new elements mixed in it.[3]

Elsewhere Saturday afternoon violence on the terraces escalated into full-scale rioting. A new social phenomenon was 'born': 'football hooliganism'. Youth cultures were often and routinely perceived by the press as dangerous threats to civilisation. Football hooliganism was particularly significant because it was a high profile display of a particular class resistance to the post-war bourgeois shaping of football culture. It is an area of deviance that merited much sociological, media and political attention over the 1970s and 1980s.

As the crisis deepened, so did the responses from across the political spectrum. Pressure groups and lobbies may have been successful in confronting racist and sexist legislation, but this did not lead to a smooth transition of attitudes within the cultural and social environments of state institutions such as the police, judiciary and education. The 1970s thus generated a 'politics of confrontation' (Hall, 2002) that led to a 'sharpening of contradictions' between the rhetoric of public life and the reality of the street. It was these 'contradictions' that fuelled so much of the investigations by Hall and his colleagues at Birmingham during this period; work that culminated in the publication of *Policing the Crisis* in 1978. But *how* to talk about these problems was also a big question. Could Marxism provide the terms of reference for such a task? Media studies at the Centre was about to enter a period of sustained theoretical focus. Hall describes this centripetal movement as the genesis of a 'complex Marxism', requiring a committed 'plunge into theory' and involving many 'detours' and struggles (1992: 280). Hall's writings on the problems of Marxism give a flavour of this struggle. These are not simply theoretical hypotheses. The scope of Hall's arguments concerning Althusserian structuralism, amongst other questions, have direct bearings on the way he advances a critique of both media practice and the use of media representation. Sim (2002) offers an excellent overview of the different paradigmatic shifts occurring within Post-Marxism at this time.

a complex marxism

Hall expresses great frustration at what he sees as the paucity of Marxist scholarship available to English readers. So many texts, available in German, were yet to be translated into English in the early 1970s. Nevertheless, there was strong evidence of a resurgent interest in variant strands of Marxist thinking, which precipitated conferences and meetings, to debate the different evolving Marxisms. In 1971, the Centre hosted a symposium entitled 'Situating Marx'. This was in response to many questions and problems regarding the utility of Marxism within contemporary culture. Could Marxism still provide the necessary means of understanding modernity?

In what Hall himself describes as 'a long rambling piece' (1992: 279), he draws attention to Marx's method of critique and in so doing, demonstrates the points of convergence and divergence with his own position (Hall, 1973). Hall's analysis of Marx's *Introduction to the Grundrisse*, is a difficult and lengthy treatise. Hall states clearly that Marx does not argue for abstraction, but seeks to identify specific historical moments and the conditions and forms that generate and permit the existence of specific labour-production relations. It is therefore better, Hall argues, to examine what enables a specific historical reality to come into being rather than trying to establish the general laws of reality. This is an attack on 'vulgar' 'political economy theory', which Hall denounces as a kind of 'essentialism' (1973: 7). The main point of argument here is that according to Marx, and to Hall, political economy has characterised the capitalist mode of production as an inevitable and natural economic state. To counter this method of analysis, Hall reminds us that there is no such thing as 'production in general', only production within a specific context and constructed out of particular historical-economic conditions. It is precisely because such conditions are historically contingent upon 'determinate conditions' that there can be no sure way of predicting the continuation of those same conditions. In Hall's own words,

> There can be no guarantee, outside history, outside its specific, concrete conditions, that those conditions will always be fulfilled, or remain constant through time. [ ] (Later, in *Capital*, Marx is to remind us that this transformation of feudal bondsmen into 'free labour',

which appears as a 'natural' precondition for capitalism, has, indeed a specific history: 'the history of ... this expropriation is written in the annals of mankind in letters of blood and fire': *Capital* I p. 715) This is one of the key points-of-departure of historical materialism as a method of thought and practice. (Hall, 1973: 9)

History is traditionally taught as a linear progression from one epoch to the next, with scant attention to the ruptures, breaks and discontinuities that determine the socio-economic conditions for each successive era. History therefore teaches us that each era of 'progress' brings us closer to civilisation. Hence a tendency to think in terms of Western Enlightenment[4] and of an increasingly liberal secular society as being an improvement on what went before. But this is kind of history is fundamentally bourgeois in its attachment to *a priori* assumptions. It is important to add here that if we wish to argue for the particularity of production, we must also necessarily rethink the generality of life. The idea of 'life' cannot be articulated either as a smooth continuum, or as the unproblematic background against which production unfolds.

Hall consistently urges that cultural studies must be *about* something. There must be something at stake: 'It does matter whether cultural studies is this or that' (Hall, 1992: 278). Indeed there is a lot at stake in Hall's work, which is what makes it so important within cultural studies and beyond. By articulating these precise details concerning Marx's method of critique, we get closer to the real questions about how knowledge is determined, how media institutions function within a dominant culture and how common-sense wisdoms about the world become embedded in real practice. This is important groundwork for Hall's cutting-edge analysis of Thatcherism, to be examined in Chapter 6.

althusser and the problem of interpreting history

Hall identifies Althusser's reading of Marx's *Introduction to the Grundrisse* thus: Althusser interprets this text to mean that conceptual mistakes can be clarified through theoretical practice alone. Hall

74

disagrees with this interpretation; he believes that this is actually the opposite of Marx's method. He pushes forward with an analysis of Marx's conception of the relations of material production, focusing on the idea of mediation. Through mediation, we see that consumption and production are not the same thing. They are however bound together in a dialectical relationship.

Consumption produces production, and production produces consumption. To give a simple example, we can say that if something is produced for consumption, it is consumed because we believe that it is a necessary product. If I take the example of soap production, we can see how the desire to be clean and hygienic was a manufactured feature of the production of soap. In short, people did not know that they were 'dirty' until soap was invented to make them 'clean'. The mass production of soap creates a need to be clean. Therefore it is production, not consumption, that creates needs and desires. Hall stresses that we tend to think that 'need' is a characteristic of the consumer. However he demonstrates that 'need' is a product of production: 'Thus the "forming of the senses" is the subjective side of an objective labour' (1973: 22). Labour within the capitalist mode of relations is objective because it is labour transformed into product/object. We can refer to this as the reification[5] of labour. To give a further example, the production of art creates the conditions for a public that is sensitive to art. So, our needs are not our own: they are manufactured in each epoch according to specific labour-production relations. Capitalism appears to reproduce itself naturally and *inevitably*, but this is not guaranteed.

It is necessary and important that we therefore think critically about such given terms as the 'individual', the 'people', 'consumption', 'need' and 'logic'. The concept of the individual, for example, is not an ahistorical universal idea. It is a concept born of a particular set of post-medieval labour-production relations. What we today consider to be the rights of the individual were unthinkable in a previous era. This is not because today we are more civilised or enlightened. This is because the conditions of labour and the structures of labour-production relations were other than they are today. We have to penetrate the 'phenomenal forms', to look at the real historically concrete processes taking place behind them. Hall is antagonistic towards what he views as a mistaken revival of Marxist thinking at an abstract level. It strikes

Hall as being a fundamental mistake to interpret Marx's method as being un-historical. The structural elements of Marx's method are certainly concerned with history, but it is not historicist (1972: 43). Historicism is grounded in the belief that social and cultural phenomena are determined by history. Historicism searches for the laws governing historical change and movement. Hall reads Marx's *Introduction* as a way of undertaking the analysis of history without falling into the trap of seeing history as a naturally occurring and sequential progression of social relations.

settling accounts with althusser

Althusser's structuralist interpretation of Marx presented Hall with some problems. Althusser employs a Freudian concept of symptoms in order to pursue a 'symptomatic reading' of Marx, which would enable him to interpret what he thinks Marx was really saying. The structuralist approach undertaken by Althusser ignores the surface textuality and instead roots around for the essential core of Marx's ideas. This, according to Hall, leads to a reductive reading of Marx. In isolating the elements of Marxist thought, Althusser effectively dissolves the historical context for Marx's work and in so doing, renders Marxism an ahistorical and universal model. It also produces an analysis that is fundamentally anti-humanist, because it denies the possibility of human agency and human will. But, as Hall has argued, it makes no sense to merely import and impose a structure on any given situation or era. To theorise is to look systematically at the precise interplay of forms and structures of the *particular* historical configuration. The point of this work is to rethink the problem 'in more adequate conceptual terms' (Nelson and Grossberg, 1988: 68). The goal of such work is 'to understand the situation you started out with better than before' (ibid.: 70). In order to do that, we have to operate critically within the environment, rather than seek refuge under cover of Marxist theory and its supposed 'guarantees'. The epistemological break with Althusser comes at the point at which Hall questions the function of theory.

the role of theory

Althusser argues that ideological questions carry within them a priori assumptions concerning the answers they apparently invite. If we take an example such as 'Would Prince Charles make a good King?', the question already presupposes that monarchy is in itself a good thing, and as such, cannot be questioned. The question thus carries the seeds of its own internal logic and beliefs about the world. According to Althusser, 'scientific' questions however, do not. Althusser thus differentiates between ideological and scientific questions.

Furthermore, Althusser argues that Marx is bound by the terms and logic of an empiricism that prevents him from articulating a genuinely new conception of production. Any articulation of the mode of production would have to be read 'symptomatically'. The result of this line of argument is to separate theory from reality. Hence a theory does not have to correspond to reality to be true. It only has to demonstrate an internal consistency. If we recall Hall's earlier statements concerning academic and theoretical work, we can see how Althusser's logic falls short of Hall's ethical position. What is the point of any theory which does not have a direct connection to the real world?

Hall asks the important question of how theoretical work is to be done. His answer comes out of his experience. It is not a question of internal consistencies or guaranteed structures. The experience is one of 'retreats and detours' (Hall, 1977: 16). The world is not an organised and cohesive whole waiting for academics to reveal great truths about it. The world is a messy and complicated place. Therefore, the problem with Structuralism, as Hall sees it, is the way it reduces everything to the bare bones, without recovering key elements in order to construct a new and useful conceptual framework for understanding those elements. It is, in this sense, fragmentary rather than constructive.

> You deconstruct a problematic, but the new problematic must retotalize the rational core of the paradigm it dethrones. Theory is a quite different thing from the leap from error to truth; it releases the problem from the terms in which the old problematic set it. But it doesn't abandon the problem. The problem has to be rethought in better, more adequate conceptual terms. (Nelson and Grossberg, 1988: 68)

Hall is also stressing the importance of theory to thinking through concrete problems. In other words, if a *particular* theory does not work, you do not abandon theory altogether. On the contrary, you have to rethink the theoretical framework in order to come up with a better theory! In terms of Marx's base and superstructure model, Althusser's insistence on Marx's economic determinism enables Hall to clarify his position concerning the superstructure and its relationship to the economic base. Althusser (1969) points out that Marx's theory of the determinacy of the economic base cannot account for the many and varied complex ways in which different class struggles may achieve sufficient harmony to produce a revolutionary moment or 'rupture'. Hall agrees that the superstructure is 'not merely the epiphenomena of the objective laws governing the "economic base"' (Hall, 1977b: 23). The superstructure represents 'an ensemble which is always the result of many determinations' (1977b: 23). He returns to Marx's *Introduction* to demonstrate that Marx himself argues that this is indeed the case. All the different moments of production, distribution and exchange articulate into a unity that is both economic and political. However, these moments are not equivalents and do not lose necessarily the force of their differences. Such a unity is not necessarily a harmonious one. Furthermore, this uneven 'complex unity' demonstrates that 'there is no necessary immediate correspondence between the economic and the political constitution of classes' (1977b: 24). In terms of Hall's analysis, this means that there is a much more complex relationship between the base and superstructure than Althusser's reading of Marx suggests. This argument also bears some of the traces of Gramsci's work, which enabled Hall to move forward: 'Gramsci gave me an alternative to the anti-historical thrust of Althusserianism. I deeply resented Althusser's conflation of historicism with the historical' (Nelson and Grossberg, 1988: 69).

Gramsci, of course, also argued that the base and superstructure were in complex relation. Hegemony is not solely the province of the superstructure. Neither does the economic base determine the world. It is how they function in tandem with the class antagonism generated by Capitalism that is the object of Gramsci's analysis. But Gramsci's greatest gift to Hall, is the ability to 'read Marx again in a new way';

> that is to go on 'thinking' the second half of the twentieth century, face-to-face with the realities of the modern world, from a position

78

somewhere within the legacy of Marx's thought, that is, not a quasi-religious body of dogma but as a living, developing, constantly renewable stream of ideas. (Hall, quoted in Simon, 1982: 9)

culture, the media and the ideological effect

Hall returns to these differences in his seminal paper 'Culture, the media and the ideological effect' published by the Open University in 1977. Hall's protracted arguments from the 'Introduction to the *Grundrisse*' achieve greater fluidity and assurance in this later piece. Hall recaps on Marx's arguments concerning the social nature of man's relationship to nature and the primarily social organisation of working and cultural relations. The basis of a materialist understanding of modern society must derive therefore from this central idea; that social relations determine forms. For instance, one particular relationship formed between people is marriage, which is an institution and a cultural practice born out of the intimacy between two people. The form of marriage does not predate the social relationship of two people. It is, rather, the social relationship that determines the need for a binding contract – in this case, marriage. But such forms are not necessarily the same within all comparable social relations. In the case of British law, heterosexual couples may marry, but homosexual couples may not. Divorcees may not remarry within the Catholic Church. Historically, marriages between royal houses have been deemed politically expedient as a means of guaranteeing succession and securing alliances with foreign powers. Therefore, we can see how sexuality, religion and class may over-determine social relations and thus also determine form.

Hall's argument reiterates the point that the economic base of society is not the sole, nor even necessarily the most determining aspect, of a modern culture. The important work is to understand the complex structures of the field within which human relations are mediated according to the demands of a dominant class position. Hall's definition of ideology therefore acknowledges the means by which ideology distorts, inflects and binds individuals, without equating the ideological with falsity. In other words, ideology functions as a kind of social cement. It holds together the society and the different conflicting elements within it. However it does not necessarily invert the reality of

79

those lived social relations. Rather it mediates those relations so that they appear to be a different kind of relation. Ideology is only false, therefore, in as much as it 'cannot express or embody the full social relations on which the system ultimately rests' (Hall, 1977a: 323).

capitalism, class and the market

What then is the relationship between capitalism and class? Culture under capitalism is fundamentally antagonistic. The social relations between classes are determined to some degree by the market but mediated in such a way as to mask the real relations of labour-production and exchange. The market does exist – people do buy and sell things – and profits are generated via the market. However, the market also serves as a way of explaining social relations in individual terms.

The emphasis falls on the exchange value of labour expressed in the consumption patterns of the individual. This, however, is only part of the story. By reducing market economics to the level of individual consumption, questions about the labour-production functions of different classes are rendered null and void. If we are encouraged to 'identity shop' according to our consumption habits, we are less likely to interrogate the conditions of those classes that manufacture such goods. Hence Hall argues that 'what is hidden, repressed, or inflected out of sight, are its real foundations. This is the source of its unconsciousness' (1977a: 325). Let us look at a modern example. If a pair of trainers costs £100 sterling and is manufactured in France at a cost of £20 sterling, then the gross profit (before the deduction of taxes) is £80. This represents an 80 per cent profit margin for the manufacturer. If consumers in the West increasingly demand cheaper products, the manufacturer will be obliged to lower the price. This will threaten the percentage profit margin. In order to produce cheaper products, and yet retain the profit margin of 80 per cent, the manufacturer will move the manufacturing process to another country where labour costs are much cheaper. In Malaysia, the same manufacturer could produce the same trainers for perhaps 50 per cent less and still retain an 80 per cent profit margin. This is one of the features of global market economics, or globalisation. It is globalisation that links our consumption habits to the market forces of most of the developing world's economies, and keeps them in a subordinated relationship.

But how are we to resist the ideological imperative if we are indeed living within a realm that is governed by ideological practices? How do we know that what is seemingly true, is indeed an inflection or distortion of the truth? By what objective criteria can we determine whether something is ideological or not?

Hall gives the example of common sense or common wisdom, which is a typical form of consciousness operating at a daily level.

> What passes for common sense in our society – the residue of absolutely basic and commonly-agreed, consensual wisdoms – helps us to classify out the world in simple but meaningful terms. Precisely common sense does not require reasoning, argument, logic, thought: it is spontaneously available, thoroughly recognisable, widely shared. It *feels* indeed, as if it has always been there, the sedimented, bedrock wisdom of 'the race', a form of 'natural' wisdom, the content of which has hardly changed at all with time. However common sense does have *a content*, and a history. (Hall, 1977: 325) (Hall's emphasis)

the function of common sense

Common sense always bears the trace elements or residual parts of older and more developed systems of ideological thinking. We think therefore of common sense as something eternal, but in reality it is what passes for truth 'in *our* particular age and society, overcast with the glow of traditionalism'. The very fact of common sense's readily available and ubiquitous nature, coupled with the fact that it defies any kind of rationalisation or contradiction, renders it 'spontaneous, ideological *and unconscious*' (Hall, 1977: 30).

> You cannot learn through common sense, *how things are*: you can only discover *where they fit* into the existing scheme of things. In this way, its very taken-for-grantedness is what establishes it as a medium in which its own premises and presuppositions are being rendered *invisible* by its apparent transparency. (Hall, 1977: 325) Hall's emphasis

81

As Gramsci terms it, 'common sense creates the folklore of the future, that is as a relatively rigid phase of popular knowledge at a given place and time' (Gramsci, 1971: 326). Common sense is often employed as the means of naturalising the world and undermining the use or practice of theory. According to Gramsci, it behoves every individual to become his own philosopher and in so doing, resist the incoherent, fragmentary and conformist views of the world imposed by an external environment. Better by far to adopt the Socratic principle, 'know thyself' in order to generate a genuine praxis by which one can take action for change.

> The starting point of critical elaboration is the consciousness of what one really is, and is 'knowing thyself' as a product of the historical processes to date which has deposited in you an infinity of traces, without leaving an inventory. (Gramsci, 1971: 324)

Gramsci observes that common sense is fundamentally aligned with an inability to recognise the historicity of one's position in relation to the world at any given time. This is very important because if we do not understand that when we speak, we do so from a particular point in history, then we misapprehend both the possibility of other positions and, even more crucially, the fact of our temporal-spatial condition. What we take today to be the common sense of the age is not and could never be, universally or eternally true. Where common sense tries to always speak of the general and the universal, it is, in fact, a fragmented and incoherent wisdom. Gramsci is suggesting that only when we can elevate our thinking to conceive of the bigger and coherent world picture, can we truly start to develop a 'praxis' – or theoretically informed practice. However if we continue with Hall's line of argument, it would seem that it is only through an awareness of disjunctures, discontinuities, contradictions and fragments that we can glimpse how ideological thinking operates to create smooth non-contradictory and self-evident statements of truth and fact. Common sense is thus a complex term within Marxist critical thinking.

the practice of dominant ideology

Hall now turns to the question of language in order to explore the practice of ideology. The domain of meaning, constructed through the various webs of codes that generate our sense of the world, functions like a map within which we naturally link some things, and naturally exclude others. The maps of meaning that are generated by a culture contain both the residual elements of previous cultures and histories as well as the emergent strains through which society comes to identify itself as modern and contemporary. But how exactly does a dominant hegemony come into being? How does it articulate its dominance, and how are alternative visions subordinated?

First, as I have already suggested, Hall makes the distinction between false consciousness and ideology (Hall, 1977: 325). Whereas ideology has more commonly been associated with hidden forces, Hall argues that it is crucial that we understand that ideology is 'what is most open, apparent, manifest' (ibid). Ideological propositions or explanations reveal themselves at the surface level. What is concealed are the real foundations of such ideas or premises. Common sense can operate therefore as an ideological tool in the way that it typically eschews any analysis of the real roots of a problem or situation. This further suggests that theoretical practice has a very important role to play here in the analysis of the culture of a civil society. It is by means of such cultural analysis that we can begin the work of identifying the ideological structures that dominate and constrain our ways of being. If ideology is thus visible, why do we not see mass demonstrations opposing it? How does dominance work to maintain power if ideology is operating so openly? Hall argues that the beliefs, points of reference and social knowledges that make up a society's world view, are construed within the 'horizon' of language and culture. Drawing on Roland Barthes, Hall speaks of the clusters of networks of meanings functioning as 'domains of meaning' within which we can see the whole class structure reproduced. We live and understand our world within the legitimated horizon of dominant ideology. As Marx claimed, this will be the scope of meaning understood by the dominant classes.

The hegemony of the dominant classes cannot, however, be secured purely at the level of the economic. As we have seen with Hall's discussions of Gramsci and Althusser, it is within civilian life and the institutionalised spheres of the state that we 'see' the function of ideology. This is because ideology is the tool by which a dominant class constitutes the limits of 'primary lived reality' for all:

83

This operates, not because the dominant classes can prescribe and proscribe, in detail, the mental content of the lives of subordinate classes (they too 'live' in their own ideologies), but because they strive and to a degree succeed in *framing* all competing definitions of reality *within their range*, bringing all alternatives within their horizon of thought. (1977: 333) (Hall's emphasis)

If we think back to Hall's analysis of the Hippie movement, we can recall how some of the more militant elements within the counter-culture of the period were intent on creating a new order where the 'rules of the game' were not even acknowledged. Hippies were not willing to be constrained by the existing structures of power and as such, refused to be contained within those same 'horizons' of thought and experience.

In the case of subordinated classes, Hall argues that if they are not sufficiently strong enough to create a counter-hegemonic force, then they may find that their own structures have been hegemonised, 'as a means of enforcing their continued subordination' (1977: 333). The trade union movement for example, though formed to defend the rights of working class labour, may find itself perpetuating class relations that subordinate their own membership. The necessary equilibrium resulting from this arrangement does not signal either an end to class struggle, nor a total capitulation to the dominant order. Instead we have a period of 'unstable equilibrium' to use Gramsci's term, 'so that, whatever the concessions the ruling bloc is required to make to win consent and legitimacy, its fundamental basis will not be overturned' (1977: 334). In the case of capitalism, concessions won by the trade union movement will not result therefore in the overturning of capitalist modes of labour-production relations because the trade union movement itself operates *within* those same ideological structures of corporate practice. It has to date been unable to raise an effective counter-hegemonic strategy to negate dominant capitalist practice.

the function of the state

Hall now turns to Althusser to explore how the state is able to reproduce these class relations and structures of dominance without insurrection or bloodshed. The state, according to Althusser is viewed (views itself) as neutral and above class interests. It operates therefore principally through the Ideological State Apparatuses (ISAs) and its power is thus exercised indirectly. As Hall expresses it,

> Althusser recognises that the ruling classes do not 'rule' *directly* or in their own name and overt interests, but via the necessary displacements, examined earlier, through the 'class neutral' structures of the state, and the complexly constructed field of ideologies. (1977: 335)

Hall asserts that Althusser's conception of civil society owes much to Gramsci's articulation of the basic paradigm of state and civil society. However Hall regards Althusser's model as still too 'functionalist'. Nevertheless, Althusser's notion of 'imaginary relations' and his concept of interpellation, enables Hall to explicate the process by which dominant ideology achieves hegemonic status. Hall also draws upon Poulantzas in order to formulate his proposition. The shaping and production of consent from subordinated classes does not rest at granting concessions. Rather, it is a case of masking the real conditions of class relations and in some cases, repressing any 'antagonistic' elements within the system. The second phase is to fragment or dissipate the collective interests of the subordinated classes through the workings of the institutions of the state. The final phase is to reunite and bind those disparate elements within a new unity, which might be called the 'nation', 'public opinion', 'society', and more commonly in the West today, 'the people'.

> At this level, unities are once again produced; but now in forms which mask and displace the level of class relations and economic contradictions and *represents* them as non-antagonistic totalities. This is Gramsci's *hegemonic* function of *consent* and *cohesion*. (1977: 337)

Thus we can see how language functions in the articulation of ideological structures and class relations. Through a process of masking/displacing, fragmenting and binding, the dominant classes of the state are able to win, secure and reproduce consent from the subordinated classes. This lends further credence to Hall's earlier analyses of ideology, namely those concerned with the mass media. In Chapter 3, we saw how Hall argued for the structured and endemic nature of media representation, in relation to news media. We can see how his argument regarding the media as producers of systematic, institution-alised, specific and ideological codes begins to gather pace. Here, he asserts that ideology operates systematically, structurally and episte-mologically. This is to say that ideology is practised *routinely*; it is the product of a particular equation of knowledge with power and lies at the root of the organisation of civil society.

The 'ideological effect' within a capitalist society masks the exploitative relationship of the dominant-subordinate class structure and instead fragments those class structures into consuming individu-als. The real nature of the state is concealed and myths of the 'classless society' perpetuate. In this way,

> [The] Exercise of ideological class domination is dispersed through the fragmentary agencies of a myriad individual wills and opinions, separate powers; this fragmentation of opinion is then *reorganised* into an imaginary coherence in the mystical unity of 'the consensus', into which free and sovereign individuals and their wills 'spontaneously' flow. (1977: 339)

The 'legitimate' consensus is then used to exercise power in the name of 'the people'. It is at this point that Hall is able to draw some conclusions about the role and function of the mass media within civil society. Although he emphasises that the media does not function exclu-sively as an ideological entity, nevertheless, it is precisely that role which he seeks to identify. The mass media have, through the emer-gence of late capitalist society, become the prime means of the distribu-tion of knowledge and information about the world to the world. The mass media as we know it would not have developed had it not been for the creation of the middle-class suburbs, the proliferation of popular culture and the establishment of mass markets and mass consumption. Thus, the inter-penetration of the mass media and state and civil society, has become one of the defining characteristics of what we would term 'modern' culture:

> Quantitatively and qualitatively, in twentieth-century advanced capitalism, the media have established a decisive and fundamental leadership in the cultural sphere. Simply in terms of economic,

86

technical, social and cultural resources, the mass media command a qualitatively greater slice than all the older, more traditional cultural channels which survive. (1977: 340)

the functions of the mass media

Hall goes even further when he states that the mass media have in effect 'colonised the cultural and ideological sphere'. Increasingly we live not in relation to each other, but in relation *to* the other. Our understanding of the society in which we live is mediated by the mass media. Hence our social knowledge is derived in the main from the mediations of the media. It is the media, in ideological mode, that produces 'the images, representations and ideas around which the social totality, composed of all these separate and fragmented pieces, can be coherently grasped as a *"whole"'*. (1977: 340) Hall identifies this as the first of the media's 'great cultural functions'.

The second function is more complex. Given the plurality of identities, lifestyles and experiences under capitalism, the media is concerned to observe and reflect upon these pluralities and in some sense, 'provide a constant inventory of the lexicons, life-styles and ideologies which are objectivated there.' (1977: 341) The media construct 'maps' of social reality in order to make the complexities of modern living intelligible and classifiable, so that they can be readily understood. This understanding, though, is already prefigured within the structures of the dominant consensus. An apparently new phenomenon, which could be anything from snowboarding to inner-city rioting, is quickly assimilated into the existing categories of received social wisdom. It may be deemed deviant. It will almost certainly be regarded as problematic. This is the site of real struggle, 'between *preferred* and *excluded* explanations and rationales, between permitted and deviant behaviours, between the "meaningless" and the "meaningful"' (1977: 341). It is, as Hall states, 'the site of an enormous *ideological labour*, ideological *work*', which the mass media undertakes expertly and routinely every day.

The third ideological phase involves the mass media in the task of reorganising and collating all those fragments of representation in order to produce a cohesive whole. It is here that the media begin to negotiate the difficult territory of representation. In the great melé of voices that demand to be heard, some voices will command more authority than others. However, the media also need to represent minority views in order to withstand accusations of bias. This is the critical moment for Hall:

> This forms the great unifying and consolidating level of the media's ideological work: the generative structure beneath the media's massive investment in the surface immediacy, the phenomenal multiplicity, of the social works in which it traffics. (1977: 342)

It is not so much the finished product of consensus that is at issue here. It is 'the whole process of argument, exchange, debate, consultation and speculation by which it emerges' (ibid) that is the key to understanding both media power and its ideological functions within society.

Hall makes clear, throughout his analysis of the mass media, and television in particular, that events are mediated. Media texts are extremely symbolic messages that are made intelligible (encoded) and disseminated for audiences to decode. The multi-layered aspects of media production, and the systematic ways in which the social world is packaged for mass consumption, should not be read too narrowly as the direct translation of world events into dispatches of false consciousness. The ideological labour undertaken by the mass media is extensive and deeply rooted in the institutional practices as much as in the professionalism of individual broadcasters. In particular, the dominant consensual rational of media broadcasting shapes both the presentation and reception of media representations. The process of encoding and decoding that Hall identifies, is part of the mechanisms of media production. The entire infrastructure of the mass media is much more closely aligned to the governance of civil society than established mass communications theory would allow. We can see Hall is positing the idea that meanings are neither generated in isolation, nor produced at random. The media does not, in democratic societies, seek to engender a monopolistic view of society. However, by its proximity to the institutions of state power, and because of its status as one of the most highly evolved institutions under capitalism, the mass media is, nevertheless, the dominant means by which dominance is won, secured and maintained. Those meanings created and proliferated by the mass media come to represent the *only* viable and intelligent means by which we can fully understand the world:

The premises and preconditions which sustain their rationalities have been rendered invisible by the process of ideological masking and taking-for-granted we earlier described. They seem to be, even to those who employ and manipulate them for the purposes of encoding, simply the 'sum of what we already know'. (1977: 343)

It is important to remember that those who work within the system are frequently at a loss to explain their own internal processes of logical deduction, except in terms of what has become established custom and practice. The assumptions which prefigure media representation

embody the dominant definitions of the situation, and represent or refract the existing structures of power, wealth and domination, hence they *structure* every event they signify, and *accent* them in a manner which reproduces the given ideological structures – this process has become unconscious, even for the encoders. (1977: 344)

Media producers are not aiming to reproduce dominance. However by their very actions they collude in the manufacture of consent through precisely these means. Whether at the level of news photographs, the reportage of a specific demonstration or event, or in the habitual representation of a geo-political space such as Northern Ireland or the Middle East, the media 'will have an overall tendency of making things "mean" within the sphere of dominant ideology' (1977: 344). According to Hall, the media producer will go even further in his desire to win consent for his own version of events, so that not only the events themselves, but also the manner of their representation will be endorsed as valid and worthwhile. Hall further reminds us that this relationship between the mass media and the dominant powers is not a straightforward question of economics or ownership. With reference to Althusser, he insists that

there is a crucial sense (it may be this which enabled Althusser to call them nevertheless, Ideological *State* Apparatuses) in which it must be said that the media relate to the ruling class alliances, not directly but indirectly; and hence they have some of the characteristics – the 'relative autonomy' – of the State Apparatuses themselves. (1977a: 345)

Hall uses the example of broadcasting to make the point that certain media institutions, in being considered above state politics, are deemed to have an autonomy based on such principles as 'impartiality',

89

'objectivity' and 'balance'. These operating tools, however, also depend on the same 'structured ideological field' as the very state systems which they seek to represent. Broadcasting, like the largely two-party political system of most western democracies, is 'fundamentally oriented "within the mode of reality of the state"'. The field itself is 'structured in dominance' and it is this that limits the available range of definitions and interpretations of events. Such work is highly 'contradictory', because in the very moment of trying to elicit a clear and faithful interpretation of the world, the media tend to reproduce the same contradictions, class assumptions, institutional positions, established meanings and dominant power structures in the process of that articulation. It is, Hall claims, 'a systematic tendency' and one that ultimately performs a strategic hegemonic function in the reproduction of a class-exploitative terrain, where the struggle for dominance is played out.

'Culture, the media and the ideological effect' represents a consolidation of many of the analyses that have gone before, in relation to an explanation of media activity and its relationship to civil society. It pivots on the Gramscian idea of hegemony as fundamentally unstable, unequivocable and in a constant state of flux. However, the argument also owes much to Althusser, not least in its recognition of the value of structured materialist practices on the part of those institutions that are in some ways aligned with state power, while apparently independent. The article also brings together Hall's long-term concerns with the manufacture of consent, and the function of the mass media in producing and reproducing the conditions by which consent is legitimated within the cultural sphere.

At this point I think it is beneficial to examine how many of these theoretical arguments find expression with regard to a concrete example. One of the characteristics of Hall's work is the way in which he is able to make interventions into public debates. Though his arguments sometimes turn on very complex theoretical points, he always aims to make use of that analysis in concrete and purposeful ways.

the case of football hooliganism

As mentioned earlier in this chapter, one of the more high profile and pressing social problems of the decade was the spectator violence associated with football matches. The rise of 'football hooliganism' as it was dubbed by the press and the judiciary alike, appeared to be a social phenomenon and inexplicable except in terms of psychopathic behaviour. In conjunction with several other academics and social commentators, Hall contributed to the debate around football hooliganism and its meaning within British post-war culture, in a volume published in 1978 by Inter Action Inprint (Ingham, 1978). Hall's essay on football hooliganism and its representation within the British media is a short but lucid analysis, which draws out questions of the ideological function of the news media, with appropriate examples.

representing football hooliganism

National and local press coverage of football hooliganism was widespread during the late 1960s and 1970s. Hall begins his analysis by insisting that 'the nature and pattern of this coverage is a phenomenon worth analysing in its own right' (1978: 15). He therefore shifts the sociological attention away from the phenomenon itself, toward the mediation of that phenomenon. This focus on the mode of representation as object, rather than the object itself, represents an epistemological shift in terms of traditional sociological investigation and was one of the features of the Centre's output during this period. Why not merely look at the social and cultural causes of football hooliganism? The focus on media representation enables Hall to explore the relationship between mass media and the wider hegemonic culture. It is therefore an opportunity to investigate the theoretical proposition that the media are engaged in systematic ideological labour which is, to all intents and purposes, unconscious. Hall reminds us that the media provide the 'principle source of information about this problem for the vast majority of the public', and therefore, is 'highly instrumental in defining, shaping and generating interest' in football hooliganism. The press construct images, explanations and definitions based on their deployment of expert witnesses, commentators and victims and, thereby, are important and significant agents in the creation of social knowledge of this phenomenon. The press are not bound by the same statutory requirements of impartiality and balance as broadcasters. They therefore function as more 'active agents' in the creation of a consensus view. However: 'once a phenomenon like football hooliganism has been widely identified as a "problem" about which "we ought to do something", even television and radio can work from the basis of a common consensus about it' (1978: 16).

Once consensus is reached, the normal rules about impartiality no longer seem to apply. This is because the terms of reference have fallen within the discursive parameters of common sense. It becomes common sense, for example, to view football hooligans as 'mindless thugs' or 'animals'. These terms no longer require interrogation since they are by common sense definition, *beyond* analysis. They have entered the lexicon of common folk wisdom which informs popular social knowledge.

the status and function of sport within the press

Whereas news is typically prioritised within the press according to its position within the pages of the paper, the sports page functions effectively as an alternative front page.

> Sport is not relegated in the league table of news, so much as set off, in a world distinct from other kinds of news, self-contained and self-sufficient – a well-defined enclave – one of whose major attractions is that it has little or no relation to the rest of the news. (1978: 18)

Hall goes on to add, 'this offers an important clue about our culture', though, unfortunately, he does not elaborate on this point. However the main point is that for a sports-related issue to appear on the front pages of the national press, it must be 'a phenomenon of very great public resonance'. Typically sports stories only hit the front page when 'sport has gone political'.

mediating violence

Hall asserts the function of the media in creating, rather than reflecting, the reality of the world for the reader/viewer. The selection of material and its positioning within a narrative account is often undertaken with scant attention to the consequences of such reportage. The media, in other words, have a responsibility towards readers and society in general. Sensationalist reporting can only inflame or exacerbate a situation that is already worrying. By isolating the most sensationalist and violent aspects of these stories, the press end up increasing the scale of the problem. Hall asserts the necessity of rigorous analysis and criticism, which, he adds, is frequently perceived as antagonistic towards the practice of journalism. There is sadly no shortage of material to justify the need for intelligent analysis. In focusing on the reporting of events, the press present themselves as passively reflecting reality. However, they are engaged in the active construction of events for the reader. By looking for evidence supporting the so-called 'trend', the press 'suppresses the true nature of the problem and in so doing, increases the scale of the social problem'. If the intention is to find a remedy for this social ill, the effect is to exacerbate it.

The criteria of news values also have their place within sports coverage. Hence 'the sports pages don't simply reflect sport, they order the world of sport in terms of a league table of significance' (1978: 21). The journalist operates according to the codes and conventions of his/her profession. This 'professional news sense' is learned on the job. It is 'habitual, instinctive, something he can operate without a moment's conscious inflexion' (1978: 21) and, consequently, beyond analysis. Hall specifies journalism's epistemology. The world is viewed as a 'flat constant background' against which things happen. It is as if the world were a static place within which changes – usually bad ones – occur every day. The role of the journalist is to inform us about those changes and their consequences. It is, of course, a common sense view of social reality. The effect of this lies in the fact that papers 'are driven to find, examine and report [ ] the big bang stories' and 'reassure the readers that the world is still intact (just)' (1978: 22). Journalists therefore perform an ideological function in their articulation of the real as a consensual and highly exclusive vision of reality. Furthermore, as Hall argues, focusing on a phenomenon may inadvertently distort its scale, and suggest that it is more widespread than is actually the case.

Hall moves on to identify a cyclical pattern which links the phenomenal effects in the real world, to the reporting of those effects within the mediated or symbolic world of representation. A social phenomenon is identified by the press, as an apparent threat to public safety. The threat of confrontation leads to increased calls for law and order policies and actions to contain the threat. This desire for greater controls leads to an increased level of confrontation between the agencies of control, and those who are deemed deviant. This results in more people being drawn into deviant behaviour which then increases the anxiety of public safety. The 'amplification spiral' thus works to promote conditions for more and more violence and social disorder. As Hall says, the press coverage of football hooliganism could never be described as 'careful, judicious, measured, inquiring, attentive to the complexities of the problem, sceptical of exaggerated claims, anxious to calm unreal fears, or demystifying.' (1978: 26) But Hall insists that this is owing to the nature of the newspaper industry, as a competitive, news-values oriented institution. The language of sports coverage is itself, aggressive and confrontational, 'studded with images drawn from the blizkrieg and the military showdown' (1978: 27) and it may not therefore be so surprising if the violence on the pitch does not seep into the terraces.

Labelling football hooligans as 'animals' only reinforces the view of spectator violence as an inexplicable psychopathy. Such explanations are sadly only too common in Western culture. We have a 'strong tendency to see everybody else's aggression as irrational except our own' (1978: 28). Furthermore, the delineation between the psychopathic violence of the football hooligan, and the coercive powers of the police, works to legitimate state violence in its myriad formations. 'We see the violence of the street brawl or the pub fight, but not the violence implicit in poverty, unemployment or racism' (1978: 29). This refusal to see the reality of endemic social conflicts and antagonisms within society effectively masks the real conditions of capitalist society – one which pitches class against class. By failing to acknowledge the rational motivations behind seemingly irrational social activity, society perpetuates the mythology that common decency, moderation and self-control are universal ethical standards, rather than middle class mores. Not only do such myths lead to increased social conflict and the experience of permanent exclusion, but they also work to justify the use of violence in order to curb violence. The terms of debate therefore rest on simplified explanations which 'cut off or pre-empt deeper or more penetrating kinds of enquiry' (1978: 30).

investigating hooliganism

By suggesting that football hooligans may have rational reasons and motivations for their behaviour, Hall posits the issue of press representation within the wider framework of cultural hegemony. In the case of football hooligans, suppose their aggressive acting-out arises, not from the withdrawal into passivity and anomie of the mindless, but from an over-involvement and over-identification with the thrills and spills and the controversies and disappointments of the game (1978: 31).

Perhaps football has become the sole terrain with which some individuals feel they enjoy an element of control. Instead of seeing how disenfranchised certain groups or classes have become within the cultural and social landscape, dominant explanations of football hooliganism only seek out short-term remedies of containment. The 'swift law and order reaction' is as 'irrational and unconsidered in the long-run as the thing it is trying to remedy' (1978: 34). The law and order approach aims to simplify causes, stigmatise those involved, whip up public panic, and stamp hard on it from above (1978: 34). Why is it that the press and the agencies of social control wish to proceed in this fashion? Hall argues that the tendency towards repression arises out of a backlash against the permissiveness of the previous decade. The chapter offers therefore some interesting insight into both Hall's application of the more theoretical points regarding complex marxism, and how he relates directly to the pressing social questions of the day. Here we see how Hall marshals his arguments through the use of specific examples, to demonstrate the ideological productivity of the media and their close proximity to the other superstructural institutions of state power. Though the analysis of the press is partial and incomplete, it does illustrate the potential work that might be usefully achieved through a longer and more sustained project.

official responses to hooliganism

With the outbreak of rioting by England fans in Luxembourg and France, football hooliganism reached a point of intense international scrutiny. The second Thatcher Government instigated an Official Working Group from the Department of the Environment, in order to 'tackle the problem' (1984: 3). The introduction from the published report makes clear the 'split logic in liberal society' (1978: 34) to which Hall refers. Though published some six years later, the Government report appears not to have been influenced in the slightest by the sociological causes and effects of football hooliganism.

We were clear that it was not now our task to consider broader social issues, although we were aware of the widely held view that this is not exclusively a football problem but one which has deeper roots in society and happens to affect football among other activities. It may be that football violence would respond ultimately to social remedies. Such considerations are outside the scope of this report. We were concerned with specific and practical effects and remedies, especially in the short term (1984: 5–6)

The report goes on to make suggestions for increased surveillance, police powers, control, containment, and better communication between the police and the Football Association. Its tone is one of weary resignation, coupled with a presaging sense of its own futility. Amongst their recommendations to the media is that they should 'highlight examples of fair play and sporting behaviour by participants or spectators, in order to give publicity to the authors of such acts and encourage their peers to emulate them' (1984: 54). The authors of the report state early on, 'We are also clear that the practical measures to counter violence recommended in Sections 5 and 6 will not eliminate violence. We consider that to be an unrealistic aim' (1984: 8). Such admissions by the authors of the report would appear to be irrational, unless one considers the wider ramifications of such an official report. We can see how the hegemonic drive toward containment, necessitated an official response. The response must be in line with demands for greater control and punishment. Though the authors themselves are prevented from investigating football hooliganism as an urgent sociological problem, they do at least acknowledge the limitations of their brief. The hard-line actions of the Thatcher administration would certainly have an impact on football hooliganism, but there would also be other casualties. The decision to fence in football fans, and the increasingly defensive nature of policing at football events were two of the major contributing factors to the Heisel Stadium disaster when the stand collapsed, killing 93 Liverpool fans in the crush.

conclusion

Hall's maturation as a post-marxist intellectual can only really be understood if we consider the detailed nuances of his arguments in relation to a variety of European thinkers, intellectuals and critics. Throughout this chapter we have seen how his engagements with Althusser and Gramsci enabled Hall to articulate a 'complex marxism' with his colleagues at the Centre, and some of the implications and consequences of that articulation in his analysis of media and the wider culture at large. Hall's consistent negotiation of dominant culture and his questioning of consent and its ideological construction, provide the building blocks for his most mature work around hegemony and Thatcherite culture.

We can summarise his critical development in the following ways. Hall achieves a considerable degree of fluency and independence from Althusserian theory, through his readings of Gramsci. He begins to articulate a more theoretically complex, yet demonstrable, practical approach to the analysis of media forms and institutions. By examining the relationship between dominance and consent Hall opens up the marxist terms of reference around the base and superstructure model. Hall focuses upon the mass media as the ideological powerhouse of western capitalist society, which enables him to pursue questions of agency and dominance in relation to real social phenomena of the day. By examining the function of ideology, Hall demonstrates how ideological structures operate systematically, structurally and epistemologically. This is to say that ideology is practised *routinely*; it is the product of a particular equation of knowledge with power and lies at the root of the organisation of civil society.

Of course, the question of legitimated consent did not rest solely with Hall's interest in the mass media. As we will see in the next few chapters, Hall's thinking in relation to hegemony would come to fruition in his analysis of Thatcherism, racism and the construction of identity. Firstly however, it is the work of Hall and his colleagues in relation to race, law and order, and gender issues which will provide the focus for the next chapter. In *Policing the Crisis*, Hall and his colleagues take the debate out to policy makers, government and the wider general public, in a deliberate and provocative manner.

further reading

Gramsci, A. (1971) *Selections from the Prison Notebooks*. Lawrence and Wishart: London.

Curran, J. et al. (eds) (1977) *Mass Communication and Society*. Edward Arnold: London.

Rock, P. and Mcintosh M. (1973) *Deviance and social control*. Tavistock: London.

the politics
of representation

Meanings have all sorts of 'effects', from the construction of knowledge to the subjection of the subject to the meaning offered. If they have an influence on 'behaviour' it is more likely to be indirectly because knowledge is always implicated in power and power implies limits on what can be seen and shown, thought and said. (Hall, quoted in Evans and Hall, 1999: 311)

introduction

Hall could see how the terms of the debate concerning representation were becoming more sharply defined throughout the 1970s. In this chapter we are going to examine Hall's relationship to the primary areas of race and gender representation. First we are going to explore the sites of Hall's interventions in debates around race and representation. Second, we will consider the impact of the Women's Movement on Hall's politics and his negotiations with feminism within the Centre at Birmingham. The anti-racist and anti-sexist movements of this period were having an enormous impact on the structures and forms governing representation.

Hall was already well aware of the problems besetting black Britons who were struggling to come to terms with the tensions associated with their complex ethnicity and their growing estrangement from white British mainstream culture. He wrote specifically about the experiences of the new black diaspora in Britain and the problems facing their children – the 'new Englanders', as he termed them.

young, black and british

The rise of Powellism as a dominant force within mainstream politics prompted Hall to speak out many times against racist ideology in politics and the media, and to argue the need for understanding the real historical material conditions that gave rise to racist discourses. In 1965 the National Committee for Commonwealth Immigrants (NCCI) was set up to advise government policy on the integration of Commonwealth immigrants. Hall's speech to the NCCI, 'Young Englanders', drew specifically on his own experiences as a West Indian school teacher in south London at the time of the Notting Hill riots in 1958. As several of the boys in his class had been directly involved in the riots, Hall encouraged discussion of the issues. He observed first hand the contradictory nature of their views on race relations.

> On the one hand they believed (often repeating the casual conversation of their parents) that West Indians were savages flooding the country, taking jobs, filling up classrooms, stealing women; that they were a lower order of society altogether and should be encouraged to 'go home'. On the other hand they had the friendliest of attitudes towards me (a teacher who, after all, had 'stolen' a job in their school) and their own West Indian classmates (a group clearly 'filling up the classrooms'). (Hall, 1968: 1)

Hall highlights the specific difficulties facing immigrant teenagers who have to negotiate the territory between the traditional family structure and mainstream British culture. It is the tension between the identity of home and the newly emergent identification with England 'towards which every new experience beckons him – school, friends, the street, work' (Hall, 1968: 8) that causes friction and uncertainty. 'Somehow he must learn to reconcile his two identities and make them one', yet as Hall points out, the 'young Englander' often discovers his way is barred by prejudice. Despite the promises of teen freedoms in Britain 'to wander and loaf, to pick up friends, to chat the girls up, to dance or listen to records or play cricket, to dress up and move into town on Saturday evenings' (1968: 10), the immigrant teenager is squeezed between the claustrophobia of the immigrant family unit trying to maintain traditional values and discipline, and the closed communities of white culture, which persist in excluding him. Tolerance is not enough, according to Hall. We must instead seek understanding of the pressures on families and young people as part of the process of integration. Hall ends on a warning note. In terms of integration, 'we are further away from that goal today than we were in the late 'fifties when heavy immigration began'. Thanks to Powellism, Smethwick and the Notting Hill riots, immigrant teenagers are 'falling back on their own reserves'. 'They are closing-in their lines of contact, re-discovering their own racial and national identities and stereotyping their white counterparts' (1968: 12). The drift towards a more aggressive defence of immigrant identity may appear to be a positive stance but will not ultimately help those young people to integrate into the host community. The overall tone of this piece suggests that Hall's audience was liberal in intention but ignorant in terms of its experience of immigrant communities. However, by 1970, Hall's tone had become more defiant. By now the issue of 'belonging' had assumed centre-stage in public debates. In the Spring of 1970, the *Sun* newspaper issued a questionnaire asking readers whether they agreed with Powell's views on immigration. Of the 20,000 respondents, half said that they were in agreement.

the 'problem' of race

Hall initially wanted to draw attention to the plight of black and Asian youth 'trying to tiptoe through society' (1968: 8). By the 1970s however, the young immigrant community had found many different ways to make itself heard. Many black teenagers were turning to violence as a means of articulating their defiance against the increasingly hard-line actions of the state. The fears shared by Hall and his colleagues at the Centre for Racial Equality gave rise to successive broadcasts and public talks, which were subsequently published by the BBC. The dangers that Hall had foreseen in the 1960s were now being realised. Against the grain of public sentiment and political rhetoric, Hall argued fiercely that the so-called 'problem of race' was neither a modern phenomenon generated by the post-war wave of immigration, nor an abstract question separate from the specific social and political contexts of British economics.

In his public talk 'Racism and Reaction',[1] Hall traces the history of British racism back to the reign of Elizabeth I. Racism is thus an internal problem of imperial economics transposed and projected onto the black community. It is therefore endemic to British social formations and underpins a particular notion of Englishness that is both exclusive and ideologicial. Even without the immigration policies of the 1950s, Hall asserts the essential importance of the '"imperialist" chain', which binds millions of colonial workers all over the world to the economic and social structures of British society: 'If their blood has not mingled extensively with yours, then their labour power has long entered the economic bloodstream of British society: It is in the sugar you stir; it is in the tea-leaves at the bottom of the next "British cuppa"' (Hall, 1978: 25).

In a series of articles, Hall attacks the core assumption that race and racial relations are problems in themselves. He argues that race is not in itself a crisis, but rather 'the lens' (1978: 31) through which fear and anxiety are distorted and refracted away from the root causes of economic crisis and projected onto a stigmatised community. This is of course the essence of Hall's argument in *Policing the Crisis*,[2] a work that draws together many intertwining issues of race, media reportage and the evolving capitalist crisis afflicting the British economy. Moreover, the tendency among certain politicians to deploy racialist arguments engenders panic on the part of the populace, and leads to an increasingly self- justifying cycle of explanations. But racism, Hall argues, is not false consciousness:

> I want to insist that racism is not a set of false pleas which swim around in the head. They're not a set of mistaken perceptions. They have their basis in real material conditions of existence. They arise because of the concrete problems of different classes and groups in the society. Racism represents the attempt ideologically to construct those conditions, contradictions and problems in such a way that they can be dealt with and deflected in the same moment. That instead of confronting the conditions and problems which indeed do face white and

black in the urban areas, in an economy in recession, they can be projected away through race. (Hall, 1978b: 35)

But how could Hall explain the mobilisation of a popular racism such as that which afflicted Britain during the 1970s and 1980s? Two things were now required. We can see in Hall's sustained activity in this area during this period, a barely contained anger as he tried to convey to politicians, broadcasters, academics and students alike the inadequacies of a liberal approach. Hall was in fact invited on one occasion to chair a television discussion between Enoch Powell and the CRE. Such a programme could only lend legitimacy to Powell's views. Besides which, Hall was unwilling to collude with the broadcaster in representing himself as a neutral party within the debate. He therefore declined the invitation.

Faced with the daily representations of race and racial issues within the public domain, Hall had to find a way to address the fundamental operations of racism within the broad spectrum of cultural production. Further, Hall needed to address the specificities of the media and the characteristically unthinking racism inherent in popular representation.

the failure of liberalism

Just as he had attempted to describe the real experiences of Black people in Britain (1968; 1970; 1978a), Hall now turned his attention to the urban crisis of black poverty. In a provocative paper given at the Polytechnic of Central London[3] to an assembled audience of students, academics and media professionals, Hall rejected what he saw as the liberal attitude to tackling racism through a focus on anti-discrimination policies. The paper is uncompromising in its insistence on the structural causes of racism. He argues that it is the insertion of black people from the colonial hinterland into the very heart of British culture that has generated the racial problems of modern Britain. Therefore the urban social and cultural problems facing black and white communities in the inner cities cannot be separated from the economic situation of black workers within British industry. The 'black underclass', as Hall terms it, is increasingly in danger of slipping into deviant and criminal activity in an effort to resist and survive the damaging effects of their subjugated position. In a bleak condemnation of the journalistic practices of the day, Hall stresses the dangers of creating and sustaining the discourse of black mugging as a crime epidemic:

> If you highlight the crime and mugging problem of the inner cities and do not deal with the expulsion of the black labour force from productive work, then you are not seriously engaged in the problem, you are engaged in exacerbating the consciousness of racism. You are laying down the objective basis on which racism thrives and I am not interested in what your good intentions may be or indeed your professional interests.

Hall goes much further when he warns of the consequences of accepting and working within the increasingly hegemonic racism generated by political leaders, intent on engendering a sense of national crisis. The discursive function of a 'moral crusade' draws upon a particular notion of Englishness that makes its ideological appeal to a weary and frightened population. In 'Thatcherism', Hall sees the beginnings of 'an official authoritarian populism' intent on legitimating the use of state power in order to deal with those areas of the populace deemed to be antagonistic towards it. We are being prepared for 'iron times' (Hall, 1978c: 21). Though Powell was dismissed from office, his ideas nevertheless have become naturalised in the debates around mugging, inner city crime and immigration policy. As Hall puts it, the terms of the debate about immigration came to assume that repatriation is the answer.

> In Thatcherism, racism comes home to be perfectly respectable and even 'responsible' English ideology. Something that will not be shifted, will not be budged from. We know it in our bones, we know what our culture is. We have forgotten why people from another culture came here or indeed how much your culture depends on having their culture somewhere else and why you brought them from where they were to be where you are now and why you would like them to go back. As if you can switch populations around at the whim of a moral anxiety. That is the nature of racism from above. Coupled with racism from below it creates the exposed political nerve on which fascism operates. (Hall, 1978c: 23)

Hall's campaigning against racism in public life took many different forms. He undertook work with the Campaign Against Racism in the Media (CARM), which looked specifically at the ways in which the use of black and Asian stereotypes fostered a racist culture within broadcasting and the media in general. In order to identify and assess the wider impact of racism within mainstream British culture, Hall and his colleagues set about a project which that culminate in a hugely influential study called *Policing the Crisis*.

policing the crisis

Policing the Crisis (Hall et al., 1978a) is a collaboration epitomising the character of work within the Centre at Birmingham. Even the most sophisticated of the Centre's projects have a 'work in progress' feel, and though *Policing the Crisis* is a thorough, extensive and detailed work, it none the less communicates a powerful sense that sociological investigations never achieve real closure. The authors of this work were Stuart Hall, Chas Critcher, Tony Jefferson, John Clarke and Brian Roberts. The volume, which stands as an important and controversial contribution to sociological enquiry in post-war Britain, is the result of a sustained collaborative analysis that gathered momentum through-out 1970s in the form of individual and group conference papers, journal articles and contributions to books. It is in effect a critical examination of British society in the 1970s, and takes as its focal point the 'phenomenon' of 'mugging', which appeared and disappeared from British public consciousness at a time when law and order issues were beginning to dominate the political agenda. As with the sociological work concerning football hooliganism, we can see in 'mugging' how the media stood in relation to other ideological state apparatuses of the period, for example the judiciary and the police. *Policing the Crisis* is important in terms of the debate around law and order and the apparent rise in violent street crime. However, it is also an important work, which intervened at a critical point in order to raise public awareness of media practice and the complicated roots of a sociological phenomenon.

By addressing a particular moment in Britain, the authors also sought to exemplify the ways in which different yet related institutions of the British establishment work together, often unwittingly, in the generation of social trends, public debate and cultural phenomena. It is however best understood with hindsight as an insightful critique of the culture that manufactured the conditions for the advent of far right policies epitomised by Thatcherism. Hall and his colleagues argue, persuasively in my view, that chief among the paradigmatic conditions for the emergence of Thatcherism was the articulation of race.

hegemony in crisis

Policing the Crisis is in essence, a book 'about a society which is slipping into a certain kind of crisis' (Hall et al., 1978a: viii). The authors are forthright in their introduction and determined that there should be no misunderstanding concerning either their position, or the seriousness of their concerns.

> [This book tries] to examine why and how the themes of *race, crime and youth* – condensed into the image of 'mugging' – come to serve as the articulator of the crisis, as its ideological conductor. It is also about how these themes have functioned as a mechanism for the construction of an authoritarian consensus, a conservative backlash: what we call the slow build-up towards a 'soft' law-and-order society. But it also has to ask: to what social contradictions does this trend towards the 'disciplined society' – powered by the fears mobilised around 'mugging' – really refer? How has the 'law-and-order' ideology been constructed? What social forces are constrained and contained by its construction? What forces stand to benefit from it? What roles has the state played in its construction? What real fears and anxieties is it mobilising? These are some of the things we mean by 'mugging' as a social phenomenon. It is why a study of 'mugging' has led us inevitably to the general 'crisis in hegemony' in the Britain of the 1970s. This is the ground taken in this book. Those who reject the logic of our argument must contest us *on this ground*. (Hall et al., 1978a: viii)

The intentions are clear. 'Mugging' is not simply a categorisation of street theft. Nor is it the invention of scurrilous newspaper journalists. 'Mugging' is 'a relation between crime and the reaction to crime' (ibid.: viii). It cannot be divorced from the conditions that determine it and the institutional agencies and structures which determine those conditions. This goes some way towards making sense of the title of the work. While the project is focused on 'mugging', it is the way in which the state effectively *polices* the perceived and emergent *crisis* that forms the investigative route through the analysis. The authors are clearly anticipating widescale opposition from a variety of sources. They express their view that the book is unlikely to please the majority of readers:

> The courts, the police, the Home Office will certainly find it wildly exaggerated about their negative role (to put it nicely), and inexcusably 'soft' on criminals, agitators and trouble-makers. The media will say it is biased. Academics will find it too unbalanced, too committed. Liberals, people of good will, active in the cause of penal reform or improving race relations, will like it least of all – perhaps because they will approach it with more positive expectations. (Hall et al., 1978a: ix)

The roll-call of readerships covertly expresses the authors' hope that the book will be *read* by such groups even if it ultimately offends or disappoints them. The book may be an intervention in 'the battleground of ideas' (ibid.: x) but the authors are adamant that it is, none the less a practical engagement, which should engender substantive and continuing change in the present state:

> We confess to have had our hearts hardened by what we have discovered. It is a widespread but fatal trap – precisely the trap of 'liberal opinion' – to split analysis from action, and to assign the first to the instance of the 'long term', which never comes, and reserve only the second to 'what is practical and realistic in the short term'. (Hall et al., 1978a: ix)

As we saw in the last chapter, the issue of football hooliganism suffered from this same dual logic. The government of the day rejected the 'long term' sociological analysis of working class alienation and disenfranchisment in favour of a number of short-term repressive measures, recommended by the Official Working Party Report. But the authors of *Policing the Crisis* make their point well when they draw attention to the very contradictory forces at work, and the constraints imposed by such logic.

> The problem is that the 'present conditions', which make the poor poor (or the criminal take to crime) are precisely the *same* conditions

which make the rich rich (or allow the law-abiding to imagine that the social causes of crime will disappear if you punish individual criminals hard enough). (Hall et al., 1978a: x)

Hence the analysis of 'mugging' as social phenomenon presented here is less concerned with 'mugging' per se, than with the culture of control (ibid.: 76) created to police it. By cutting crime 'adrift from its social roots', the signifying culture comprising of newspaper reportage, police documentation, public debates, television news, crime statistics and the orchestration of public opinion, strives to close down the meaning of 'mugging' so that it can be readily identified, targeted and stopped. However, the irony of such intensive scrutiny by these agencies is that the phenomenon itself achieves ever greater stature, power and command within the public imagination. Furthermore, as 'mugging' becomes increasingly subject to common sense definitions and explanations, it escapes the boundaries of discourse and becomes a phenomenon that defies rational explanation. It becomes relatively easy at this point for the split in liberal thinking to occur – long term analysis can be jettisoned in favour of harsh and repressive short-term measures.

moral panics and the threat from america

Hall and his colleagues argue convincingly and with passion that 'mugging' was in reality a moral panic:

> Cohen defines this in terms of a shift of attention from the *deviant act* (i.e. 'mugging'), treated in isolation to *the relation between the deviant act and the reaction of the public and the control agencies to the act.* This shift of focus alters the nature of the 'object' or phenomenon which needs to be explained. (Hall et al., 1978a: 18)

Hall et al. recognise that a different epistemology is at work when a social activity becomes a moral panic. The moral panic becomes, in fact, more significant and authoritative in determining the response of the state to the deviant act, than the act itself. Moral panics effectively mobilise other discourses, fears and anxieties, which in turn are highly productive and result in action that often ignores the root causes of the original deviant act, in favour of admonishing individuals in order to allay public unrest. 'Mugging' becomes synonymous with the decline of civilised society, and the end of freedom: 'Use of the label is likely to mobilise *this whole referential context*, with all its associated meanings and connotations' (ibid.: 19).

'Mugging' is readily identified by the American press as an assault on democratic liberal values. It is this associative meaning that drives much of the British press coverage, and contributes to the crisis of public confidence in law and order on the streets of British cities. If, as according to the authors, 1960s America epitomised a capitalist nation state in crisis, it was in 1970s Britain that the effects of such a crisis were being felt. The experiences of New Yorkers seemed to translate effortlessly to the streets of London so that by 1973, when press reportage of 'mugging' was at its height, the meaning of the deviant act had extended to embrace 'race, crime, violence and lawlessness' (ibid.: 28). The term 'mugging' was imported from the American experience replete with a political and social rhetoric, which functioned as an '*anti*-crime, *anti*-black, *anti*-riot, *anti*-liberal, law-and-order backlash' (ibid.: 28).

> If the career of the label made a certain kind of social knowledge widely available in Britain, it also made a certain kind of response thoroughly predictable. No wonder police patrols jumped in anticipation, and judges delivered themselves of homilies as if they already knew what 'mugging' meant, and had only been waiting for its appearance; no wonder silent majorities spoke up demanding swift action, tough sentences and better protection. The soil of judicial and social reaction was already well tilled in preparation for its timely and long-prepared advent. (Hall et al., 1978a: 29)

In their first chapter, Hall et al. are able to deal deftly with the issue of crime statistics and the 'rising crime rate equation' that appears to justify stern measures in policing and sentencing. The hard facts of statistical evidence point to some creative statistical manoeuvrings on the part of the Home Office. One of the reasons for this identified by Hall et al. is the non-existence of 'mugging' as a category in the Metropolitan Police Annual Reports. Statistical evidence is one of the favoured sources of media reportage:

In short, the statistics such as we have do *not* support the 'rising crime rate' equation. An 'unprecedented' rise in robberies with violence was *not* new in 1972. Sentences for serious offences were growing *longer* rather than shorter, and *more* people were receiving them; acquittal rates seemed *not* to have changed. And these tough policies were *not* deterring. (Hall et al., 1978a: 30)

Hall et al.'s scathing analysis of the role of the police, the media and the judiciary in misrepresenting, augmenting and combating the phenomenon of 'mugging' did not go unheeded. Despite compelling arguments demonstrating that the rise in public consciousness of 'mugging' could not derive from either the police's own records, nor from the experiences of innocent victims, the research was savaged by critics. Hall et al.'s chief argument lies in the fundamental relationships between the ideological state apparatuses of modern society and how they work together, sometimes unwittingly, in order to generate consensus. As with football hooliganism, 'mugging' performs an ideological function and is used to legitimate particular social, political and penal responses, which, in turn, closes down alternative or dissident viewpoints and achieves a new hegemony.

At no point do the authors however deny that 'mugging' had a real and tangible impact: 'It is *not* our view that the police or some other agency of the state has simply conjured "mugging" and street crime up out of thin (ibid)'. The issue is not whether individuals robbed other individuals, or that people were hurt as a result. They clearly did, and many were. Hall et al. do not pass moral judgement on victims or 'muggers', nor do they seek to trivialise 'mugging'. The authors are at pains to point out that their position in relation to the 'mugging' debate is to refuse to 'orientate ourselves in the accepted and conventional accounts of the "mugging" panic'. In other words, they wish to critique the whole common-sense framework in which the 'mugging' phenomenon is discovered, articulated and contained. To do this, they need to look at the multiple and complex layers and networks of symbolic production that, in turn, constitute the superstructural field. Hall et al. must turn to Gramsci in order to enlarge upon their thesis, that the State's reaction to 'mugging' epitomises a particular ideological strategy, which fragments class consciousness even as it binds. The phenomenon of 'mugging' enables the state to exercise new and extended powers of coercion. In the case of 'mugging', the racialised nature of the phenomenon enabled working-class Black and Asian youths, who were *already* perceived as dangerous and alien figures, to become the targets of increased police surveillance and prosecution. This move on the part of the police to identify deviants and, in many well-publicised cases, to anticipate a 'mugging' by arresting loitering individuals, corrodes relations between the police and black communities. 'Mugging' becomes typified as a crime largely committed by black unemployed youths. 'The "mugging" panic emerges, not from nowhere, but out of a field of relations between the police and the black communities. Crime alone does not explain its genesis.' (Hall et al., 1978: 181) But how has this situation arisen? Why should a capitalist state be in need of such strategies? What are the roots of the British paradigm, which equate lawlessness with blackness, and street crime with the end of civilisation?

capitalism in crisis

Chapters 8 and 9 of *Policing the Crisis* focus on the question of British state power in the 1970s, arguing that 'mugging' is 'one of the forms in which this critical "crisis of hegemony" makes itself manifest' (Hall et al., 1978a: 217). Hall et al. argue that the political and economic conditions in Britain in the 1970s indicated a capitalist society in crisis. Capitalism, as we have seen, stratifies whole classes. However, if capitalism itself begins to fail, the state will rally in order to manage capital. The interventionist power of the state effectively manages the class struggle:

> As the limits to the system have increasingly become apparent – a sharpening in competition for declining world markets, shifts in the terms of trade against the metropolitan capitalist countries from the primary-producing developing world, a tendency of the rates of profit in the developed countries to fall, deepening cycles of boom and recession, periodic currency crises and growing level of inflation – so the *visibility* of the state has increased. (Hall et al., 1978a: 214)

In terms of Britain's ailing economic fortunes, both the Wilson and the Heath governments were compelled to make bargains with a striking workforce, and broker all manner of deals in order to secure some form of economic stability. It is at this point that the working-class, identifiable in 1970s Britain as the various organisations of the Trade Union movement, are encouraged by the state to take the long term view, and equate their workers' interests with the interests of capital. Appeals to 'the nation' and 'the people' multiply. But as Hall et al. argue, the more the state makes such appeals,

> the more they appear as ritual gestures, invocations, whose meaning and purpose is not to refer, but to invoke, create and bring into being a consensus which has almost in fact entirely evaporated. (Hall et al., 1978a: 261–2)

By effectively convincing the workers that they have 'a "stake" in the system', the state is able to corporatise the labouring classes. Ultimately the aims of the state are perceived to be the same as the working classes. Hence, a new hegemony has to be won, whereby the class interests of the dominant class are now endorsed by the subordinated class. We can see in the ranging battleground of strikes, pay bargaining and work to rule of the 1970s, how such instability resulted in a crisis of management for the state itself. As the state steps in to manage the capitalist system, so it places itself in jeopardy. The stakes are higher, the cost of failure, so much greater. In such circumstances, Hall et al. argue, securing popular consent becomes even more crucial, since consent of the majority represents the state's '*only* basis of legitimacy' (ibid.: 214). It is therefore at times of greatest crisis that the manufacture and manipulation of public consent becomes so crucial to the maintenance of power:

> A crisis of hegemony marks a moment of profound rupture in the political and economic life of a society, an accumulation of contradictions. If in moments of 'hegemony' everything works spontaneously so as to sustain and enforce a particular form of class domination while rendering the basis of that social authority invisible through the mechanisms of the production of consent, then moments in which the equilibrium of consent is disturbed, or where the contending class forces are so nearly balanced that neither can achieve that sway from which a resolution to the crisis can be promulgated, are moments *when the whole basis of political leadership and cultural authority becomes exposed and contested.* (Hall et al., 1978a: 217)

111

In addition, the 'masks of liberal consent and popular consensus slip to reveal the reserves of coercion and force on which the cohesion of the state and its legal authority finally depends' (ibid.: 217). In the case of 'mugging', the authors of *Policing the Crisis* aim to chart the shift that occurred in the early 1970s when the state began to exercise its considerable powers of coercion, in relation to a moral panic about street crime.

the signification spiral

Drawing on Poulantzas, and acutely aware of the limitations of their analysis, Hall et al. propose a relationship between the autonomy of the state and the drive toward consensus. They identify what they see as the crucial modes of ideological labour undertaken by superstructural agencies such as the police, the judiciary and the media. They coin the term 'signification spiral' to describe the process by which a specific concern centring around a subversive or antagonistic minority is mapped onto a matrix of other fears, concerns or anxieties. Once mobilised, the 'convergence' of specific concerns escalates the effect and consequently the reaction of social classes to the phenomenon. As it gains momentum and crosses the 'threshold' of anxiety, so the signified event spirals ever more threateningly towards the next 'threshold' and so on, becoming by turns, increasingly significant and in need of stern measures to curtail it (Hall et al., 1978a: 224).

'Convergences', such as we see in relation to 'mugging', occur 'when political groups adopt deviant life-styles or when deviants become politicised' (ibid.: 224). As police efforts to anticipate and contain the 'mugging' increasingly alienated groups of young black men, so 'mugging' becomes associated with militancy, anti-social activity and deviant lifestyles. The experience of America determines to a significant degree the linkage between 'mugging' and the black ghettos of New York, Washington and other major US cities. 'Mugging' is increasingly perceived as a black problem and efforts to contain it therefore focus on the policing of black communities. As the state reaches economic crisis point, right wing factions find it easier to exploit racial tensions. Thus in the case of 'mugging', the signification spiral works as a centrapetal force, feeding on the resonating fears of indigenous white communities who experience their loss of community, employment and security as a direct result of black immigrant communities.

Of course, in addition to the ideological rhetoric, the state in crisis will ultimately fall back on its coercive powers in order to secure its position. Hall et al. quote Gramsci,

> As soon as the dominant social group has exhausted its function, the ideological bloc tends to crumble away; then 'spontaneity' may be replaced by 'constraint' in even less disguised and indirect forms, culminating in out-right police measures and *coups d'état*. (Gramsci in Hall et al., 1978a: 273)

It is no coincidence then, that a period of mass resistance by the workforces of Britain should provoke a crisis of management for the state. There were even rumblings of a police strike by 1979. Unofficial strikes and industrial action by a growing population of disillusioned and angry workers (teachers, dustmen, hospital ancillary workers, miners, electricity-supply workers, post office workers, ship builders, seamen, dockers, civil servants) resulted in the state's introduction of hardline legislation, use of army and police to manage industrial disputes and the systemic dismantling of union power by the early 1980s. The escalation of the state's repressive and coercive measures in response to the 'mugging' phenomenon, represents one element within the whole deepening crisis. But most important of all according to Hall et al., when put under the microscope, the key determining factor in this reconstitution of state authority, was that of race.

policing the black community

Rather than just examine the phenomenon of 'mugging' as a product of specific historical, political and cultural junctures, Hall et al. see it as relational to the deeper crisis of state control: 'A sharp judicial reaction to 'street crime' *could* have occurred at other moments in the post-war period' (Hall et al., 1978a: 305). It is also the case that a state in crisis will utilise the law to shore up its power, becomes therefore by definition 'legitimate' 'even if it is not "right"; and *whoever threatens the*

113

consensus threatens the state' (ibid.: 310). What is no longer achievable by consent, is achieved through recourse to the law and as a consequence, the law stands in opposition to violence. Those who use violence in whatever form, are increasingly perceived by the state as a threat to state authority. In the case of 'mugging', police harassment of black youth led to an increasingly organised and politicised response from the black community. Pitched battles between black groups and the police occurred during the early 1970s.

Hall et al. identify the period immediately after the 'mugging' phenomenon reached its peak, as the beginning of a more sustained attempt on the part of the police to manage the state's crisis:

> Policing *the blacks* threatened to mesh with the problem of policing *the poor* and policing the *unemployed*: all three were concentrated in precisely the same urban areas [ ] The on-going problem of policing the blacks had become, for all practical purposes, synonymous with the wider problem of *policing the crisis*. (Hall et al., 1978a: 332)

How did this come about? According to Hall et al., the growing economic crisis hit the particularly vulnerable black workforce, which together with a young generation of black school leavers, constituted 'an *ethnically distinct class fraction* – the one *most exposed* to the winds of unemployment' (ibid.: 331). The politicisation of blacks coupled with their economic situation made for a volatile relationship to the state, and those agents of the state, namely the police, who were charged with containing the revolt, such as it was. The National Front were not slow to jump on the bandwagon, levelling attacks against the black community and whipping up support for compulsory repatriation. Race had become the 'objective correlative of crisis' (ibid.: 333) mobilising all the anxieties, tensions and fears generated by the crisis in hegemony and the loss of economic stability.

> 'Mugging' is now unquestioningly identified with a specific class fraction or category of labour (black youth) and with a specific kind of area: the inner ring zones of multiple deprivation. (Hall et al., 1978a: 338)

When Hall et al. spoke in their introduction of race as the 'ideological conductor', they were intent on analysing the conditions that enabled 'mugging' to be fore-grounded in terms of black immigration, black poverty and black crime. The accumulative and spiralling representation of 'mugging' as a predominantly *black* issue, lends credence to Hall et al.'s analysis of the state's increasingly tough measures to combat 'the enemy within'. That black communities should bear the brunt of the state's crackdown becomes inevitable given both the visibility of black people in London and other major metropolitan centres, and their particular economic, social and political vulnerability. The idea of 'the enemy within' becomes a resonant ideological 'truth' when articulated by the state, and therefore has profound consequences for civil society.

the enemy within

When the state finds itself in crisis, it tries to police the crisis by containing any disruptive elements, vilifying dissenters, mobilising ideological constructions such as 'the nation' and 'the people' in order to reclaim a legitimacy for its actions. In short the state must generate an 'authoritarian consensus' (Hall et al., 1978a: 339) enabling it to make more concerted and coercive use of the agencies of law and order, police, judiciary, and exceptionally, the army. Most notably for Hall et al., the crisis allows the state to operate ideologically, pitching working class whites against working class blacks, so 'that each can be made to provide the other with its negative reference group, the "manifest cause" of each other's ill-fortune' (ibid.: 339). Racism has much mileage according to the authors, and feeds National Front rhetoric. However it is important to recognise the extent to which racism informs the mechanisms of ordinary civil society:

> So the crisis of the working class is reproduced, once again, through the structural mechanisms of racism, as a crisis *within* and *between* the working classes. [ ] In these conditions blacks become the 'bearers' of these contradictory outcomes; and black crime becomes the *signifier* of the crisis in the urban colonies. (Hall et al., 1978a: 339)

But the inevitable discrimination that arises as one of the effects of the crisis is also subject to ideological definition. Racism is usually (common-sensically) understood as an exceptional circumstance. This, Hall et al. argue, arises from the mistaken premise that blacks and whites start from the basis of a level playing field. However, Hall et al. argue for an understanding of racism and colour discrimination as endemic to capitalist structures and institutions. The apparatuses of the state effectively reproduce the same conditions and exclusions over and over. This capitalist reproduction not only reproduces class positions but also the same racial schisms. Such stratifications are also clearly visible in relation to gender divisions, both in relation to expectations and labour. Hall et al. point to the experiences of young blacks in education, who are routinely excluded by being stigmatised and stereotyped.

Language in particular is the battleground where culture and identity become fused. Hall comments how, 'Instead of standard English being added as a necessary second language to whatever is the version of patois or Creole spoken by the child, the latter are often simply eliminated as sub-standard speech' (ibid.: 341). The situation in schools is but a microcosm of what follows in the world of work. Black and Asian labour in the 1970s was largely concentrated in heavy manufacturing industries, low-paid work and the transport and service industries. Even in the more competitive and productive industries, black workers were more acutely at risk from mechanisation of the work-force, and subject to de-skilling across the British economy. Moreover, Hall et al. remind us that the immigration so threatening to Enoch Powell is directly related to the ebb and flow of British capital (ibid.: 343). Caribbean and Asian labour was solicited in the 1950s in order to supply the needs of an expanding post-war industrial nation. Blacks and Asians constitute the labour force that powered the Empire, and continues to supply the needs of British industry. They are therefore the engine of industry, and consequently, also most vulnerable at times of economic slow-down and recession.

race, capitalism and employment

Hall et al. argue that the 1970s and 1980s saw the emergence of an increasingly racialised British politics. In their final chapter, 'The politics of "mugging"' they make a compelling case for understanding racialised politics and racism as crucial material and social factors in the production and reproduction of capitalist class relations in Britain. Young black people are objectified by this process and find themselves ethnically and socially marginalised and victimised. What happens in the case of such symbolic and actual violence?

> But race performs a double function. It is also the principal modality in which the black members of that class 'live', experience, make sense of and thus *come to a consciousness* of their structured subordination. It is through the modality of race that blacks comprehend, handle and then begin to resist the exploitation which is an objective feature of their class situation. (Hall et al., 1978a: 361)

Thus race is more than a matter of some individuals experiencing occasional discrimination. As Hall has argued earlier in relation to class, race operates hegemonically in the structuring of both dominance and resistance. The ideological positioning of black working-class youth within British society in the 1970s determined the real relations of black experience, *and* its mode of resistance against the state:

> It is in the modality of race that those whom the structures systematically exploit, exclude and subordinate, discover themselves as an exploited, excluded and subordinated class. Thus it is primarily in and through the modality of race that resistance, opposition and rebellion *first* expresses itself. (Hall et al., 1978a: 362)

And it is black youth that Hall and his colleagues are most concerned about because they are the first generation of black children born into British society. Black Britons educated in Britain are likely to feel the presence of British racism for the following reasons:

> Better equipped in terms of educational skills to take their place beside the white peers of their own class in the ranks of the skilled and the semi-skilled labour, they feel the closure of the occupational and opportunity structure to them – on grounds not of competence but of race – all the more acutely. English racism, both as a material structure and as an ideological presence, cannot be explained away to them as a temporary aberration, the result of a fit of white

absent-mindedness. It is how the system works. In their experience, English society *is* 'racist' – it *works through race*. (Hall et al., 1978a: 363)

Hall's experiences as a secondary school teacher in Brixton at the time of the Notting hill riots of 1958 laid some of the groundwork for these later arguments. He is able to speak with knowledge about the conditions confronting black youth, and of the strategies utilised by black communities to achieve stability and acceptance within British society. Equally, Hall's knowledge of the generation divide between the immigrant parent generation who first came to Britain in the 1950s and their children born in Britain during the 1960s and 1970s, allows him some insight into the ways in which race functions *within* the black community itself. Where the older generation may seek integration and stability, the younger generation is increasingly radicalised by its experiences of structured and endemic discrimination. Unable to find work and unwilling to follow the example of their parents' generation, which they see as kow-towing to white authority, Hall et al. argue that black youth is increasingly at risk; petty crime, hustling, and falling foul of overzealous policing strategies. Whereas working classes have traditionally acquired class consciousness through their struggles in relation to capitalist labour relations, in the case of working-class blacks, their consciousness-raising is largely as a result of their exclusion from labour relations. As Hall et al. see it, such a circumstance can be read as a politicisation that is articulated at times as a *refusal* to work (Hall et al., 1978a: 370).

a marxist theory of crime?

But can crime itself be a political act? Does the 'mugging' phenomenon indicate a rise in the tide of black political consciousness as a section within the proletariat? Hall et al. cite Hirst's argument (Hall et al., 1978: 364–367) that one cannot theorise working class criminality as a political strategy against capital for a number of reasons. First, 'theft' is unproductive in the sense that it is outside of the relations of production and adapts to the capitalist system through the organisation of criminal enterprises. Second, the dangerous and possibly criminal classes, or what Marx termed the *lumpenproletariart*, live parasitically off the working classes through such activities as gaming, prostitution, extortion and theft. Third, it is the same criminal element that will, if circumstances are favourable, turn informer or engage in meaningless acts of violence, which do no more than perpetuate the capitalist system of labour relations. This is a pertinent argument, however Hall et al. are not convinced and turn back to Marx's definition of the *lumpenprole-tariat* in order to quizz the idea of productive and unproductive labour. Their argument hinges on one particular point of interpretation: 'who and what corresponds to the *lumpenproletariat* in contemporary capital-ist social formations' (ibid.: 365), and how does this relate to the expe-riences of black working class youth who engage in 'mugging'?

Hall et al. read Marx's definition of the *lumpenproletariat* as fundamentally historical, though not necessarily 'out of date' (ibid.: 365). In order to justify their reading, Hall et al. stress the importance of Marx's later work, the unfinished *Capital*. We are reminded that it is here that Marx reconstructs his theory of capitalist exploitation of the proletariat, in terms of the *relations* of production that always dominate and through which all other social relations ultimately have to be understood (ibid.: 366). According to Marx, it is only by re-organising the modes of production that we can move from a capitalist system to a socialist state.

When Marx articulates the nature and function of profit within the capitalist system, he demonstrates the gulf between what owners pay and the real value of labour. Owners strive to keep wages down, in order to maximise profit. Workers struggle to demand higher wages in order to prevent further exploitation by the owners. This struggle between owners and workers is thus endemic to capitalism. But what of the classes which do not participate in this relationship? Do those who make up the *lumpenproletariat* exist outside of this mode of rela-tions? According to Hall et al., they do not. Since the modes of produc-tion permeate all aspects of social life, those who are wageless are no less party to the capitalist mode of production than those who are waged. In other words, the criminal classes, the unemployed, and the dissolute are all still subject to the same conditions as the waged. Unproductive labour is the term used by Marx to describe labour that is unwaged or unsalaried. Such a category may nowadays include those engaged in housework, family members who care for an elderly

119

relative, or those who are otherwise financially supported by family or friends. Such 'workers' may be unwaged, but they none the less generate 'value'. This is because such workers are still integral to the capitalist modes of consumption and, therefore, part of the capitalist mode of production. They are in effect structured by capitalism as an unrecognised and unofficial workforce, or a 'reserve army of labour' (ibid.: 369). Hall et al. draw upon the work of Selma James and Mariarosa Della Costa who make the link between women's work in the home as fundamentally productive, because women are central to the constitution of social power within the family, and the political potential of those who refuse to work: 'If your production is vital for capitalism, refusing to produce, refusing to work, is a fundamental level of social power' (ibid.: 369). They extend this argument to address the position of blacks who articulate their relative powerlessness against the capitalist state by refusing to work. Hall et al. point out how influential this thesis has become among politically active black groups living in Britain in the 1970s:

> Police activity, which is primarily directed against this 'workless' stratum of the class, is defined as an attempt to bring the wageless back into wage labour.

Furthermore, because of the organised political nature of this refusal,

> The 'wageless' are not to be equated with the traditional disorganised and undisciplined 'lumpenproletariat'. This false identification arises only because the black working class is understood exclusively in relation to British capital. But, in fact, black labour can only be adequately understood, historically, if it is also seen as a class which has already developed in the Caribbean – vis-à-vis 'colonial' forms of capital – as a cohesive social force. (Hall et al., 1978a: 370–1)

What Hall et al. are stressing is the specific cultural and political formations of black working class experience *prior* to their arrival in Britain. Hall et al. are acutely aware of the complexities of black identity in relation to the question of work. They cite Darcus Howe and the *Race Today*[4] collective's arguments, which stress the political and social structures of a black working class that does not apparently work. Howe argues that 'hustling' is a way of life for many young black men living in Trinidad and other Caribbean Islands. This wageless black class has historically been able to negotiate real power in Trinidad. Howe argues therefore that the exercise of the 'wageless' refusal to work within Britain constitutes a political stance. When Hall et al. comment on the antagonism between the older parent generation who first settled in Britain in the 1950s and the younger second generation of blacks born in Britain, they are describing two different black working-class formations. The older generation who, as Hall has described his own father, observed the colonial hierarchy and sought a place within it, and the younger generation who refuse to accept their place as colonised and dependent upon the structures of white capital. The struggle that ensues is a bitterly contested one in which the younger black citizens of Britain will begin to express their anger and disillusionment at their native country with 'a new confidence and boldness' (ibid.: 371) that may result in the refusal to work. In some cases this may also generate a tendency towards 'hustling', petty crime and even 'mugging'.

There is no doubt that such arguments were viewed as highly contentious. Hall et al. point to the contrary arguments posed by Cambridge and Gutsmore who argue that such rebellion is ideological, rather than political. According to this line of argument, the black 'wageless' do not operate in any organised sense as a political class against capital. Rather they represent the surplus reserve labour that British capital at present cannot fully utilise. Hence their 'wageless' condition is evidence of their containment by capitalism, not their rebellion from it.

the function of the black working class

Hall et al. now go beyond the class antagonism endemic to capitalist relations of production in order to consider the specific geo-political situation of the black working class within the context of Empire. They clearly draw key elements from the differing arguments advocated by Selma and Della Costa, Howe, Cambridge and Gutsmore.

They unite the concept of the 'wageless' with the subordinated condition of the colonised proletariat who are both exploited by

British capital, and ideologically positioned as subordinate in relation to the indigenous white proletariat. It is the exploitation of colonial labour that enables the colonial power to subsidise and 'placate the proletariat at home' (Hall et al., 1978a: 377). According to this argument, overseas labour becomes a readily exploitable resource for capital, thus shoring up the home economy in times of recession and enabling extra productivity in times of increased competition. The antagonism played out between workers and owners is demonstrable in the antagonism between these two proletariat work forces when they both meet. In practical terms, the threat of cheaper overseas labour is often utilised to contain militancy within the labour force. Equally, the colonised workforce is held in check by the relative requirements of the mother country's economy, and this relationship often eclipses the needs of the local economy, so that local colonised communities become dependent upon overseas trade. The Developing World, as it is nowadays termed, consists primarily of formally colonised nations that are structurally bound to this kind of economic relationship. In the 1970s, many countries in Africa, the Caribbean and Asia were still colonial territories. The workforces in these countries cannot be said to have achieved the class consciousness so well embedded in Western Europe. As a consequence, such work forces might be termed 'unproductive' and described as the 'lumpenproletariat'. However, as Hall et al. point out, identifying the nature of the black 'wageless' in Britain depends on the particularities of each working-class formation. Caribbean labour is a product of a specific relationship between the Caribbean nations and Britain. When black migrant workers first started arriving in the 1950s, one of the key distinctions that was lost was their sense of national identity. Far from being identified as Trinidadian or Jamaican, such migrants were viewed as merely black. Similarly the class distinctions apparent in places like Jamaica were also 'lost' on the British. Their relationship to Britain was one predicated on the idea of 'the mother country', where they would be welcomed into the existing labour force.

Hall et al. are also concerned to address the present circumstances that may have a direct bearing on the position of the black proletariat. They argue that a necessary reserve army of colonised labour has become a permanent feature of post-war capitalism. Migrant labour was, in the late fifties and sixties:

sucked into production from the Caribbean and Asian sub-continent. Gradually, as economic recession began to bite, a more restrictive practice was instituted – in effect, forcing a part of the 'reserve army' to remain where it already was, in the Caribbean and the Asian homelands. Now, in the depths of the economic crisis, we are in the alternate pole of the 'reserve army' cycle: the phase of control and expulsion. (Hall et al., 1978a)

Where the government has tried to curb rising inflation and spiralling debt by wage freezes and increased borrowing, the effect has been the collapse of British industry and massive job losses. Hall et al. conclude that one of the chief residual effects of what they term 'the political assault on full employment' during the early and mid 1970s has been the rise in black unemployment. In terms of the 'reserve army', which British capital has created, 'the black youths roaming the streets of British cities in search for work are its latest, and rawest recruits' (Hall et al., 1978a: 381).

black resistance

Hall et al. are conscious of the double history that created the conditions of the black working class in Britain in the 1970s. Caribbean workers in Britain are subject to the needs of British capital and are positioned within British urban society as secondary unskilled workers within the economy. Hall et al. are also acutely aware of the complexities of the different theoretical arguments that constitute the debate around black oppression and the function and nature of black street crime, or 'mugging'. On the one hand we have a black labour force that, in times of recession, must find its own ways of surviving. The more self-aware elements within this labouring class articulate their resistance to this relationship of secondary status, in a refusal to work. This is the position advocated by the editor of *Race Today*, Darcus Howe.[5] What emerges is an 'underclass' consisting of the marginalised and surplus workforce who are therefore 'wageless', and, crucially in 1970s Britain, increasingly without hope of employment. Furthermore, the colonial history binding the Caribbean workforce to British capital is another means by which younger black Britons come to understand their powerlessness as a kind of structured racism. It is also the means by which they articulate their resistance to the dominant structures of social and economic society.

Hall et al. refer to the experience of black communities in the ghettos of American cities in order to draw parallels between the increasing criminalisation of black youth and its corollating patterns of black resistance. In the case of America, black separatist movements such as the Black Panthers made significant interventions into the structures of black communities in order to incite revolutionary fervour. Their commitment to the black struggle called for armed resistance against the forces of white oppression. However the movement's primary aim was to unite the disaffected and the marginal elements within the black working class – the black *lumpenproletariat* – in order to organise resistance to what they saw as the structured and endemic racism of capitalism. The work of Franz Fanon was extremely important in the mobilisation of this movement and informed the belief that it was indeed possible for 'key social classes' to become revolutionary.

> But the adoption and adaptation of Fanonism within the *black* movement in the United States is more directly germane: first, because of its impact on the developing consciousness of black people everywhere, including those in Britain; second, because it suggested that a political analysis, initiated in terms of colonial society and struggle, *was* transferable to the conditions of black minorities in developed urban capitalist conditions. (Hall et al., 1978a: 386)

Fanon saw organised violence as a direct and necessary means of building self-respect and overcoming fear of the structures of white oppression. However, the rising of a peasant or urban collective could not be achieved without the leadership of informed revolutionary figures. The Panthers raised consciousness by going into the ghettos of America and transforming them. Central to this work was the role and function of the black 'hustler', who,'provided one of the few role models for young blacks on the block: one of the few not cowed by oppression, not tied to the daily grind of low-paid poverty' (ibid.: 387). Such figures were actively recruited by the Panthers as a means of awakening a latent consciousness among black groups. Such a strategy relied upon the relationship of black 'brothers', rather than black workers, and as such constituted 'a lumpen politics' (ibid.: 387) that sanctioned the role of the hustler, even as it attempted to convert criminal activity into political activism. Hall et al. draw attention to this movement as they believe it has a direct bearing on the crisis of black urban youth in Britain and their criminalisation within the structures of a law and order society. They do not, however, agree entirely with Fanon's thesis. Nevertheless they see important parallels with the way Fanon's work has been used to mobilise a particular politics of black identity both in America and elsewhere.

reproducing inequality

Hall et al. argue that the very structures that reproduce the secondary racial status of black workers within capitalism are the same structures that enable those workers to achieve a level of political consciousness in relation to race, and in some cases, to seek redress through violent or criminal actions. In this context, 'mugging' assumes 'an ambiguous relationship' (Hall et al., 1978a: 390) to certain forms of consciousness. Crime, though no answer to these structured ineqaulities, can at times operate as a 'muffled and displaced expression to the experience of permanent exclusion' (ibid.: 391). This is the crisis of race relations Hall et al. identify as endemic to British society in the 1970s.

But, as the authors readily acknowledge, the situation is not so easily theorised. The pattern of black responses to the political, social and economic situation in British society is as uneven as it is varied and contested. As such black workers are positioned in relation to ideological, social, political and economic structures of inequality. Those structures are themselves extremely complex and may be char-acterised by their 'discontinuities', 'discrepancies', divergences' and non-correspondences' (ibid.: 393). In short, there is no single simplistic manner in which we can identify and categorise the range of black working class experience. Despite this, Hall et al. are very clear that one logic emerges out of this tangle:

> Race is intrinsic to the manner in which the black labouring classes are *complexly constituted* at each of these levels. [ ] The constitution of this class fraction as a class, and the *class relations* which inscribe it, func-tion as *race relations*. The two are inseparable. Race is the modality in

which class is lived. It is also the medium in which class relations are experienced. (Hall et al., 1978a: 394)

However, the 'political knot' the authors identify, 'cannot be untied here' (ibid.: 393). The apparently simple identification of the black mugger in 1970s Britain is dismantled in its entirety by Hall and his co-authors. The work undertaken in *Policing the Crisis* exemplifies some of the best kind of sociological enquiry because it raises awareness of complex social formations, rather than trying to fit the world into one particular sociological model. At the same time as they try to dissect the operations of ideological and economic structures, they expand their discussion of the theoretical in order to make a specific intervention into the debate escalating within the public sphere. The authors clearly speak to the terms of the wider debate, rather than retiring safely to the sidelines.

Policing the Crisis tried to address the problems besetting a generation of disenfranchised young black men. Though the authors did not discuss representation in aesthetic terms they were extremely aware of the consequences for the articulation and representation of black masculinity within British culture. The authors wanted to demonstrate the impact of social and economic structures on these subordinated classes, and gender could not be left out of that equation. If *Policing the Crisis* focussed on the experience of black men, elsewhere a parallel project was underway that fore-grounded the experiences of women.

the impact of feminism

Although most people associate Hall's relationship to feminist scholarship with the turbulent years at the Centre, Hall's first experience of feminism did not begin with Birmingham.

> I looked after children at the first meeting of the History Workshop in Oxford. I was in the crèche, holding the babies! So that whole experience, the feminist conscious-raising group, the reading group, you know, it was a terrifying experience for a man, I mean what can I say, that it was absolutely great!? It was horrendous! – because they said 'shut up', you know, 'don't come' or 'no, you can't come'. 'Don't tell us what to do, don't tell us what to read, you know – it's not your

business!' It was a most aggressive moment. Of *course* it *had to happen*. But I'm not going to tell you I thought it was wonderful! But I was transformed by it. Absolutely transformed by it. I was certainly transformed against my better nature, against my patriarchal nature, against my wanting an easy life and against the image, my image of marriage.[6]

Like most men of his generation, Hall was feeling the effects much closer to home. Living with a feminist challenged all of Hall's preconceptions, particularly in relation to marriage. With the onset of parenthood, many women scholars at Birmingham were finding it tough trying to juggle the demands of career and family. The Birmingham feminist network began as a childcare group, enabling women scholars the opportunity to meet and support each other in what otherwise had become an isolating experience of motherhood. Hall is candid as he reflects on his response to the new politics: 'Of course I resisted! I don't believe any man who says they didn't resist it, you know. What would feminism be worth if the men didn't fight it! If we said, "Oh yes – fine – press on!" Of course we resisted it! But you had to live through it.'[7] The impact on Hall however went beyond the politics of the home and into the workplace. He and his colleague Michael Green recognised that things would have to change at the Centre. The rise of feminism needed to be acknowledged in terms of its impact on cultural studies:

> we said, well we must get some people who are doing this into the centre. It was not a demand from the women in the centre. They were not yet very much into it. They were younger, graduate students, they hadn't been through what the other women in Birmingham were going through – namely the sudden on-set of children, motherhood descending on an active career and the only place they could get to talk to anybody was to get together with other feminists in the crèche. The young women grad students were not terribly into it. We said we must get someone in. We said we should be doing more work in this area, so there wasn't a resistance to the idea like that. What there was a resistance to was the lived experience again of people again saying 'well we don't want to read Marx, we would like to read French feminism.[8]

women take issue

Hall's famous description of feminism's intervention into cultural studies conveyed both the disruptive force *and* the necessity for the interruption to what had become yet another patriarchal space: 'As the thief in the night, it broke in; interrupted, made an unseemly noise, seized the time, crapped on the table of cultural studies' (Hall, 1992: 282). Some of the women working within the Centre decided to address the fundamental problem of female subordination within cultural studies. The Women's Studies Group was formed in October 1974. Their work resulted in the important and influential volume of work, *Women Take Issue* (1978), a collection of essays that fore-grounded feminist debates and issues in relation to cultural consumption, agency and identity. But the dynamics of the Centre itself were also taken to task. As Director of the Centre, Hall found himself caught up in the struggle. There were essentially two issues that Hall had to negotiate. The first was the demand from members of the Women's Studies Group that they be allowed to meet as a separate group, without men being present. The Women's forum was established in 1976, but it was a difficult and strained period for Hall and his colleagues.

> Even I had to read French feminism! How can I understand you when I don't know what Irigiray is saying, so 'do I really have to?' 'Do we have to revise the MA?' 'Yes we do!' and that is very difficult in a democratic place. You could ignore it in an authoritarian place, but when everyone had equal power where everyone could have a say in what they were studying, had a say in who we should read next, of course you couldn't say 'no', and what's more it [saying no] was threatening to the style we had tried to develop of a kind of political consensus.[9]

Hall had worked hard to ensure that the Centre operated as an open space that was never overtaken by the politics of one particular group over another: 'We were not an off-shoot of the Communist Party, we were not an off-shoot of the Trotskyist Party, we were not an off-shoot of any party, you know, we couldn't have a direct mediation of party politics in that way'.[10] Hall was also mindful of the university's interest in the Centre's activities, and fully aware that any overt politicisation of the student body threatened the future of the Centre:

> What united us was a basic political critical orientation, but you know, we couldn't mobilise, we were not at the service of various discriminations along the political spectrum. Well as you can imagine that

created a sort of commonality, not a uniform party line, a kind of commonality. Well into that come the feminists who say 'we want to meet on our own'.[11]

The problem facing Hall was how to manage the situation so that the feminists could meet without either upsetting the balance of influences within the centre, and without the university finding a reason to intervene in the Centre's internal affairs.

> There was a feminist reading group, there was a Freud reading group because the feminists were very into psychoanalysis, you know and so on. I had no problem with that. I had a problem in relation to the delicate political balance, the attempted informal political democratisation, collectivism that we were trying to run.[12]

Hall's function within the structure of the Centre was no doubt a contributing factor in the struggles that resulted.

> My feeling was, in the end, they could only operate by stereotyping me as the father. And since I wasn't the father, and didn't want to act the father, I couldn't step out of it. I was the father in the sense that there were only two members of staff. I was supervising them, I was running the seminars, you know, what can you do? I tried to flatten the hierarchy as far as possible, but you can't flatten them entirely, and it was an impossible position for me. I was represented as being more hostile than I actually was.[13]

There is a sense of inevitability in Hall's acknowledgement of his own personal and professional relationship to feminist politics during this period, yet as Charlotte Brunsdon (1997) recognises, Hall does not seek self-justification. He fully acknowledges his own resistances and the extent to which his position within the Centre had to be challenged: 'I think they wanted to transform me, but they couldn't transform my position, structurally there were limits. And I think they wanted to transform me in terms of my intellectual leadership, but I don't know that they wanted to get rid of me'. There is no question that Hall's engagement with feminism and post-structuralism was transforming. Not only did his own work take a turn towards the thorny questions of identity and subjectivity, but he had experienced the reality of the gulf between intentions and practice, and the hidden resistances that surfaced without warning. He has described this as 'the point at which power bites',[14] acknowledging the tension between structure and agency, desire and action. It was at the crucial intersection between power and knowledge that Hall understood the reality of gendered power relations: 'Long, long after I was able to pronounce the words, I encountered the reality of Foucault's profound insight into the individual reciprocity of knowledge and power. Talking about giving up power is a radically different experience from being silenced' (Hall, 1996: 270).

conclusion

Hall's encounters with race and gender politics were deeply formative during his years at Birmingham, and the increasingly confrontational mode of his interventions are certainly indicative of the extent to which the politics of identity and representation were becoming sharper and more polarised during the 1970s. Whatever optimism might have been engendered in the 1960s had evaporated in the face of much tougher defensive actions on the part of the state, and its movement towards a law and order society.

But the end of the 1970s also signalled the end of Hall's time at Birmingham and a move to a new post at the Open University. Hall's decision to leave the Centre has often been linked to the inception of feminist politics. However I think this both overstates Hall's resistance and underplays the extent to which his role as Director was itself a critical barrier against the machinations of the university. Had he left any earlier, it is certain that the university would have closed the Centre down. Only when the Centre had achieved a degree of external recognition could Hall move on, confident in the knowledge that there was sufficient support *outside* of the university to merit its continuation.

further reading

Brunsdon, C. (1996) 'A thief in the night. Stories of feminism in the 1970s at CCCS' in Morley and Chen (eds) *Stuart Hall, Critical Dialogues*. Routledge: London.

CCCS, University of Birmingham (1982) *The Empire Strikes Back.* Hutchinson: London.

Barker, M. and Beezer, A. (1992) *Reading into Cultural Studies.* Routledge: London.

Cohen, S. (1980) *Folk Devils and Moral Panics.* Basil Blackwell: Oxford.

Willis, P. (1977) *Learning to Labour: How Working-class Kids get Working-class Jobs.* Saxon House: London.

Women's studies group, CCCS, University of Birmingham (1978) *Women Take Issue: Aspects of Women's Subordination.* Hutchinson: London.

6

taking the risk
of living dangerously

> If you deny the existence, the interdependence which is registered in the terms 'society' and 'community', if you refuse to accept the principles of the gift, if you subscribe to any other philosophy than that which is articulated in the poet's words 'no man or woman is an island', if you go down that road, there is nothing left to defend but your salaries'. (Hall, 1989: 17–18)

introduction

Hall left the Centre in 1978 in order to take up a professorial post at the Open University. Hall's move was symptomatic of his desire to bring cultural studies to a new constituency of students. This move to a greater inclusivity appears to be further marked by Hall's shift in writing. For the next ten years or more, he would voice his antagonism towards the New Right and his disaffection with the Left, not through the conventional means of academic publishing, but through the organ of a journal that occupied a particular space vis-à-vis the British political landscape. In this chapter we will examine Hall's key writings from *Marxism Today* and in particular his work on Thatcherism, which has engendered so much debate and argument throughout the 1980s and beyond.

marxism today

Marxism Today was originally the journal of the British Communist Party. Under Martin Jacques' editorship it acquired a new lease of life. Angela McRobbie (1996: 239) however has described *Marxism Today*, as a publishing project, as opposed to a political project. Hall disagrees:

> There was a real political project there. A political project that identified with the communist university in the 1970s, which was major and very big and very broad, very inclusive. Race and feminist agendas, sexual politics in there along with discussions on class and political parties and so on. [It was] a very heady time, and all this was inserted into the *Marxism Today* project, which had a quite specific politics.[1]

One of the conditions of Hall joining the editorial board was that neither he nor his colleague David Edgar should be required to join the Communist Party. This was an unprecedented move and marked the beginning of a much more inclusive project of left-wing politics within the journal, than had historically been the case. *Marxism Today* provided an important space for the critique of established Marxist positions, and encouraged new thinking regarding the role and function of the state, strategies for opposing the rising tide of New Right politics and the need for a new kind of socialism. During the 1980s, it became a high profile and successful vehicle for left wing debate. The contributors even included the occasional Conservative politician, as well as many emergent and leading figures on the left, from Tony Benn to Tony Blair. Hall's arrival at the journal marked a new era and opened the journal up to a broader audience. Hall's involvement with the journal gave him space to articulate and develop his critical analysis of the New Right and make considerable interventions into the political debate concerning Thatcherism and the crisis facing the Left in Britain.

The work undertaken by the *Policing the Crisis* collective represented a sustained critical analysis of the conditions affecting Britain and the foundations of the rise of a new and radical kind of Conservatism. Over the next ten years Hall would continuously assert the need for the left in Britain to understand the particular nature of what he termed Thatcherism in order that the Left might mount a successful counter-position. Villified by many on the left, and ridiculed by the Far Right, Hall's position during this period was never comfortable. He was often charged as being (unnecessarily) pessimistic; an accusation to which he responded with characteristic frankness.

The groundwork already undertaken by Hall in his analysis of the British political climate in the 1950s, through the heyday of student revolution in the 1960s and the economic collapse of capital in the 1970s, proved valuable and insightful as his critique of 1980s Far Right Conservatism gathered momentum. Where Hall differed from many other commentators of the period, was in his emphasis on the relationship between the failure of Labourism and the astonishing degree to which the Far Right was able to capture the working class vote. He signalled how impossible it would be for the Left to return to power unless they understood the real fundamentals of the new wave of Conservatism sweeping through Britain. In January 1979, Hall published 'The great moving right show'[2] in *Marxism Today*. In it, he outlined the significance of the shift in power and 'the crisis of the left which it has precipitated' (1988a: 1). It was a landmark article and marked the beginning of an analysis that would have profound consequences for the formation of the left in Britain, and would ultimately shape our understanding of Thatcherism as a new phenomenon in British politics.

problems with the left

Hall saw the Left as a political faction in total disarray. Still more worrying than the drift to the right, was the left's apparent inability to understand the full scale of the crisis, as Hall saw it. This failure of imagination would result in nearly 18 years of Labour opposition in the wilderness. The main problem confronting the left was, according to Hall, its unwillingness to address the failure of labourism and the organic nature of the crisis for socialism. Consequently, critics on the hard left such as Tony Benn addressed the issue of far right Conservatism as just another example of capitalist rhetoric. They therefore underestimated the appeal of Thatcher's new politics to the traditional labour-voting members of the working-class. It seemed to many on the left that such voters were suffering from a false consciousness which could be overthrown through committed attempts to restate the socialist ethic. However, as Hall grasped early on, the 'swing to the right' was not to be so easily resisted.

the failure of labourism

Hall and his colleagues at the Centre pointed to the mesh of problems confronting the governments of the 1970s, and their successive moves to intervene in all aspects of social, civil and economic life. The effective collapse of the social democratic contract between the working classes as represented by the trade unions, and both Labour and Conservative government during the 1970s, meant that by 1974, consensus politics and its corporatist strategies were undone. Heath's government fell as a direct result of the miners' strike. In times of crisis, the state will increasingly fall back on the rhetoric of inclusivity in order to marginalise and isolate those factions that are antagonistic to its position. Having failed to win support for its policies, the Heath government directed its energies against organised labour, which it termed 'the enemy within'. Heath's appeal to the population at large fell on deaf ears. But the Callaghan government was no more successful in breaching the deep chasm that now existed between government and the unions. The relationship with organised labour once enjoyed by Wilson is commonly referred to as the era of 'beer and sandwiches at No 10'. But Hall argues that the failure of the Labour government to deliver the radical programme of social change in the late 1960s was the beginning of the creeping disillusionment and sense of betrayal felt by the working classes. The Labourist strategies undertaken by postwar governments in Britain were in the process of collapsing, for, as Hall reminds us,

> It is important here to remember that this version of social democracy – 'Labourism' – is not a homogenous political entity but the complex political formation. It is not *the* expression of *the* working class 'in government', but the principal means of the political representation of the class. (1988a: 45)

In other words, the management of government depends on the corporatist bargaining of the Labour government, who supposedly represent the people, and the trade unions who represent the working classes: 'This "indissolvable link" is the practical basis for Labour's claim to be the natural governing party of the crisis. This is the contract it delivers' (ibid.: 45–6). However, at times of crisis, the social-democratic state will subjugate working-class interests in order to sustain capitalism. The resulting conflict lays government open to the charge of 'statism' and poses a deep contradiction for the working population. Once in government, how can the party of social democracy overthrow the interests of the labouring classes? As the crisis deepens, the government introduces greater measures of regulation and control, which are experienced by the working classes as direct assaults on their working conditions and income levels. The crisis effectively 'required Labour to discipline, limit and police the very classes it claimed to represent – again the mediation of the state' (1988a: 50). Furthermore,

> The actual experience which working people have had of the corporatist state has not been a powerful incentive for increases in its scope. Whether in the growing dole queues or in the waiting-rooms of an over-burdened National Health Service, the corporatist state is increasingly experienced by them not as a benefice but as a powerful bureaucratic imposition *on* 'the people'. (1988a: 51)

It is at this point that the issue of 'false consciousness' becomes pertinent. If the people experience the disparity between their needs and interests on the one hand, and the workings of the state on the other, then this can hardly be said to be an effect of false consciousness: '"Thatcherism"', far from simply conjuring demons out of the deep, operated directly on the real and manifestly contradictory experience of the popular classes under social-democratic corporatism' (ibid.: 50). Furthermore, the failure of the left to appreciate the manner and degree in which 'Thatcherism' was able to win support for its proposals, 'greatly underestimates both the rational core on which these populist constructions are situated, and their real, not false, material basis' (ibid.: 49).

the swing to the right

Given the particular structure of relations and subject positions under Labourism between government and the governed, the key challenge to Thatcherism was to re-articulate these subject relations in such a way as to bring about a unity between itself and the people it sought to represent. Hall points to the rhetorical discourse employed by Thatcher herself as evidence of this shift in subject relations.

> 'Don't talk to me about "them" and "us" in a company,' she once told the readers of *Woman's Own*: 'You're all "we" in a company. You survive as the company survives, prosper as the company prospers – everyone together. The future lies in co-operation and not confrontation.' This displaces an existing structure of oppositions – 'them' vs 'us'. It sets in its place an alternative set of equivalents: 'Them *and* us equals *we*'. (1988a: 49)

But this is not simply a trick of language. As Hall goes on to elaborate,

> Then it positions we – 'the people' – in a particular relation to capital: behind it, dominated by its imperatives (profitability, accumulation); yet at the same time, yoked to it, identified with it. 'You survive as the company survives'; presumably also, you collapse as it collapses. .... Co-operation not confrontation! The process we are looking at here is very similar to that which Gramsci once described as *transformism*: the neutralisation of some elements in an ideological formation and their absorption and passive appropriation into a new political configuration. (1988a: 49)

In this way, class relations themselves are re-forged and re-presented. But what is it that enables such a transformation to occur? How can a working class population be persuaded to align their interests with those of an aspiring Thatcherite party of government? In order to answer these questions we must look to Hall's use of Gramsci and his attention to the specific historic conjunctures of late capitalism.

gramsci and the 'historic bloc' thesis

As we have already seen in relation to Hall's analysis of the failure of Labourism and the corporatist management of capital, the 'swing to the right' cannot be explained as 'a reflection of the crisis, but as a response to it'. Thus, 'the rising fortunes of Thatcherism were tied to the tail of Labour's fading ones' (1988a: 2). Where state intervention had failed, Thatcherism required a new language in order to advance a new discourse that people would understand and could relate to their situation. The success of Thatcherism lay primarily in its ability to harness popular support – constructing a new 'common sense' and the people 'into a new populist political subject: *with*, not against, the power bloc' (1988a: 49). The construction of such a unity works in order to legitimate and cement a new field of subject relations where the traditional social-democratic concepts of the collective or the 'welfare state' have little jurisdiction. The state comes in fact to be seen as the enemy, and the scene is set for the dismantling of state power in favour of individualism, enterprise, and the free market.

Hall argues that Thatcherism constituted an historic bloc since it arose out of 'an organic crisis' (1988a: 43). The terrain is defended by those who wish to maintain the status quo, but

> If the crisis is deep, – 'organic' – these efforts cannot be merely defensive. They will be *formative*: aiming at a new balance of forces, the emergence of new elements, the attempt to put together a new 'historic bloc', new political configurations and 'philosophies', a profound restructuring of the state and the ideological discourses which construct the crisis and represent it as it is 'lived' as a practical reality. (1988a: 43)

Thatcherism, according to Hall, is able to redirect working class allegiances because it positions itself as antagonistic to the Labourist vision of the state. 'This abstract state', so enshrined in Labour politics as a benign and neutral entity, 'now appears transformed in the discourses of Thatcherism as the enemy' (ibid.: 52). Whereas Labour is firmly entrenched in the discourse of the state, Thatcherism aligns itself with the people's need to be free of it. In short, the terrain on which the struggles for power and position are taking place, has in part been reconstituted according to the new logic of Thatcherism. The 'creeping

authoritarianism' (ibid.: 126) of the state under the consensus governments of the 1970s effectively helps to create the conditions for a new
insurgent political force. As we have already seen in Chapters 2 and 3,
Hall's understanding of the conditions for hegemony depend upon the
intersection between the present conditions *and* the deeper long-term
structural shifts that *together* constitute a new historic bloc. Hall is
acutely aware of the more general left wing arguments that
Thatcherism is simply an assertion of capital and therefore unremark-
able. He counters this with his insistence on looking at the particular
conjectures that have occasioned the 'swing to the right', through a
consideration of Britain's specific historical peculiarities. That is to say,
only by understanding the extent to which the post-war state has exercised its power in relation to capital, can we fully appreciate Gramsci's
point about 'the terrain of the "conjectural"' (ibid.: 131). It is not merely
a question of party politics – rather the whole of civil society forms the
terrain where the 'war of position' is waged. Thus Hall argues that
it is fruitless to ignore the material conditions out of which the new
polemical reality is constructed and articulated. It is not a question of
ideology and false consciousness, or the dominant power of a ruling-
class élite.

> What is in question, is the issue of the ethical state: the ceaseless work
> required to construct a social authority, throughout all the levels of
> social activity, such that a 'moment of economic, political, intellectual
> and moral unity' may be secured, sufficient to 'raise the level of the
> state to a more general plane'. (1988a: 133)

These 'moments', according to Gramsci, are brought about through
constant attention to polemic and activity that aims to win consent. The
struggle for hegemony therefore operates not simply at an economic
level, but at all levels of civil society.

What was clear to Hall was the reforming zeal of Thatcherism
and its commitment to change in all arenas of public and domestic
life: 'It regards the current crisis as providing, not a passive status quo
to be defended, but a strategic political field of force to be reconstructed: reconstructed, of course, to the right' (ibid.: 125). This is
the beginning of Hall's analysis of what he termed 'authoritarian
populism' (1988a).

thatcher's appeal to the working classes

The weakness of the social-democratic workings of the state under labourism can be broken down into two aspects: the issue of class representation at the level of government has been displaced, if not eclipsed by the interventionist nature of the state. Thatcherism was able to exploit the 'contradictions in social democracy', which though apparently promising social and economic change, actually, in times of crisis, became increasingly interventionist and coercive in its dealings with the people who it supposedly represented. We have seen some of the evidence put forward by Hall and his colleagues to justify this argument in Chapter 5. The 'law and order' society that Hall identifies as symptomatic of this widening gulf between government and the governed, is further grist to the Thatcherite mill:

> The themes of crime and social delinquency, articulated through the discourses of popular morality, touch the direct experience, the anxieties and uncertainties of ordinary people. This has led to a dovetailing of the 'cry for discipline' from below into the call for an enforced restoration of social order and authority 'from above'. (1988a: 136)

The 'long-term effect' of such a crisis, however, 'is to legitimate the swing towards a more authoritarian regime' (ibid.: 138). But lest we forget the material conditions for this state of affairs, Hall refers again to Gramsci's insistence that in order to make a succesful intervention in the 'war of position', the leaders of the 'new reality' must forge a new common sense that works upon the assumptions of common discourse. Common-sense does not arrive fully-fledged as a decisive break from the old; rather it succeeds through fragmenting existing lexicons and lending weight to certain ideas while constructing itself anew. Common sense, as we saw in Chapter 4, is ideologically and therefore materially, extremely productive. The historical and material yoking of the idea of 'the state in the service of the people' to Labourism for example, is an idea Thatcherism needed to break down and reassemble. This important ideological labour was in large part successful for many reasons. Thatcherism brought politics within reach of the vast majority, condensing complex ideas into apparently sound common-sense wisdoms about the world. The approach was immediate and gathered support from across the spectrum of working class and *petit bourgeois* voters.

In November 1979, Thatcher appealed directly to the families of trade unionists in order to curb strike action. She abandoned Heath's centrist politics and carved out a distinctive economic strategy that Heath later characterised as 'the dogma that barked on the right' (Heath, 1998: 574). An extract from Margaret Thatcher's autobiography gives a flavour of the problems facing Britain and the terms in which they could be readily understood:

> Council housing is the worst source of immobility. Many large council estates bring together people who are out of work but enjoy the security of tenure at subsidised rents. They not only have every incentive to stay where they are: they mutually reinforce each other's passivity and undermine each other's initiative. (Thatcher, 1995: 671)

Thatcher's own history as the daughter of a Grantham shopkeeper also played an important ideological role in the formation of her commonsense attitude to market economics and international trade. Thatcher's style and personality were also important elements in the success of the restructuring of popular consent. Her media and political persona was highly effective in its mobilisation of many conservative 'philosophies', which were rooted in and constitutive of a respectable bourgeois subjectivity.

> The success of this venture must be seen in the context of what it is replacing and displacing: the fragmentation of many of the traditional 'us/them' discourses of the working class (which sustained the people/power bloc contradiction, although in a corporatist form) as a consequence of the 'social-democratic solution'. (1988a: 141)

By aligning working class interests with radical Conservatism, Thatcher was able to neutralise the established relationship between the people and the state, and re-articulate it as one of the state *against* the working man. Thatcherism was thus able to champion the working class position by appealing to a wide repertoire of historical populist sentiments; 'the British people', 'Great Britain', and in so doing, map out an alternative set of subject relations that cut across and destabilised the traditional, and perhaps too readily *assumed* subject relations that existed between the Left and the working classes. Where once there would have been class positions, now there was an alternative set of subjectivities, which could lay claim to moral truths about the world. As Hall argues,

> The point about popular morality is that it is the most practical material-ideological force amongst the popular classes – the language which, without the benefit of training, education, coherent philosophising, erudition or learning, touches the direct and immediate experience of the class, and has the power to map out the world of problematic social reality in clear and unambiguous moral polarities. It thus has a real and concrete grasp on the popular experiences of the class. (1988a: 143)

This argument brings the question of the 'law and order' society full circle. If increased authority by the state in the areas of the police or the judiciary can be read as indicative of a deep crisis in capital, then such a situation can be exploited in order to undermine the state's legitimacy, by an appeal to the concerns of ordinary workers. It is the party that can most successfully identify, articulate and represent those concerns, *irrespective of traditional party-class allegiances* that will win power. This is the basic fact, Hall argues, not understood by the majority of the Left, who still think that 'in the last instance' the working classes can be brought round to a socialist way of thinking. In other words, it is the very populism of Thatcherism that marks it as a significant moment in the re-figuring of class and subject relations.

But it is at this point that we should address some of the chief criticisms levelled at Hall's analysis, and examine alternative positions mounted, among others, by Jessop et al. and Larrain.

the limitations of 'authoritarian populism'

Jessop, Bonnett, Bromley and Ling (1988) offered a counter argument to Hall's position in which they disagreed with what they term his 'uncritical use of Gramsci's rather descriptive accounts of hegemony' (1988: 69), to analyse the specifics of a political strategy. They pose the question of whether it is sufficient to debate the relative success or failure

142

of Thatcherism as a political-ideological phenomenon. To what extent is it necessary to examine existing state structures in order to situate Thatcherism as an historical rupture within the structural and conjunctural formations of the state? Jessop et al. argue that Hall's analyses are too discrete and cannot yield sufficient understanding of what they term the 'compenetration' of social moments. In their view, Hall's work fails to take adequate account of the complexity of different influences on the emergence of political ideas or action. Therefore they return to an articulation of Thatcherism that situates itself between the ideological-political formations of Hall's work and the more material conditions of social production and social structures.

Jessop et al. offer six possible ways of analysing Thatcherism and emphasise that these approaches need not be mutually exclusive. Their studies indicate the necessity of moving away from what they see as Hall's straightforward political analysis towards a multifaceted account of Thatcherism(s). The thrust of their argument is that it is the very uneven and sometimes contradictory quality of Thatcherism that renders it worthy of analysis. This separates them from the work of political science, which they describe as too narrowly concerned with electoral models, and from *Marxism Today*. Indeed they criticise Hall for his over-insistence on 'authoritarian populism' as a way of explaining Thatcherism's dominance, given the degree to which it has also engendered bitter and sustained resistance from various sections of the electorate.

Jessop et al.'s critique of Hall's analysis appeared five years later, when Thatcherism had become 'bedded in' and appeared to be an unstoppable political force. While the initial article is very long, very detailed and very sure of its ambitions, the authors later conceded the degree to which theirs' and Hall's analyses had converged over a period of time. Although they reject Hall's idea of authoritarian populism in 1985, by 1987, they had revisited their arguments and concluded that,

> in claiming that AP [authoritarian populism] could not explain important features of the Thatcher government's first years in power, we tended to draw the illegitimate conclusion that it was also irrelevant to the rise of Thatcherism. (Jessop et al., 1988: 67)

That does not undermine their analysis, but it does point to the longevity of Hall's original argument and the extent to which his first appraisal of the Thatcher phenomenon has held sway over the field of debate ever since. But Jessop et al. begin by accusing Hall of an 'apparent ideological celebration of Thatcherism' in which he offers 'grudging admiration because Thatcherism took the ideological struggle more seriously than the left and has reaped the reward of popular support' (ibid.: 69).

The idea that Hall celebrates Thatcherism is difficult to sustain in the light of his writings over a considerable period of time, and is perhaps one of the weaker criticisms directed at his work. It is the yoking of 'populism' and 'authoritarianism' that provide a richer and more interesting source of criticism.

the limitations of ideology theory

Jessop et al. argue that the term 'authoritarian populism' is ambiguous because Hall uses it in different contexts to mean different things. It therefore 'mystifies the real sources of support for Thatcherism' (Jessop et al., 1988: 72), and is too rooted in ideology to enable really useful analysis. Furthermore, Hall's specific points about the language of Thatcherism and its construction of a new common-sense through the discursive operations of the mass media are viewed by Jessop et al. as 'excessive' (ibid.: 73), because they do not take adequate account of the real material and structural conditions underpinning this phenomenon. They complain that 'there is barely any reference to the material rewards accruing to those sections of society, within and without the power bloc, who have supported the Thatcherite camp' (ibid.: 73). As a consequence of Hall's approach, they argue, important questions go unasked and unanswered.

Given Hall's own work on encoding and decoding, how can he say with any certainty which messages formulated by the Far Right have been understood and accepted and which have not? Just because Thatcher espouses a particular view, does not mean that it will be picked up by the target working class audience. Thus Jessop et al. point to what they see as an overly homogenised view of Thatcherism that overestimates its universal appeal:

> The AP approach focuses on the ideological message of Thatcherism and thereby endows it with an excessively unified image. It sometimes

implies that all sections of society support Thatcherism for the same (ideologically induced) reasons. This neglects possible internal cleavages within the social basis of Thatcherism. One wonders whether the 24 per cent of the unemployed and the 55 per cent of professional middle class men who voted Conservative in 1983 really did so for the same reasons. (Jessop et al., 1988: 74)

This is a reasonable point but Jessop et al. are not comparing like with like. Their overt criticisms of Hall come at a strategically different point in the succesive Thatcherite administration. By 1983, it is almost certainly the case that the discrepancies between voting rationales imagined by Jessop et al. would be concrete enough. However, in January 1979, five months prior to her election as Britain's first female Prime Minister, it is clear to Hall that her appeal was becoming increasingly successful in harnessing the support of *many different factions* within the electorate at an hegemonising politico-ideological level. In other words, what Thatcherism set out to do, was win populist support. But Hall does not shy away from the material roots and consequences of Thatcherism. Hall answers Jessop et al.'s central point concerning AP in the following way.

I have repeated *ad nauseam* Gramsci's argument about hegemony being impossible to conceptualise or achieve without 'the decisive nucleus of economic activity'. It is therefore particularly galling to be accused of advancing an explanation of Thatcherism as exclusively an ideological phenomenon, simply because I have drawn attention to features of its ideological strategy which are specific and important. (Hall, 1988a: 105)

He goes on to state how 'absurd' it is to imagine that 'because one works at that level, one therefore assumes economic questions to be residual or unimportant' (ibid.: 105). The strategic use of a new ideological formation of subject positions and discourses is, according to Hall, precisely the dimension of Thatcherism that the left has failed to comprehend. Hall's determination to address this specific aspect is therefore deliberate and aligned with Thatcherism's other hegemonising strategies – economic, political, structural and social. The question of hegemony however remains a moot point. Hall is adamant that the hegemonising tendencies employed by Thatcherism

145

are evidence of the Far Right's understanding of the value of bringing all aspects of society under the reforming political banner. But this does not mean that Thatcherism ever achieved hegemonic status. Nor does it mean that Thatcherism is only a discursive phenomenon.

accusations and recriminations

Jessop et al.'s reply to Hall's response demarcates three areas of engagement; points of clarification, differences of position and the acknowledgement of error. If we take the last category first, we can identify those areas where Jessop and his colleagues admit the extent to which they have mis-identified or mis-understood the relevance of certain key ideas. They acknowledge his point that they fundamentally mistook Hall's 'more delimited project for their own, more ambitious one' (Jessop et al., 1988: 99), and that the inclusion of the mass media as a site of ideological activity is both advantageous and appropriate (ibid.: 117). Despite this, they insist on traducing Hall's argument regarding the necessary strategic work of the left: 'Intentionally or not, he is prioritising a long-term ideological struggle to articulate a new common sense' (ibid.: 119). But it is the very contradictions in Thatcherism's common sense that Hall seeks to clarify, and the continual attempts to 'recruit people to its different, often contradictory, subject positions' (Hall, 1988a: 106). While it is true that Hall is very concerned with this particular strategy, he does not advocate discourse theory as a way of analysing 'whole social formations', yet discourse theory is clearly of interest to Hall. Hall's use of discourse theory is precisely geared to articulate the concrete material *relevance* of discursive practice, *not* to privilege discourse over and above material conditions. Discourse can indeed be read as a 'critical aspect' of the function of ideology. As Hall reiterates in his response to Jessop et al., Thatcherism's ideological practice operates through the attempt to condense many contradictory subject-positions: 'I don't see how at all that could conceivably be construed as endowing Thatcherism with "an excessively unified image"' (Hall, 1988a: 107). When Jessop et al. continue to criticise Hall's apparent failure to connect the hegemonic with the deep structural context for Thatcherism's dominance, they appear to unwittingly

146

commit the same alleged folly. It is however in their assertions concerning the use of Hall's work by un-named others, that Jessop et al. appear most to be on shaky ground:

> However, whatever his own stated intentions in underlining the wider implications of *hegemonic politics*, others have certainly read his conjectural analyses and strategic conclusions as more narrowly *ideological* in focus. We argue that Hall's continual emphasis on the successes of Thatcherism has encouraged such readings. (Jessop et al., 1988: 110) (Jessop's emphasis)

This accusation is an interesting one as it recognises Hall's position in regard to the left, as one of considerable influence. At the same time, Jessop et al. seem to be suggesting that Hall should be more careful and circumspect so as not to lead others astray. It is also interesting that the criticism here rests on Hall's apparent celebration of Thatcherism's successes rather than its failures. Is this what Hall refers to as his 'apostasy'? (Hall, 1988a: 107). It is as if the very fact of recognising where Thatcherism has been successful in mobilising support constitutes a betrayal of left wing principles. But Hall's point is surely to draw attention to precisely those areas where the left can understand the terrain on which the political game is being fought. It may be, therefore, that the left need to appeal to the working classes in a different way. Jessop et al., however, suggest that the left should instead be drawing more attention to the contradictions between what Thatcherism claims and what it actually delivers. The left should therefore 'try to intensify the difficulties of the Thatcherite state' (Jessop et al., 1988: 119). The key areas for resistance are to be found within the spaces between. The left therefore need, according to Jessop et al., to exploit the gaps in Thatcherism both through long-term and short-term strategies. Chief among their suggestions is that the left needs to produce an alternative economic strategy (AES), which redefines corporatism and looks towards the restatement of 'a new socialist *general will* within which conflicting economic-corporate interests can be negotiated and mutual sacrifices agreed' (ibid.: 124).

Two things become clearer from looking at this debate between Hall and Jessop et al. First, despite their intellectual differences, it is the *urgent* need to really understand Thatcherism that is driving both parties: 'For if one cannot understand the opposition then attempts to

147

construct a political alternative will remain critically debilitated' (1988a: 182). Thus, all are concerned with finding an appropriate strategy to enable the left to defeat Thatcherism. As part of their conclusion, Jessop et al. even acknowledge the necessity for recognising and understanding 'the strengths of Thatcherism' (Jessop et al., 1988: 183), something for which Hall came under considerable criticism in 1985.

Second, we need to consider the audience for this debate. Hall's initial article appeared in *Marxism Today*, a polemical journal directly engaged in the full fray of political debate. As such, Hall's article and those that followed, are not highly theorised pieces of academic writing. It is urgent, passionate even, and essentially aimed at a readership fully aware of the internal divisions within the left, and the problems of unity. In short, Hall is writing for a left readership, but in a populist mode. *Marxism Today* aimed to present radical and controversial material that would challenge conventional and orthodox ideas about socialism. It is much more in the spirit of the early *New Left Review*, which, under Hall, brought together an eclectic group who sought to combine radical politics with intellectual debate. *New Left Review* however, was not orchestrated around a particular notion of strategic intervention in the way in which *Marxism Today* can be understood. Martin Jacques and Stuart Hall made a formidable team at *Marxism Today* and spearheaded the assault on Thatcherism, and later, New Labour. As Kenny (1995) has pointed out, Hall's involvement with the early New Left and his subsequent later involvement with *Marxism Today* provide a certain continuity, both in the development of his thinking and the acceptance of Gramscian ideas into the British left. We can see that within this given context, Hall's article is pitched at a moment of profound crisis for the left as Thatcher accedes to power.

Jessop et al.'s response appears nearly five years later with Thatcherism bedded in for a second term. The crisis for the Left has deepened considerably and there is a general and widespread feeling at large that any turn to the left will be a long time coming. Jessop et al.'s response was carried in *New Left Review* – the very journal which Hall himself edited in its first incarnation. *New Left Review* is of course, as the title suggests, also concerned with leftwing thinking, but from 1962, under the editorship of Perry Anderson it underwent significant alteration in tone and perspective. Anderson led *New Left Review* to focus increasingly on the international scene. What Kenny describes as 'an unspoken unease about nationalism' underlying the early New Left's position on internationalism, develops under Anderson into a 'more explicit anti-nationalism':

> Whilst exploration of the movement's international agenda progressed rapidly therefore, scant attention was paid to related developments nearer home, partly because of an unthinking conflation of English and British identity, but also because these touched upon sensitive and unresolved questions within this movement. (Kenny, 1995: 182)

Jessop et al.'s reply to Hall is thus a far more extended, theoretical and detailed essay more in keeping with the intellectual academicism of *New Left Review*. It attempts to broaden the field of analysis by introducing the idea of 'two nations' – which roughly equates to the haves and the have-nots. Thatcherism, for Jessop et al., has an 'authoritarian element', but this is no more than a response to the 'problems of economic and political crisis-management' (Jessop et al., 1988: 88, 89). Yet despite its claims to 'complement' Hall's concept of Authoritarian Populism, Jessop et al.'s exegesis on Thatcherism is obviously far more ambitious. Hall's reply and Jessop et al.'s final response also appeared in *New Left Review*. The debate around Authoritarian Populism may have started on the fringes of the academic quarter, but it was effectively brought into the fold during 1985.

against false consciousness

But Jessop et al. were, of course, not the only ones to bring Hall to account. In a short but energetic paper given at the University of Illinois in 1983 and later published in a collection entitled *Marxism and the Interpretation of Culture*, Hall returns to the question of Gramscian hegemony as the most potent and appropriate means of identifying and understanding the specific rise and command of Thatcherism. In 'The toad in the garden: Thatcherism amongst the theorists', Hall uses the example of Thatcherism in order to demonstrate the paucity of development in Marxist thinking around the concept of ideology. He also discusses in brief some of his misgivings about Foucauldian discourse theory as it has been used by Foucault's followers. He articulates the need for the Left to give up the notion of false consciousness, which he believes to be a poor diagnostic tool for analysising the condition of the working classes under Thatcherism.

Hall begins by stating the purpose, as he sees it, of theoretical endeavour;

> The purpose of theorizing is not to enhance one's intellectual or academic reputation but to enable us to grasp, understand, and explain – to produce a more adequate knowledge of – the historical world and its processes; and thereby to inform our practice so that we may transform it. (Hall, 1988b: 36)

The question then becomes, what would constitute the best method of achieving such an ambition? This reiterates Hall's position as one of the necessity for intervention, rather than argument for the mere sake of intellectual exercise or academic kudos. His description of the Thatcherite phenomenon pivots on the ideological terrain that Thatcherism appeared to master. He explains Thatcherism's ideological task of dismantling and fragmenting established 'taken-for granted' knowledge about the world, while erecting a new common sense borne of an organic marriage of *some* elements of old-world conservatism and new-world market-economics.

> 'The mission of Thatcherism' involved the transformation of society at every level. This was conceived on no narrow economistic basis. The aim was to reconstruct social life as a whole around a return to the old values – the philosophies of tradition, Englishness, respectability, patriachialism, family and nation. The most novel aspect of Thatcherism was indeed the very way in which it combined the new doctrines of the free market with some of the traditional emphases of organic Toryism. (Hall, 1988b: 39)

Consequently it is the remarkable degree to which Thatcherism has been able to muster popular support that requires consideration. So far then, we can see the bones of Hall's argument for coining the term 'Authoritarian Populism'. He next takes issue with what he terms 'the classic Marxist theory of ideology', which locates ideology firmly within classes. It follows from this position that the ruling class will determine the ruling ideology. According to this position, ideology is not contested or won. It is not arrived at through a process of struggle.

But, as Hall argues, the very composite nature of Thatcherism cannot be reduced in this way. Thatcherism itself was a way of thinking, a mode of being that overthrew not only the Labour government of 1979, but more crucially, the Conservative Party. Thatcher had begun to exert a hegemonic tendency in politics even before her accession to power. From Hall's point of view, a theory of ideology that does not recognise the penetrating, fragmentary and fractured articulation and condensation of subject positions and relations, cannot adequately explain Thatcherism (Hall, 1988b: 42).

Hall reminds us of the failure of the false consciousness model to account for the popular support among working class people for Thatcher's new programme. This, he comments, is a particular problem for Marxism in trying to explain the consciousness of working-class labour in advanced capitalist society. He rejects absolutely the idea that some are duped and others are not. He is highly dismissive of what he regards as the traditional Marxist position that depends upon the working classes waking up to a sudden realisation of their real situation. The argument rests on the premise that if things are bad enough for long enough, then finally people will become conscious. This is a line of argument pursued by Tony Benn through the 1980s and indicative of the particular split in left wing thinking of the period. Hall cites the example of mass unemployment reaching three million as evidence of the failure of this viewpoint to grasp the complexities of ideological subject relations: 'The unemployed, who might have been expected to pierce the veil of illusion first, are still by no means automatic mass converts to labourism, let alone socialism' (Hall, 1988b: 43).

the critique of ideology

Nevertheless Hall is adamant that ideology is a useful tool because despite the problems of the false consciousness argument, social knowledge is unequal and skewed towards different sectional and class interests. Power, class, gender and race all constitute areas in which symbolic power is accumulated in order to explain and define the world. But where Hall differs in his emphasis from the traditional left, and where Jessop et al. accused him of celebrating Thatcherism, is

151

in his assertion that we need to examine the truth of the ideological experience rather than its falsity. In other words, we need to look at what is experienced by people as true and meaningful in order to gauge both the reach and the limits of Thatcherism's social project.

So far, Hall's definition of ideology is both neutral – not tied to a particular class position, and contested – subject to fluctuations and power struggles for supremacy. It is also premised on the relationship between people's subjectivities and their real experiences. In this sense then, Hall is arguing for a definition of ideology that is concrete rather than abstract or false, and which is hegemonic in the ways in which it requires popular support in order to marshal power. He does not, as some have alleged, confuse the idea of 'ruling ideas' with 'ideology'. In an essay written in the same year[3], he interprets the relationship between 'ruling classes' and 'ruling ideas' in the following way:

> On the other hand, to abandon the question or problem of 'rule' – of hegemony, domination and authority – because the ways in which it was originally posed are unsatisfactory is to cast the baby out with the bath-water. Ruling ideas are not guaranteed their dominance by their already given coupling with ruling classes. Rather, the effective coupling of dominant ideas *to* the historical bloc which has acquired hegemonic power in a particular period is what the process of ideological struggle is *intended to secure*. It is the object of the exercise, not the playing out of an already written and concluded script. (Morley and Chen, 1996: 44)

This positioning of hegemony with the idea of 'ruling ideas' enables Hall to retain some of the elements of classic Marxism, while working within a profoundly Gramscian way. It opens the door to the idea of 'common-sense' and its ideological functions.

problems with interpellation

As we saw in Chapter 3, according to Althusser, it is the articulation of state power that informs his explanations of ideology in action. However, as Hall points out (Hall, 1988b: 48), when we turn to the example of Thatcherism, we can see that ideology is working not merely at state level, but at the civil level of the social. Thatcherism is intent on transforming all of society, not just those areas falling within state control. Indeed, Hall points out that Thatcher's exertion of ideological power was already forming in civil society *before* her election to Prime Minister. This then sharpens the distinction that Hall wishes to draw between Althusser's theory of the reproduction of existing ruling ideological formations, and the actual practice of Thatcherism's struggle to create a (new) hegemony.

But Hall's considered rejection of an Althusserian theory of ideology also derives from his conflict with the Lacanian ideas underpinning Althusser's formulation. If ideological positioning pivots on interpellation – that we are always already subjects waiting to be hailed – then does that mean that there is a little bit of a Thatcherite in all of us, waiting to be brought forth? If we enter into ideology as fully formed subjects, then how is it possible for Thatcherism to overwhelm our already-formed and existing subjectivities?

> What Thatcherism poses is the problem of understanding how already positioned subjects can be effectively detached from their points of application and effectively repositioned by a new set of discourses. This is precisely a historically specific level of application of the interpellative aspects of ideology that is not adequately resumed or explained by the transhistorical speculative generalities of Lacanianism. (Hall, 1988b: 50)

At this point it is pertinent to look at the criticisms mounted by Jorge Larrain in response to this and other essays regarding Marxism, Thatcherism and ideology. Larrain contests Hall's dismissal of classic Marxist theory of ideology on the grounds that Hall is not actually referring to Marx's theory at all, but Lenin's version of it. We can recall from the arguments cited in Chapter 3, how closely Lenin's concept of ideology informed Althusser's thinking. Thus Larrain proposes that, although Hall is right to argue against a theory of ideology that fixes ideologies to certain classes, Hall has missed the point about Marx's original premise; that ideology is not a neutral term, but one which refers to a bourgeois political position.

hall's definition of ideology

Hall's essay 'The toad in the garden: Thatcherism among the theorists' does not really do justice to his considerations of the Marxist problem.

In a famous essay reprinted for the 1986 *Journal of Communication Enquiry* he outlined with greater detail and caution his reasons for abandoning Marx's negative conception of ideology, the limitations of the false consciousness model, and the creative critical uses of Gramscian theory. Hall's position is stable, but attracted a welter of criticism from the Left, who read his rejection of classic Marxism as a failure of his political commitment.

It is in the realm of false consciousness that Larrain believes Hall to be most at fault. Whereas Hall states his opposition to the idea of false consciousness on the grounds that the real material conditions of Thatcherism have failed to transform the consciousness of the working classes, Larrain points out that Marx understood only too well that capitalism was by no means a transparent system. For Marx, the labouring subjects under capitalism

> were not passive either. They were actively engaged in practices which, in so far as limited and merely reproductive, enhanced the appearances of the market, in so far as transformatory or revolutionary, facilitated the apprehension of real relations. (Larrain, 1996: 60)

Marx, according to Larrain, did not expect the proletariat to rise up on the basis of their experiences of capitalism, but only as a result of political education. Furthermore, Larrain argues, there is no real reason why Hall could not still make good use of Marx's theory of ideology as a complement to the Gramscian model favoured by him. Marx's theory of ideology was negative, Gramsci's definition is neutral. As well as exploring how an ideology functions successfully, Larrain asks, why couldn't we also look at its negative features?

Once again we can see the pursuit of an argument that hints at Hall's isolation within the left. Larrain is careful but pointed in his reminder,

> Mrs Thatcher was not presiding over any change in the mode of production, she was propping up and defending the same capitalist system at a different stage of development. The novelty of her position should not therefore be exaggerated. (Larrain, 1996: 58)

The final blow rests with Larrain's assertion that Hall is insufficiently critical because he does not use Marx's negative definition of ideology. This blow is softened by Larrain's addition that Hall's use of Gramsci is undeniably useful. However, we can sense Larrain's discomfort here. He is staunch in his view that Hall's work on Thatcherism is empirically sound, and refutes absolutely those critics who see in Hall's work a 'celebration' of Thatcherism. Nevertheless, he is determined to 'rescue' the role that classic Marxism can play in analysing Thatcherism. But one wonders whether this is not also an opportunity to extend a helping hand to Hall, whose isolation on the Left is compounded by his apparent rejection of classic Marxist theory.

When Larrain states, 'I am convinced that Hall, having appreciated the hegemonic form of Thatcherite politics has also been critical of its content, even though his emphasis has probably been on the former aspect' (1996: 66), he sounds like a character witness for the defendant. His conclusion is muted. Perhaps a classic Marxist analysis can only produce, in his words, a 'skimpy' account, but it seems Larrain is intent on harmonising Hall's maverick position on the one hand, and the established academic and political left, on the other.

new times

Undeterred by the often negative reception of his work at this time, Hall's success with *Marxism Today* and his burgeoning friendship with Martin Jacques are best reflected in their joint publishing ventures. Their analysis of *New Times* reflected a certain cautious optimism around the possibility of a new opportunity for the Left to capitalise on the economic and political climate. However, as McRobbie, a critic herself of *New Times* has pointed out,

> it was a vulnerable target because the articles were written in a deliberately journalistic, accessible and, to some extent, provocative tone. However this stepping outside of the academy and bringing into the world of politics, both a new set of concepts for understanding social change, and simultaneously a strong defence of the 'politics of theory', as Stuart Hall has put it, remains, in my mind, an important task. (McRobbie, 1996: 240)

Grouping together the work of various critics, Hall and Jacques displaced and fractured the more traditional modes of sociological and political enquiry. In his description of the character of *New Times*, Hall points to the necessity of deconstructing the notion of the unified subject. Instead of 'self' comes the realisation that identity comprises increasingly complex, fragmentary and contradictory 'selves'. The dissolving of seemingly stable categories into competing and eliding subjectivities is both frightening and challenging. It represents not only an enormous shift in terms of political theory, but also an enormous opportunity to create a new and productive politics. Yet despite this, at the close of the 1980s, the Left was still in a state of total dissaray. How could a left wing politics reassert itself in the continuing presence of Thatcherite dogma? How could any left wing strategy manage to co-opt the working classes into a new formation that would radically challenge the status quo?

strategies of difference

The mistake, as Hall sees it, is to assume a complete continuity between Thatcherism and *New Times*. Rather than suppose that Thatcherism constitutes and manufactures the modernity experienced in the late twentieth century, it is important that we understand the levels of contingency in operation. That Thatcherism represents an important transition is not really in any doubt. But analysing the nature of the transition is essential, particularly if we are to mount some form of alternative. The modernity of Thatcherism is only one particular direction in which *New Times* can be said to evolve. There are, of course, other possibilities: 'Once we have opened up this gap, analytically, between Thatcherism and *New Times*, it *may* become possible to resume or re-stage the broken dialogue between socialism and modernity' (Hall and Jacques, reprinted in Morley and Chen, 1996: 232). In order to recognise the productivity of such an analysis, Hall advocates a thorough understanding of the culture in which we live and operate. It is through the organisation and practices of culture that different and contesting subjectivities come into play. The Left needs to adapt and update if it is to compete with the dominant modes of address and signification on offer under Thatcherism. In short, the Left, according to Hall, needs to understand the function of ethnicity. 'Ethnic' identity does not mean the specific marker of a marginalised or under-represented group. To work from the premise of ethnicity means understanding that *all* identities are historically and culturally contingent. There can be no privileged access or point of view that does *not* proceed from some specific matrix of identifications, prejudices, experiences or assumptions. Under Thatcherism, identities are fixed and relegated to specific hierarchies that privilege some identities over others. Hence, the centrality of a particular notion of 'Englishness'. Thatcherism excludes the possibility of a black British subjectivity. Similarly, despite the advances made by feminism, the left seems reluctant to accept the extent to which gendered practices inform all aspects of political, economic and social life.

Hall and Jacques' clarion call to the Left demands that we recognise the primacy of identity as a means of speaking specific subject positions. Understanding Gramsci's 'war of position' thesis demonstrates the relative instability of seemingly fixed and enduring identities, clustered as they are, around notions of racial, class, sexual and gendered exclusivity. This not only undermines their apparent fixity, but also suggests the possibility of creating and mobilising alternate and radical positions and identities. A modern socialist politics could then arise out of a recognition of difference and alterity.

new labour, new problems

Although Hall makes no apology for his persistent battles with the Left, there is one uncomfortable legacy that is often laid at Hall's door. To what extent did Hall's sustained critique of Labour party politics contribute towards the rise of New Labour under Tony Blair? While *Marxism Today* provided some of the fertile ground for New Labour to sow its ideas, is it really fair to suggest that Hall's arguments concerning modernity, welfare and the state, opened the door to New Labour policies of deregulation and the continued privatisation of public sector services?

> We were in very unexplored territory and I wouldn't want to defend everything I wrote. I wrote a piece in *Marxism Today* about the state.

It's called 'the old caretaker'. I think that piece probably goes too far in the notion of dismantling regulation, or rather it doesn't make clear that the regulatory state is much stronger than the Blairite one. As you explore things like that, you can't see to the end of what you are doing, so we took the risk of living dangerously for a while. I think we made some mistakes, I wouldn't want to defend all of it. I do want to say that there was more than one tendency in *Marxism Today*, and I think what I wrote has to be distinguished from the overall position. I do think at one point that *Marxism Today* did stray into 'there is no difference between left and right'. I defy you to find that sentence in anything I wrote, yes? I never wrote that. That is the kind of Demos position, Demos is the *Marxism Today* position on the way to becoming Blairism.[4]

Hall recognises that there were dangers in putting the case for change so bluntly. But Hall is not a politician, and certainly not the architect for New Labour. The Conservatives may have been ousted, but that did not automatically guarantee that the incoming Labour administration would set right all the wrongs incurred under Thatcher. Blair's 'managerial' style has always troubled Hall. In an interview with Martin Jacques in November 1997, Hall reflected on the emergence of Blair's New Labour vision.

Philosophically he [Blair] thinks it would be wrong to redistribute opportunities even if we could afford it. He believes that it is not the purpose of government to look after those who cannot look after themselves. The main purpose of government is to help the individuals stand on their own two feet. That's not Thatcher's rampant individualism but a version inbetween which still sees the individual as the fulcrum of social action and has no sense of society as more than the sum of individual interests. That's a very profound philosophical shift and it puts a limit on the degree to which Blair has transformed the notion that there's no such thing as society. (Jacques, 1997: 28)

Nevertheless had it not been for *Marxism Today* and Hall's analysis of Thatcherism, there would have been no need for the Labour Party to re-invent itself as it did.

conclusion

The critics who attacked the *New Times* initiative were often savage, seeing in Hall's work both a reluctance to return to the old certainties of classical Marxist analysis, and an unseemly focus on the popular. They were correct on both counts. Hall makes no apology for addressing the primarily popular elements of modern culture, nor does he shrink from arguing the redundancy of the 'false consciousness' thesis. He even dared to suggest that the left might learn something from Thatcherism (Hall, 1988a: 271). But if the analysis of *New Times* truly was 'a controversial turning-point for the Left and for those concerned with the politics of culture' (MacRobbie, 1996: 247), then it was the issue of identity that assumed centre stage. In the next chapter we will examine the development of Hall's work on the politics of identity and his self-exploration as a 'disasporic intellectual' (Morley and Chen, 1996: 484).

further reading

Nelson, C. and Grossberg, L. (eds) (1988) *Marxism and the Interpretation of Culture*. University of Illinois Press: Urbana.

Hall, S. and Jacques, M. (eds) (1989) *New Times*. Lawrence and Wishart: London.

Heath, E. (1998) *The Course of My Life*. Hodder and Stoughton: London.

Jessop, Bonnet, Bromley and Ling (1988) *Thatcherism*. Polity: London.

McRobbie, A. (1996) 'Looking back at *New Times* and its critics', in Morley, D. and Chen, K. (eds) *Stuart Hall, Critical Dialogues in Cultural Studies*. Routledge: London.

Thatcher, M. (1995) *The Downing Street Years*. Harper Collins: London.

in the belly of the beast

More recently I write a lot about the diaspora, writing about the Caribbean and so on, but I am writing about the Caribbean in relation to the problem which is here, and not there. I need to clarify all the questions about African-ness because I need to understand what happens when Rastafarianism arises in Isleworth. And when Babylon is not Norman Manley, but Roy Hattersley.[1]

introduction

In this penultimate chapter we turn to the questions of identity and subjectivity that have been the focus of Hall's most recent work. We have explored the connections between Hall's analyses of class, classlessness and Marxist theory and his contributions to the emergence of British media and cultural studies. We have examined his analysis of British capitalism, and the impact of Thatcherism in particular, on British social and political formations, most notably, class ethnicity and race.

We will look at the arguments and debates that have been the focus of Hall's latest projects and interventions. Hall's reflections on social attitudes to race and ethnicity and his deep concerns about multiculturalism in Britain have been a feature of his work over many years. He has also come under attack for 'abandoning' his Althusserian roots in favour of discursive interpretations of identity. This is particularly problematic as it goes to the heart of Hall's theorisation of identity. This chapter therefore examines Hall's analysis of identity, with particular reference to questions of ethnicity and multiculturalism in Britain.

hall and postmodern approaches to identity

Let us consider first the criticism that Hall has rejected class as an object of analysis. Rosemary Hennessy (2000) argues that recent postmodernist explorations in cultural studies have tended to abandon, if not erase, the fundamental links between culture and capital: 'We can see this trajectory quite distinctly in the work of Stuart Hall himself, who finally abandoned his always somewhat tenuous endorsement of historical materialism by the late 1980s in favour of the post-Marxism of Foucault and Laclau and Mouffe' (Hennessy 2000: 82). This separation of Marxist from post-Marxist accounts of media and cultural practice is often seen as endemic within cultural studies. When Hennessy quizzes the centrality of culture rather than capital within cultural studies, she asks 'whether abandoning all causal connections between culture and material relations outside of culture has strengthened cultural studies' critical edge?' (ibid.: 83) She alerts us to the dangers of a cultural studies which elides those real relations that inform both the production of culture, and the striated class formations within it. But the abandonment of capitalist critique is something that Hall has neither advocated nor practised. When Hennessy cites Hall's work as evidence of this tendency, she overstates her case. Whilst it is true that Hall's later work on identity often draws attention to the shortcomings of classic Marxist theory, he has always insisted on the importance of class and capitalist relations within cultural analysis (Hall et al. 1978; Hall 1980; 1986). Indeed, Hall's use of the term 'articulation' (1980) demonstrates his fundamental point that class, race, ethnicity, gender and sexuality cannot be understood as discrete identities. It is not a question of ignoring class in favour of race. To suggest therefore that Hall rejects or abandons class and capitalist-cultural relations in his later work is extremely misleading.

Within British cultural studies, serious rifts and conflicts have developed over the last 20 years between those engaged in the analysis of institutional structures and formations, and others who have focused attention on the interplay of text and audience. Postmodernism has been frequently designated the guilty culprit in this war of attrition, seducing scholars away from the 'serious' business of analysing capitalist relations of production. While it is indeed the case that Hall's later work engages with a number of writers associated with post-structuralism and postmodernism, such as Laclau, Mouffe, Bakhtin, Derrida and Foucault, it is a mistake to imagine that such a shift has occurred at the expense of an engagement with issues of class and capital. For one thing, Hall refuses to give up ideology as a critical term:

> I use ideology as that which cuts into the infinite semiosis of language. Language is purely textuality, but ideology wants to make a particular meaning. I want to break the chain of meaning here. I want to have this meaning, not every other meaning. So, politically, I slightly separate those two out. I think it's the point where power cuts into discourse, where power overcuts knowledge and discourse; at that point you get a cut, you get a stoppage, you get a suture, you get an overdetermination. The meaning constructed by that cut into language is never permanent because the next sentence will take it back, will open the semiosis again. And it can't fix it, but ideology is an attempt to fix it. (Hall, quoted in Cruz and Lewis, 1994: 263–4)

Hall is describing the way in which ideology operates through language and in so doing, contains and displaces meaning so that the ideological statement wears the guise of being the *only* possible meaning of a text. This is only possible if we think in terms of the way power is exercised through language. Clearly Hall is working with and through the influences of Derrida and Foucault, but he still maintains a hold on ideology as a determining factor in language, and therefore in social practice. Hall is not about to relinquish structure and agency in pursuit of an identity politics that is founded purely on an idea of self-determination. We are *not*, according to Hall, simply whatever we want to call ourselves. Identity is *not* simply a question of identity-shopping. Identity is in constant production and exists at the point of intersection between the individual and other determining structures and institutions.

Nevertheless, Hall's characterisation of his activities has undoubtedly caused consternation within Marxist scholarship. He describes his process of having 'radically amended [ ] some Marxist concepts' in order that they might be 'rescued for critical work' (Essed and Goldberg, 2002: 451). This is not likely to go down well with scholars and critics working within the classic Marxist paradigm. Although sometimes understood as an attack on historical materialism, Hall's work in fact operates on the cusp of two seemingly irreconcilable areas of analysis. He attempts to bridge the spaces between economic and sociological theories by harnessing concepts such as articulation, dominance and ideology to elements of posmodern theory such as discursivity and difference. Once again it is the totalising of Marxism as 'a closed theoretical universe' to which Hall is objecting. Conversely Hall is not persuaded by the oft-repeated arguments that postmodernity liberates individuals from the traditional trajectories of modernity and their associated ideological baggage. There may be much to celebrate in the recovery and re-presentation of alternate and competing histories, the articulation of 'new' identities and the disclosure of complex subjectivities. However, these acts do not in themselves guarantee liberation from the economic and social structures that continue to bind individuals within different classes and strata of society. Whereas Hall has tried to establish the grounds for an integrated approach to cultural analysis that recognises the importance of structure *and* form, agency *and* discourse, capital *and* culture, critics on both sides of the divide have eschewed such attempts by returning to the relative safety of either camp. This is by no means the only sore point within cultural studies, but it is one of the most deeply felt areas of conflict within the field.

the cultural turn

It is within this context that we can begin to appreciate the problems associated with Jameson's phrase 'the cultural turn'. The fundamental movement within the humanities away from the classic Marxist paradigm was due in large measure to the eruption of social and political issues in the late 1960s and the 1970s. Feminism contradicted the patriarchal assumptions and principles governing gendered relationships on both domestic and public fronts. Racial relations at home and abroad came under fresh scrutiny as a dismantled Empire fragmented into the post-colonial settlement of new and emergent nation-states. The need to talk about these enormous changes necessitated new languages to express them such as psychoanalysis, post-structuralism, post-colonialism and postmodernism. Cultural studies became the successor to established fields such as history, literature and linguistics. As Simon Watney puts it,

> Available theories of class could not even acknowledge the existence of desire, let alone explain it, as a constitutive force. Marxist cultural theory had traditionally tended to regard cultural production in direct instrumental terms as an agency of class consciousness, supposedly 'true' or 'false'. This Manichaean[2] vision has proved increasingly vulnerable in its refusal (and inability) to offer an account of subjectivity on the side of consumption which is anything like as sophisticated as its explanations of the rest of the process of commodity production. In this respect Marxism offers a social picture of what amounts to an 'empty machine' – empty, that it, because uninhabited by desiring, motivated human beings, who have been theorised away as no more than agents of class struggle. (Evans and Hall, 1999: 142)

In light of this description, Hall's attempts to 'rescue' those more 'useful' elements of Marxist theory could be read as courageous and necessary work.

The 'turn' towards the analysis of culture through an engagement with feminism and anti-racism proved to be both radical and enlarging. Yet for many, the issue of class was and still is, extremely pertinent (Fiske 1995; Caughie 2000). Hall defends his own exploration of poststructuralism as a means of analysing race, within a new 'conceptual space', which still recognises class as important, but not exclusively so:

> class, as the 'master category', was obliged to take its place alongside other 'primordial' social divisions, like race, ethnicity, gender, and sexuality. These had been treated as subordinate or dependent variables in classic Marxist analysis – subeconomic or superstructural. This was impossible, theoretically, after the rise of the anti-racist, gender, and sexual liberation movements of the 1970s. (Hall, cited in Essed and Goldberg, 2002: 451)

But what exactly did the 'cultural turn' propose and how did Hall's analysis of race and identity emerge in the light of his readings of, among others, Foucault and Fanon? Hennessy correctly identifies the influence of Foucault on Hall and others during the 1980s. Foucault's term 'discourse', though never actually defined, has become one of the most oft-quoted terms in media and cultural studies. However, perhaps because of the term's ubiquitous application, it is sometimes forgotten that 'discourse' does not exist purely in the realm of the symbolic or ideological. That is to say, a discourse is not simply an idea. Discourses are concrete in so far as they emanate from specific points of view. They are historically specific, though sometimes their enduring quality makes a specific discourse appear to be both natural and transcendent. This is often the case with racism. Despite the specificity of particular racisms, racism is usually discussed as if it were a transcendent human condition afflicting all people in the same way. Discourses however do not merely hang in the ether as disembodied ideas, though they may come to be regarded as such, and in turn be appropriated within the 'common-sense' wisdom of the age.

To give an example of how discourse operates, we may observe that specific discourses around religion, ethnicity and race are currently achieving widespread circulation and acceptance within the US and Western Europe. The discourse of 'the war against terrorism' pits the US administration against the Iraqi regime. As politicians, media producers, religious leaders and other opinion-formers take up this particular discursive position, so the likelihood of action against a specifically targeted nation-state becomes increasingly real. This in turn has an impact on world markets, currency controls, spending levels, patterns of consumption; even people's choice of holiday destination.

Discourses are material in the sense that they emanate from specific classes or social relations and they have material consequences because they mobilise support for some actions and suppress others. The 'war on terrorism' discourse was already having an impact on the lives of millions of people worldwide long before an official state of war existed between these two countries. We could argue that the discourse itself had already generated sufficient power to make political and economic change possible, if not inevitable, without either side ever launching a single missile. When we make meaning, we create real effects in the material world. We therefore ignore the materiality of discourse at our peril.

As Hall argues,

> The cultural or discursive 'turn' proposes that *all* practices (including the economic) have to be reconceptualised as 'working like a language'. *Not* that everything *is* language, but that no social practice

works 'outside of meaning' and in *that* sense, every social practice is 'written discourse' – i.e., it depends on meaning for its effectivity. (Essed and Goldberg, 2002: 453)

If we take the example of the debate around Marxist methodology and capitalist relations, we can see that the very terms of that debate operate discursively. On the one hand, classic Marxist scholarship, which is generated by scholars of the classic Marxist model – classic Marxism does not exist on its own as a naturally occurring phenomenon – cite the debate about class in classic Marxist terms. However, class as a term, an idea or even more significantly, as a lived reality, exists beyond and outside of the classic Marxist paradigm. In other words, you do not have to be a Marxist to understand and experience class divisions and/or acts of solidarity. The discursive power of 'class' operates in different ways depending on which group is mobilising the term, and for which particular reasons. When scholars operating within the classic Marxist paradigm criticise Hall's work for rejecting the significance of class and capitalist relations, they are actually only in a position to comment on his rejection of that particular method of analysis. Hall has tried to demonstrate that class and capital are indeed instrumental in the formation of culture, but he has done so without recourse to the classic Marxist paradigm. This may constitute heresy for classic Marxists, but it does not mean that Hall has renounced the significance of class within his analysis. He has merely rejected classic Marxist accounts of the significance of class. This is where Hall's use of Gramsci's 'hegemony' thesis and Althusser's term 'articulation' come into play in relation to his analyses of both class and race.

implications for the analysis of race

If discourse is material, then it follows that racial discourses will have real material impact on the conditions and experiences of people who are rendered subjects within them: 'Race, in that sense, is a discursive system, which has "real" social, economic, and political conditions of existence and "real" material and symbolic effects' (Hall, cited in Essed and Goldberg, 2002: 453). Hall goes further in his insistence that 'this does *not* imply that race is purely ideological or cultural, whatever that might mean.' (ibid.). How could race or class exist merely as ideas, when people everywhere are fragmented and bound in their daily lives by their immediate experiences of class and racial structures of dominance? If these were only ideas, then simply by changing your mind, you could change your reality. But the institutions that create and regulate the cultures in which we live, are also determined by the social and political relations operating throughout society. In some high-profile cases, this recognition has led to the accusation of 'institutional racism'. 'Institutional racism' acknowledges the extent to which organisations are, in spite of their equal opportunities policies, governed by the same racist attitudes that pervade the entire society within which they function. The most recent admission to date has come from the British judiciary reporting on the metropolitan police's handling of the Stephen Lawrence murder inquiry.[3] In 1999, The MacPherson Report concluded that a culture of racism existed within the police force, 'born out of an inflexible police ethos of the "traditional" way of doing things'. The report went on to add, 'Furthermore such attitudes can thrive in a tightly-knit community, so that there can be a collective failure to detect and to outlaw this breed of racism. The police canteen can too easily be its breeding ground' (Cathcart, 2000: 413).

If racism is a structured presence within culture, then it follows that the adoption of anti-racist strategies must be carefully examined so as not to fall into the same discursive paradigm. Anti-racism must avoid the tendency of sounding anti-white. Similarly, the assertion of black identity as a legitimate subjectivity sometimes runs the risk of eclipsing ethnic and social difference. Under the banner of 'black is beautiful', the same terms of reference are deployed as within racist ascriptions – that black people are really all the same.

reclaiming the personal

Whereas Hall's earlier work around class, media and the analysis of Thatcherism was undertaken without direct recourse to personal experiences, Hall's later approach to questions of racial representation brought the personal and the political into a new kind of fusion. This move was in part made possible by the influence of Feminism on academic scholarship. The Feminist rally cry 'the personal is the political' together with the impact of Foucault's notion of discourse threatened the apparent stability and authority of knowledge. Where Marxist scholarship had made the case for re-examining the history and formation of modern economic societies, Feminism voiced its dissent with histories and theories that outlawed, ignored or suppressed the roles, experiences, and achievements of women. Foucault scandalised the liberal intelligentsia with his insistence on the integral relationship between knowledge and power. It thus became possible, and indeed imperative that one acknowledge different speaking positions and subjectivities. By speaking of truths rather than searching for *The Truth*, all aspects of social and political life could in theory be recovered and expressed through reference to ones own lived experiences. This is not to suggest that there were, and are, no inherent problems with such an approach. Is it legitimate, for example, to speak of women's experience as if all women are the same? Regardless, this new discursive energy infused cultural studies and gave rise to new work that questioned the very tenets of the field itself (Gilroy, 1987, 1993; McRobbie, 1981).

This search for a way to understand the expression of new subjectivities and identities paralleled Hall's close contact over many years with black film-makers and artists working in Britain and the US. Hall's support for organisations such as the Black Audio Film Collective and The Sankofa Workshop reflected a particular concern with funding for black British cinema. Hall's many collaborations with Isaac Julien included narrative voice-overs and cameo appearances as well as interviews on screen. Working with the BFI, Channel 4 and the Open University, Hall also generated numerous television and video projects including *Black and White in Colour*, sociology programming for the Open Univesity and *Redemption Songs*. As McRobbie (Gilroy, Grossberg and McRobbie, 2000: 217) has pointed out, the majority of Hall's activities could never be categorised as mere academic research. In comparison with many of his colleagues and peers within the political and sociological fields, Hall's approaches to intellectual practice have been enormously varied.

Throughout his work on race and ethnicity we can understand Hall's point about identities being in dynamic relation to each other. We can no longer point to one aspect of our identity as being somehow discrete from the whole. Class, race, ethnicity and sexuality all function in relation to each other, as much as they do in relation to other identities. Hall's decision therefore to speak of his own ethnic and racial identity marks an important point of enunciation into the debates around race, identity and black popular culture.

In a sense the work Hall produced for UNESCO (1980, 1985) tried to build a bridge between the high octane theoretical engagement with Althusserian principles so characteristic of his earliest explorations of the Marxist problematic (Hall's exploration of the *Grundrisse*) and a more concrete means of understanding questions of race. In addition to this we find an impassioned advocacy for the use of Gramsci as a means of identifying and working on the very specific problems of different racisms and the framing of ethnic and racial identity (Hall 1980, 1985, 1986). The transitional nature of this work hinges on Hall's focus on Althusser's term 'articulation' since it enables a more complex theorisation of determination than classic Marxism would seem to allow. As Hall puts it, ' "Articulation" [is] a non-reductionist way of formulating how an overdetermination of factors could produce a historical conjuncture' (Essed and Goldberg, 2002: 450). 'Articulation' enables us to grasp the complexity of different forces within the social, political and economic fields that shape and impact upon the creation of civil and economic society. In this sense, 'articulation' overcomes the problem of classic Marxism as Hall sees it – the compression or reduction of culture to economic determinism. For Hall, the appeal of Gramsci lies in precisely this expression of complexity. Gramsci's theory of hegemony describes the tensions between the forces of dominance and resistance. The practice of hegemony demonstrates the turbulence and frictions of social formations. It is a theory premised on the ideas of schism and rupture. Hegemony presents a way of understanding social formations as conjunctural rather than totalising. Gramsci understands that the world is a messy place, and Hall understands this too.

When Hall yokes together the concept of hegemony with post-structuralist concepts such as discourse and difference, he produces a radical methodology for the analysis of race. Hall's use of Gramsci to talk about race seemed daring indeed, given the specificities of Gramsci's historical and political analysis and Hall's own avowal that Gramsci should not be used as 'a general social science' (Morley and Chen, 1996: 411). However, by 'rescuing' the more 'useful' Marxist ideas and putting them together with post-structuralist concepts, Hall attempts to map out a different route. *Gramsci's Relevance for the Study of Race and Ethnicity* set the terms for a debate that sought to explore in concrete ways the problems facing multiracial Britain. Originally delivered as a paper on the analysis of racism and ethnicity to a colloquium organised by UNESCO in Paris, the paper was reprinted in the *Journal of Communication Inquiry* in 1986. Aside from the important theoretical and conceptual impact of this work, we can also trace a certain continuity between Gramsci's writings and Hall's own complex formation.

David Morley and Kuan-Hsing Chen outline the process by which Hall came to feature as the subject of a special issue of the American *Journal of Communication Inquiry* in 1986. As a visiting Ida Beam Professor, Hall made a big impact on the students and professors at the University of Iowa. The readers and editors of the *Journal* were intrigued by his 'passion, intensity and intellectual generosity' (Morley and Chen, 1996:1) and decided to open up the critical field by inviting Hall to debate the impact of postmodernist theory on cultural studies:

> What was generated was a dialogue between postmodernism and cultural studies. When we look at it retrospectively, it can be seen as a starting-point, from which cultural studies moved on, through another round of configuration, during the next decade, in succession to its previous engagements with humanist Marxism, structuralism, feminism, post-structuralism, etc. (Morley and Chen, 2000: 2)

This intervention proved to be highly influential within British and American cultural studies. Hall's article *Gramsci's Relevance* maps out this crucial point of intersection and enables Hall to make important conceptual movements forward into his later work on ethnicity and cultural identities.

understanding racism

Hall begins by placing the issue of racism squarely in the frame. It is, he declares, a 'poorly elucidated' phenomenon, which if not properly understood, can never be adequately countered. Gramsci's particular emphasis on the formation of 'popular consciousness' goes to the very heart, as Hall sees it, of the problems of racism in modern Britain. For it is not just the messages from above, with which Hall is occupied, but also the ways in which a specific historical and social conjuncture – namely

170

Thatcherism – has given rise to a working-class racism that, regrettably, 'has proved extraordinarily resistant to analysis' (Morley and Chen, 1996: 439). To understand the very nature of the contradictions inherent in working-class racism is only one of the pressing tasks facing society. As Hall and his colleagues at the Centre made clear throughout their analyses in the 1970s, race is the prism through which British capitalism has reproduced its striated social class formations. But what Gramsci offers us is a way of understanding how the victims of racism themselves are subjected to 'the mystifications of the very racist ideologies which imprison and define them' (Morley and Chen, 1996: 440). The contradictory nature of ideology can be seen actively at work in the construction and maintenance of Black and Asian subjectivities that are locked into the network of racist assumptions, expectations, actions and prohibitions afflicting Black and Asian communities. This is not, Hall stresses, the work of false consciousness. We are not dealing with a totalising monolithic conception of thought control. This is not George Orwell's *1984* in action.

We can paraphrase the argument in the following way. What is notable about social relations in 1970s and 1980s Britain is the extent to which the racially constructed subject operates *discursively* within the frame. The black subject is constructed as sometimes successful, sometimes deviant, but *always* ultimately constrained by racial ascription. We can see how this argument works in practice by taking a concrete example.

'englishness' and the 'tebbit test'

In April 1990, Norman Tebbit, former Chairman of the Conservative Party, declared that the 'test' of whether someone was English or not, was whether they supported England or the West Indies at cricket. This infamous statement requires black people living in Britain to choose whether they wish to align themselves with English culture or West Indian culture. If they chose 'wrongly', they cannot be regarded as truly English. Apart from the obvious centrality of *English* identity to Tebbit's formula, despite him being a member of the *British* Parliament, the implications of the 'test' are clear. According to Tebbit, you cannot be one of 'them' i.e. 'black', and still be one of 'us' i.e. 'white'. Englishness is thus figured by Tebbit as an exclusively 'white' identity. This polarisation of ethnic identity along racial lines emerges out of what Martin Barker termed 'the New Racism' of the Far Right as exemplified in the racist views of Enoch Powell (Barker, 1982). So where do black Britons stand in relation to Tebbit's cricket test? Would it be possible to make a similar declaration about football fans? If you live in Macclesfield and support Real Madrid, does this mean you must renounce your English identity?

We cannot simply explain Tebbit's test as arising out of the economic circumstances of British capitalism, although Tebbit's reference to the West Indies is simultaneously an acknowledgement, and a disavowal of the imperial economic relationship between Britain and its colonies. For Tebbit, the very transportation of people from 'over there' to 'over here' poses a real problem. The presence of blacks in Britain appears to offend and threaten his sense of cultural identity. Racist statements of this kind have a connection to the economic, but they are also socially and culturally powerful, drawing on anger and resentments that are not explicable solely as economic phenomena. To take another example, Enoch Powell led a barely-disguised campaign for the forced repatriation of Commonwealth immigrants in the 1970s, yet as Health Minister under MacMillan, he advocated the recruitment of West Indian nurses into British hospitals (Heath, 1998: 292). How can we explain this apparent contradiction? Was Powell in the grip of false consciousness when he made his decision to recruit black nurses? It would instead be more accurate to say that in the booming years of the British post war era, the colonies were viewed by the state as reservoirs of surplus labour that could be mobilised and harnessed for British industry. The hegemonic ideological discourse in operation at that time legitimated such a policy. In successive years such a workforce was no longer required. These people had however by this time settled, started to raise families and had begun the process of integration into the host community. When Powell later attacked immigrants on the basis that they were stealing jobs and houses by taking up space belonging, by right, to English men and women born and bred, he spoke from a reconstituted discursive position that sought to deny the real economic and cultural histories of immigration in British towns and cities. He also denied his own part in bringing about that situation. Powell, Tebbit and others like them have espoused public attitudes to racial groups that operate from a presumption specific to post-war British racism; it is blacks themselves who are the problem, not the attitudes of the England in which they find themselves suddenly demonised and unwelcome. In fact the very idea of 'not being welcome' implies that black and Asian Britons have somehow 'just arrived'.

Thus we can begin to see the instability of identity. As discourses change and shift, so identities are reconstituted. Identity cannot be guaranteed. Gramsci shows us 'how the so-called "self" which underpins these ideological formations is not a unified but a contradictory subject and a social construction' (Hall, in Morley and Chen, 1996: 440). Gramsci's insistence on the intersection of ideological, political, cultural, social *and* economic factors presents us with a complicated and sophisticated matrix rather than the traditional pyramid structure of the base and the superstructure model. The concept of hegemony enables us to understand the inter-relationships between, for example, ideology and class, gender and age, economics and culture, sexuality and race.

gramsci's relevance for marxism

The nuanced and detailed description of Gramsci's conceptual and theoretical landscape is by far Hall's best explication yet of Gramsci's relevance to social enquiry. It brings an immediacy to Gramsci's work and helps us to feel the modern concerns of an Italian Marxist intellectual whose situation in 1930's Turin was in many respects so very different from contemporary Europe. Hall also takes great care to explain and explore the place of Gramsci's scholarship in the wider context of Marxist theory. He criticises Poulantzas and Althusser for over-theorising Gramsci's under-theorised texts. For Hall, it is precisely the concrete nature of Gramsci's fragmentary writings that make them of interest as they demonstrate the 'conjectural' possibilities of analysis. Making use of Gramsci requires that his ideas be 'delicately disinterred from their concrete and specific historical embeddedness and transplanted to new soil with considerable care and patience' (Morley and Chen, 1996: 413). Such work requires patience. It also requires understanding of the nature of the work itself. There is little point in re-potting if you are using the wrong soil. One of the biggest mistakes one can make, as Hall sees it, is to confuse Gramsci's historically concrete application of Marxist principles, with Marx's higher levels of abstract theory. In other words, Gramsci is not in some sense failing because his works do not scale the lofty heights of Marxism.

> Gramsci remained a 'Marxist', as I have said, in the sense that he developed his ideas within the general framework of Marx's theory: that is, taking for granted concepts like 'the capitalist mode of production', the 'forces and relations of production' etc. These concepts were pitched by Marx at the very highest level of abstraction. (1996: 414)

The significance of Gramsci's work then, lies in his specific explication of these abstract theoretical principles within a specific historical era. Abstract theory is often thought of within media and public life as having little use. This view misunderstands the importance and relevance of theory to concrete practice. In the case of Marxism, we can see that his analysis of capitalism offers a general framework for the analysis of modern economies. The specific mechanics and operations of capitalism in its multiple forms across the globe however, requires the careful application of those principles, with due regard to concrete historical contexts. To return briefly to Hall's analysis of Thatcherism, we can see how British capitalism shifted and evolved at a specific conjuncture between Far Right ideologies of the market and a new surge of working-class support. However, the very fact of Thatcher's success with the working-class vote, demands analysis of the precise nature and configuration of economic, cultural and ideological factors, since capitalism is demonstrated by Marx to be a system that fundamentally oppresses the working classes. On the face of it, this would seem to render Marxism obsolete or mistaken. Yet, by using a similar approach to Gramsci, Hall has been able to demonstrate both the utility of a Marxist conceptual framework and the specific dynamics of the cultural-economic relationship mobilised under Thatcherism.

The piecemeal fragmentary nature of Gramsci's writings is another oft-criticised, yet essential feature of Gramsci's achievements. Writing on scraps of paper smuggled into prison, Gramsci was hardly in a position to produce a sustained text to rival Marx and Engels' theoretical treatise. But what he did produce, as Hall describes it, were

> New conceptualisations at precisely the levels at which Marx's theoretical work was itself at its most sketchy and incomplete: that is, the levels of the analysis of specific historical conjunctures, or of the political and ideological aspects – the much neglected dimensions of the analysis of social formations in classical Marxism. (1996: 415)

So it is at the 'conjunctural level' within Marxist theory, rather than at the level of abstract theory that Gramsci's work needs to be understood and appreciated.

gramsci's relevance for hall

Since Gramsci did not write about racism or ethnicity, what is it in his writings that Hall finds so useful and stimulating for the analysis of these areas of social enquiry? One of the answers lies in the continuity between Gramsci's and Hall's own formations. Hall discusses Gramsci's history and situation in some detail:

> Gramsci was born in Sardinia in 1891. Sardinia stood in a 'colonial' relationship to the Italian mainland. His first contact with radical and socialist ideas was in the context of the growth of Sardinian nationalism, brutally repressed by troops from mainland Italy. (Hall, in Morley and Chen, 1996: 416)

Hall goes on to outline Gramsci's move to Turin where he 'abandoned his early nationalism' yet always maintained a concern and an involvement in the issues and problems of the poorer South. The regional, class and cultural differences between North and South were further complicated, as he knew well, by the uneven development associated with regional and national development. His work as a trade union official and his leading position in the Italian Communist Party later rendered him an enemy of Mussolini's fascist state. In short, Gramsci was an intellectual who had first-hand experience and knowledge of the conditions and situation of the peasant classes in Sardinia and the modern industrial working classes of Turin. Thus, in a sideswipe at Perry Anderson[4], Hall suggests that Gramsci's work bears the hallmarks of a more substantial engagement with issues pertaining to racism, colonialism, globalisation and imperialism than have sometimes been allowed.

Hall makes a good case for Gramsci's credentials. It is also increasingly apparent that like Gramsci, Hall's own background has equipped him for the task of investigating race. As a young man, Hall too was engaged in the politics of nationalism and looked forward to the day when Caribbean nations might join together to form an independent federation. Journeying from the largely agrarian, colonised and racially complex, ethnic and class oriented society of Kingston in Jamaica, to a predominantly industrialised homogenous society of England in the early 1950s, must have induced a series of profound reflections. We can see the importance of race, colour, class and ethnicity to Jamaican society in Hall's analysis (1977). The relative hothouse environment of Oxford followed by periods in poorer areas like Brixton and Birmingham certainly contributed enormously to Hall's sense of displacement. Paradoxically, these moves simultaneously afforded him greater awareness of and access to the different levels and institutions of British culture.

Just as Gramsci homed in on the less-developed aspects of Marxist theory in order to generate a means of analysing concrete situations, so Hall has made a life's work out of excavating the foundations of Marxist thinking in order to analyse the here and now. In fact, Gramsci's determination to work at the level of the factory floor and his passionate commitment to grass-roots activism is surely another dimension of his pursuit of intellectual work, which Hall himself would recognise as urgent, necessary and extremely productive. We need perhaps to remind ourselves of the basic motivations for analytical work. What is the point of analysis? Why bother to do the intellectual work? The answer lies in the example of Gramsci's life. It is only by understanding a situation for what it really is, and the complexities of the circumstances that caused it to arise that one can intervene. An intervention is not the same thing as a revolution, nor is it necessarily anarchic. Interventions can be blunt boisterous affairs, or they can be subtle. An intervention may ultimately fail. It may be suppressed or dismissed, but the important thing is to take some kind of action, to question or challenge the prevailing orthodoxy.

Sometimes, even by taking very small steps, it may be possible to bring pressure to bear, to influence, or overturn, to mediate or otherwise be the instrument of change or innovation. It is in this sense that we can understand Hall's advocacy of Gramsci, not on merely intellectual grounds, but also on the basis of Gramsci's activism. Unlike Althusser, whose reading of Gramsci yielded a theoretical, almost clinical interpretation of structure and agency that was genuinely shocking, Hall finds in Gramsci's theories of hegemony and the dynamics of the national-popular, a profound engagement with the struggles of everyday people. And Hall, like Gramsci, sees the need to intervene.

understanding hegemony and resistance

In the third and final section of his paper, Hall makes the case for bringing Gramsci's 'distinctive theoretical perspective' to considerations of how we analyse racism. Hall is indicating here that current methods of analysis are not up to the job, largely because they fail to take into account the specificity of racism within particular historical conjunctions and have a tendency to lump all identities together under the rubric of class.

Drawing on Gramsci's theories of hegemony and ideology, Hall stresses the importance of understanding 'the culturally specific quality of class formations in any historically specific society' (Hall, in Morley and Chen, 1996: 436) adding,

> we would get much further along the road to understanding how the regime of capital can function *through* differentiation and difference, rather than similarity and identity, if we took more seriously this question of cultural, social, national, ethnic and gendered composition of historically different and specific forms of labour. (1996: 436)

It is the very complexity of social relations and the plethora of discourses generating different subjectivities that is occupying Hall's thinking. Hall warns us that while class is not exactly a redundant term, it is in danger of becoming so if we do not begin to understand the contradictory and sometimes antagonistic subjectivities clustered within it. To clarify this point, let us take for example the case of a working-class woman who decides, once her children have left home, that she wishes to go to university in order to gain a degree. How might her working-class husband react to such a decision, particularly if he senses that her desire for self-improvement might lead her to seek the company of other like-minded women? Once educated to degree level, has the woman forfeited her right to be a member of the working class? In the current climate of government policy, returning to education may fit comfortably within prevailing discourses of female independence and enterprise, yet her actions may be perceived by family and friends as an assault on working-class values. In such cases as these, many women find their new identities very difficult to negotiate. Is it the case that a working-class man seeking higher education will experience the same degree of ostracism from friends and family?

Gramsci helps us to understand that subjectivities are not fixed. If we take the example above, the intersection of identities under modern British capitalism suggests that there should be no conflict between being a woman, being working-class and having a university education. Yet the experience of thousands of such women suggests conflict abounds in relation to their situation. Subjectivity is born out of struggle and conflict. If we apply this to the idea of whole classes we can see how persuading a working class that university education is of benefit to them may be an uphill struggle. Initially there may be economic implications. Cultural, gendered, racial and political factors may come into play too. Equally, within working class formations, religious, ethnic and racial differences may be extremely important factors in determining whether a university education is even desirable for young women who are expected to make a good marriage rather than go out to work. So we find that even once the argument has been 'won', and a degree of hegemonic consent has been achieved over the extension of higher education opportunities to working class communities, we may still find areas of tension and dissent such as described above, not just between classes, but also *within* them. The hegemonic moment is founded therefore on 'strategic alliances' and is therefore a moment of unification, not unity (ibid.: 437). Hegemony does not guarantee stability, nor does it need one hundred per cent agreement on the part of the population.

hall and ethnicity

Having established the grounds on which he intended to construct his analysis of the operations of racism and the construction of racial and ethnic identity, Hall set about the question of representation with characteristic boldness. In an address to the members of the ICA conference, 'The Real Me', in the autumn of 1986, Hall spoke of his own migrant black identity:

> Thinking about my own sense of identity, I realise that it has always depended on the fact of being a *migrant*, on the difference from the rest of you. So one of the fascinating things about this discussion is to find myself centred at last. Now that it is the postmodern age, you all feel so dispersed, I become centred. (Hall, 1987: 44)

Hall ponders the question of who we really are, by describing his own process of self-identification – his own chosen narrative: 'I was aware of the fact that identity is an invention from the very beginning, long before I understood any of this theoretically' (ibid.: 44). In this sense, identity is an 'arbitrary closure' that creates a relatively fixed point at the intersection between the 'self' and various often conflicting or competing histories or narratives. Within the narrative history of post-colonialism, being an 'immigrant' and being 'black' are two (often compounded) identities predicated on displacement and difference. Whereas being an immigrant poses real problems for integration, being 'black' affords a powerful sense of difference, which Hall recognises as having been part of his own 'long, important, political education'(ibid.: 45). But there are also problems implicit in the process of 'becoming' black:

> Constituting oneself as 'black' is another recognition of self through difference: certain polarities and extremities against which one tries to define oneself. We constantly underestimate the importance, to certain crucial political things that have happened in the world, of this ability of people to constitute themselves, psychically, in the black identity. It has long been thought that this is really a simple process: a recognition – a resolution of irresolutions, a coming home to rest in some place which was always there waiting for one. The 'real me' at last! (Hall, 1987: 45)

179

But as Hall goes on to explain, this idea of 'coming home' to an identity that has always been, is a myth. 'Black' identity is no less of a construction than any other. Hall explores the difference between his experience of Jamaica and the 'black' society that it has become:

> In reality [Jamaica] is a society of black and brown people who lived for three or four hundred years without ever being able to speak of themselves as 'black'. 'Black' is an identity which had to be learned in a certain moment. In Jamaica that moment is the 1970s. (Hall, 1987: 45)

Hall resists the idea that being 'black' is the recovery of an essence of self. He argues instead that such an identification, premised primarily on difference from white cultural tastes, behaviours, habits and customs, is indeed an imaginary construction at the level of the symbolic. Citing Benedict Anderson's thesis of the 'imaginary community'[5], Hall stresses the complicated and multi-layered nature of identity. Identity, according to Hall, is the 'dialogue' between subjectivity and culture. It is the space where the unified self speaks in relation to the culture. Cultures are of course real, not just symbolic, because they arise out of concrete historical conjunctures. The postmodern condition however, suggests that it is the experience of displacement, migration and diaspora that is having one of the largest influences on the construction of contemporary identities. In the rush toward the apparent safety of an essential notion of identity, Hall detects a failure to address both the problems and the potential opportunities of a new kind of politics. Rather than relying on a mythological idea of centred stability, Hall advocates a rethink of the political possibilities of embracing a more self-reflective concept that recognises the contingency of identity. How would this work in practice?

Hall is proposing a 'politics of articulation' rather than clinging to traditional notions of fixed identity. Racist assumptions are frequently predicated on fixed notions; for example the idea that black people only excel at sport and music. The presence in Western culture of many successful black artists and sportsmen would *seem* to attest to this racist 'truth'. However, if it is the case that Western society has an expectation that black children are only gifted within certain areas, then other opportunities to achieve may well be closed to them. Given those circumstances, it is not surprising if blacks are under-represented in areas such as politics or broadcasting. If we let go of our prejudices and assumptions about what is possible, and loosen our grip on the seemingly natural and universal 'truths' about identities – women are the weaker sex, black homosexuality is a myth, real men do not cry – we may be able to articulate new, powerful and effective selves rather than experiencing the world in terms of what is closed to us.

Identity, as Hall sees it, is not universally fixed. Just like language, which constantly evades our attempt to pin down the world, so identity slips through our fingers, evading absolute closure: 'Potentially, discourse is endless: the infinite semiosis of meaning. But to say anything at all in particular, you do have to stop talking' (ibid.: 45). It is the point in discourse where we make our intervention, that we draw attention to our constituted selves. To give an example; feminism is a kind of full stop (though not a final one) in the discursive flow of patriarchy. The rupture that occurs at the point of intersection between one identity and the free-flow of discourse, presents us with enormous challenges and opportunities. But Hall does not fall back on the idea that all identities are of equal relative value or power. If we go down that route, then no intervention is possible, no politics is possible because nothing is at stake if all things are the same. There are times when some identities matter more than others, and the relationships between different identities demand constant negotiation and dialogue. Taking all these ideas together we can see how Hall is using both elements of postmodern theory and Gramscian concepts of hegemony to arrive at a position where a new kind of politics becomes possible, desirable and empowering;

> Now, it seems to me that it is possible to think about the nature of new political identities, which isn't founded on the notion of some absolute integral self and which clearly can't arise from some fully closed narrative of the self. A politics which accepts the 'no necessary correspondence' of anything with anything, and there has to be *a politics of articulation* – politics as a hegemonic project. (Hall, 1987: 45)

The resulting action of such a politics could be, for example, the disentangling of race from nationalism so that we begin to think in terms of ethnicity and difference rather than the exclusive claims of a racialist national identity. If we apply Hall's ideas to the common conceptualisation of British nationalism for example, we can see how an acknowledgement of many different ethnicities might contribute to and define a modern idea of Britain in the world, rather than the hackneyed and racist definitions so beloved by overtly nationalistic organisations such as the British National Party.[6]

new ethnicities

There is however much more to the question of identity than how we define ourselves. Identity is never solely a matter for the individual but constitutes a dynamic relationship between self and others. In addressing the specificities of black identity in media and film, Hall is concerned to clarify the situation faced by black artists and 'cultural workers' in their struggle for representation. The 'Black is beautiful' strategy employed by many throughout the 1960s and 1970s challenged the marginalisation, objectification and fetishisation of blacks in Western culture. As such it was a powerful means of organising black resistance. However, Hall argues, 'I have a distinct sense that in the recent period we are entering a new phase' (Hall, in Baker, Diawara and Lindeborg, 1996: 164). Hall reflects on what he sees as the cultural racism that flourished under Thatcherism. He invites black and asian film makers and others engaged in the politics of representation to address the transformative constitutive aspects of discourse, rather than relying explicitly on the expressive. Hall is arguing that since discourse is the place where meaning is generated and disseminated, it makes no sense to go in quest of the authentic black experience. By judging films and other artistic work against this criterion, we are missing the point. This phase in the struggle for representation, Hall suggests, marks an end to the idea of the innocent black subject. This work is necessary because an understanding of ethnicity brings us to the radical realisation that we *all* come from *somewhere*.

Hall expands this idea of ethnicity beyond the way it is normally employed. Black and Asian artists have been designated 'ethnic' or members of 'ethnic minorities' as if ethnicity were itself a feature of black identity. This is a teleological argument that proceeds from an assumption that being 'white' is not consistent with a recognition of ethnicity. Hall's own experience and his analysis of race and class in Caribbean society (1977) discusses the extent to which class power is linked to skin colour. The more white you look, the more likely you are to be accorded power, prestige and status. The blacker your skin, the

182

greater the cultural and political distance from the status of the plantation class, and by inference, the culture of the 'mother country', Britain. In other words, as Richard Dyer has shown, 'white' becomes a non-colour, and is therefore presumed to be the 'norm' against which gradations, or *degradations* of colour are judged to be both inferior and undesirable. 'Thatcherism' is a prime example of the workings of just such a conception of Englishness, that 'does not represent itself as ethnic at all' (Baker et al. 1996: 169).

Working with this revitalised notion of ethnicity delivers us from the problem of racist and anti-racist strategies that are essentially premised on the same assumptions; the binary opposition of one colour against another. In a desire to articulate the concerns of black and Asian communities, film makers have been concerned to make films precisely about those issues and have, as a result, found themselves occupying a minority status away from the wider contexts of cinematic representation.

Hall argues for

> A recognition that we all speak from a particular place, out of a particular history, out of a particular experience, a particular culture, without being contained by that position as 'ethnic artists' or film-makers. We are all, in that sense, *ethnically* located and our ethnic identities are crucial to our subjective sense of who we are. But this is also a recognition that this is not an ethnicity which is doomed to survive, as Englishness was, only by marginalising, dispossessing, displacing and forgetting other ethnicities. This precisely is the politics of ethnicity predicated on difference and diversity. (Baker et al. 1996: 170)

Such a politics enables black and Asian film-makers to resist the pressure to produce 'monolithic, self-contained, sexually stabilized and always "right-on"' films (ibid.: 171). Hall cites Hanif Kureishi's film *My Beautiful Launderette* as a case in point, quoting Kureishi from an interview with *Time Out* magazine:[7] 'If there is to be a serious attempt to understand Britain today, with its mix of races and colours, its hysteria and despair, then, writing about it has to be complex. It can't apologise or idealise. It can't sentimentalise and it can't represent only one group as having a monopoly on virtue' (ibid.: 171).

Hall argues that working within this idea of ethnicity as a point of entry into discourse, as an enunciation, allows representation that engages with difference rather than trying to suppress it. All identities cannot be subsumed into the category of 'black'. Such coercion simply replicates the racist agenda. By adopting Gramsci's idea of the 'war of position', Hall explores how it is still possible to achieve a sense of solidarity without being dependent on certain fixed notions of racial and ethnic identity. A multiculturalism based on a 'war of position' would acknowledge the ways in which 'central issues of race always appear historically in articulation, in a formation, with other categories and divisions and are constantly crossed and recrossed by the categories of gender and ethnicity' (ibid. 1996: 166). Conceptualised in these terms, multiculturalism can achieve hegemonic status without recourse to liberal intentions such as 'tolerance' or 'celebration'. It would also enable genuine criticism to move beyond the idea that films made by black film-makers must be deemed good, for fear of appearing racist.

Hall develops these ideas further in his discussions about burgeoning 'world' cinema, such as that emerging from the Caribbean, and the ways in which they tackle the experiences of hybridity and diaspora.

the production of identity

Psychoanalytic approaches to film recognise and explore the correspondence between the speaking subject of the film and the point of enunciation. Where we place the camera therefore expresses our position in relation to the object. This is the basic idea of Laura Mulvey's theory of 'the male gaze'.[8] No matter what the sex or sexual orientation of the viewer, the subject of the gaze is born of the enunciating subjectivity of male heterosexuality. This assumes that the moment of enunciation and 'the subject who is spoken of' (Baker et al. 1996: 210) occupy the same space. Hall challenges this view by suggesting that identity is never as fully fledged or complete as this might suggest. Hall proposes instead a view of identity in constant flux: 'Perhaps instead of thinking of identity as an already accomplished historical fact, which the new cinematic discourses then represent, we should think, instead, of identity as a 'production', which is never complete, always in process, and always constituted within, not outside, representation' (ibid.: 210). The problem with this view however is that it 'problematises the very authority and authenticity to which the term "cultural identity" lays claim' (ibid.: 210). Despite this, Hall proceeds with this line of argument with reference to Frantz Fanon and Michel Foucault, as he explores the implications of identity as 'displacement'.

imagining 'home'

'Cultural identity' can be thought of as an historically located set of shared experiences that need to be recovered in order to fulfil the desire to become one nation or one people. In this regard, Hall argues, Caribbean cinema has an important function in the discovery of Caribbean history and the common cultural codes that provide 'continuous frames of reference and meaning, beneath the shifting divisions and vicissitudes of our actual history' (Baker et al. 1996: 211). Such is the need generated by many displaced postcolonial societies. Hall places the Pan-African project, which sought to unite all black people under the banner of African identity, in the context of Fanon's thesis. Whereas the experience of the post-colonial diaspora has typically been one of displacement and hardship, communities will search for a vision of a more perfect era – a more beautiful vision of themselves before the distortion and oppression of the colonial period. But rather than see this in terms of a genuine discovery, Hall suggests that this reclamation of the past is actually a process of production. It is an *imaginative* act of discovery, which gives an imaginary coherence to a broken and fragmented sense of identity. Memory, fantasy and myth all conjoin in the shaping and expression of a Caribbean identity through film, photography, music, and other art forms. Through recognising the contingency of identity in this way, we can explore modern black identity without relying on the security of certain older, apparently fixed, identities. Whereas the search for an authentic Caribbean subject seeks continuities with the past, Hall argues for the positioning of identity as a way of understanding *dis*continuities with the past. Placing Hall's argument in the context of modern representation, we can see how this move would go some considerable way towards the loosening of stereotypical representations of black people as slaves, primitives and victims.

None of these arguments deny the importance of, or seek to replace the work of coming to terms with, the real historical conditions of

Caribbean social relations: 'Africa must be reckoned with, by Caribbean people. But it cannot in any simple sense be merely recovered' (ibid.: 217). Africa is another 'imagined community' and is not a 'home' to which Caribbean people can simply return. Hall stresses the hybridity of Caribbean identity itself. We can never get back to some pure sense of where we come from. The pursuit of identity takes us in Lacanian fashion through an endless chain of signifiers that cannot bring us any closer to the 'real me'. But such conclusions do not, as far as Hall is concerned, leave us all at sea in our sense of relativity. It does not mean that we are powerless. Contrary to Derrida's playful articulation of difference, Hall insists that positions are strategic and motivated, rather than arbitrary and free-flowing. The decision to articulate a position is precisely that – a decision, an intervention, a motivated break into the discursive flow. Thus, in Hall's own experience, being 'African', was an identity that only erupted onto the Caribbean scene in the 1970s as a result of civil rights and other mediating signifiers impacting on the local collective consciousness. Prior to that period, 'I never once heard a single person refer to themselves or to others as, in some way, or as having been at some time in the past, "African"' (ibid. 1996: 216).

policing black identity

So far we have explored Hall's journey through his articulations of race, identity and ethnicity. We turn finally to the issue of multiculturalism and Hall's concerns around the forms and strategies employed by artists, politicians, broadcasters and academics in relation to black popular culture. Hall becomes increasingly impatient with what he perceives as a reliance on the essentialist black subject. This prompts a new question about the apparent authority of 'black' subjectivity in black popular culture (1992). In 'What is this "black" in black popular culture?', Hall suggests that 'the essentialising moment is weak because it naturalises and dehistoricises difference, mistaking what is historical and cultural for what is natural, biological and genetic' (Morley and Chen, 1996: 472). Not only does this lead to an arbitrary 'fixing' of identity, but more worryingly for Hall, it becomes a method of policing 'the straying brothers and sisters who don't know what they ought to be doing' (ibid.: 472). The dangers of such a politically correct strategy only serves to reproduce the same kinds of oppression as racist strategies. In addition, the essentialising of black experience along fixed lines of identification can all too easily result in misogynistic and homophobic attitudes: 'The way in which a transgressive politics in one domain is constantly sutured and stabilised by reactionary or unexamined politics in another is only to be explained by this continuous cross-dislocation of one identity by another, one structure by another' (ibid.: 473). Hall points to the problems inherent in privileging black identity without due consideration of how other identities such as gender, class and sexuality intersect with it. In short, acting out a particular kind of liberated black experience is no guarantee against other forms of cultural repression. The only defence seems to be a recognition of the dialogic nature of popular culture.[9] Hall refuses the comfortable and traditional ideas of binary oppositions; black versus white, high culture versus low culture, incorporation versus marginalisation. His vision of popular culture, and black popular culture is no exception, is a space with many competing voices and many varieties of discursive strategies and identities. Within the cacophony of the carnivalesque,[10] we can discover the confluence of different orders of signification, different cultural traditions, and many hybrid identities.

But what is at stake here? Why should it matter how we understand and respond to popular culture? The problem and the challenge is to examine what kind of society we really want compared with the evidence of the society we really have. Popular culture is the space within and through which we understand the nature of our social and political relations. The challenge to British culture, rests primarily for Hall, in its capacity to recognise the possibilities of multiculturalism. But even that term is prone to mis-understandings: 'Just as there are different multi-cultural societies so there are very different 'multiculturalisms'' (Hesse, 2000: 210). These different multiculturalisms range from the commercial to liberal, from pluralist to corporate:

> Far from being a settled doctrine, 'multiculturalism' is a deeply contested idea. It is contested by the conservative Right, in defence of the purity and cultural integrity of the nation. It is contested by liberals, who claim that the 'cult of ethnicity' and the pursuit of difference threaten the universalism and neutrality of the liberal state, undermining personal autonomy, individual liberty and formal equality. (Hesse, 2000: 211)

187

If we look at British culture in particular, we can see how multi-culturalism is regarded as a relatively new phenomenon. But, as Hall has been at pains to point out, 'Britain' has had a relatively short history, and indeed 'the so-called homogeneity of British culture has been massively overstated' (Hesse, 2000: 229). How then could British culture begin the process of defining itself in terms of a (long overdue) radical form of multiculturalism? A multiculturalism that recognised the real cultural diversity which is the essential condition of the modern world?

british identity in a multicultural society

Hall makes specific recommendations. It is time, he argues, for a new vocabulary. Given that liberalism has consistently failed to address issues of social justice and racial equality, as evidenced by the case of Stephen Lawrence, we need instead to open up to the infinite possibilities of being 'British'. But this is no easy matter and Hall can see the dangers implicit in such a strategy:

> It might be possible to be Black-and-British or Asian-and-British (or even British and gay!) however the idea that *everyone* should have access to the processes by which such new forms of 'Britishness' are redefined, coupled with the loss of empire and decline as a world power, is literally driving some of its citizens crazy. (Hesse, 2000: 238)

This madness can be seen in the proliferation of 'new racisms that are abroad everywhere and gaining ground' (ibid.: 238). The case of Stephen Lawrence and the celebrations of the anniversary of the arrival of the SS *Empire Windrush*[11] are two sides of the same coin – Britain's problematic relationship to the question of is multicultural status as a modern state.

the parekh report

The question of racism and its broader inflections within British society are further deconstructed by the influential report 'The future of multi-ethnic Britain', also known as the *Parekh Report*, named after the chair of the Commission,[12] Bhikhu Parekh. It is a landmark text that examines every aspect of British culture from policing to sport, in order to 'analyse the current state of multi-ethnic Britain and to propose ways of countering racial discrimination and disadvantage and making Britain a confident and vibrant multicultural society at ease with its rich diversity' (Parekh, 2000: viii).

The Commission was launched by the Home Secretary, Jack Straw, in January 1998. The members of the Commission were drawn from across many areas of public life including the media, education, police, judiciary, government, politics and health. Hall's membership of the Commission and his contribution to the Report can be seen as simultaneously the culmination of a long and active engagement with the politics of race and representation, and as a significant point of intervention. This is not simply an account of 'the way things are' but an active challenge to the status quo. The Report published its findings and recommendations in October 2000. It pulls no punches and delivers cogent recommendations. An extract from the section on 'media bias' gives an insight into the scale of the problem that the *Parekh Report* is seeking to address:

A study by the *Guardian* of its own coverage of Islam in a particular period in 1999 found that the adjective 'Islamic' was joined with 'militants' 16 times, 'extremist' 15 times, 'fundamentalism' eight times and 'terrorism' six times; in the same period the adjective 'Christian' was joined, in so far as it appeared at all, to positive words and notions or to neutral ones, such as tradition or belief. Constant juxtapositions such as these have a cumulative effect on the consciousness of all readers alike, to the point where it is exceedingly difficult, for journalists and readers alike, to unlearn the assumptions and stereotypes they perpetuate. (Parekh, 2000: 169–170)

The *Guardian* is a *liberal* daily national British newspaper. But it does not stand outside of the dominant hegemonic discourses of race that infuse British culture. If evidence were required to substantiate what Hall means by the failure of liberalism, then here it is. When Hall talks about how Britain imagines itself to be a multicultural nation, he points to the myth of the liberal state: 'All so-called modern, liberal nation-states thus combine the so-called rational, reflective, civic form of allegiance to the state with a so-called intuitive, instinctual, ethnic allegiance to the nation. That heterogeneous formation, "Britishness" grounds the United Kingdom, the political entity, as an "imagined community" '(Hall, 2000: 229). If liberalism is the founding basis for British culture, it is also the means by which Britain has been able to colonise, subjugate and repress. As Hall argues emphatically, 'the neutrality of the state works only when a broad cultural homogeneity among the governed can be assumed (Hall, 2000: 228). Multicultural populations challenge those broad assumptions about cultural identity and practice. Multicultural populations are, by their very nature, defined by difference – heterogeneity – rather than homogeneity. The liberal neutral state finds itself over-stretched and increasingly unable to mediate between different communities. It risks becoming incoherent in its pursuit of 'the common good' unless it can define what that means exactly for individuals and communities everywhere.

The *Parekh Report* endorses and appropriates many of Hall's arguments concerning the failure of broadcasters and cultural agencies to represent racial and cultural diversity as a positive asset. Specifically the report draws upon many of Hall's recommendations from an earlier document (Hall, 1999) in which Hall argues for a greater emphasis on cultural inclusion, rather than the continued representation of Britain's cultural heritage as the legacy of a homogenous white community:

> Historical events have to be seen through more than one pair of eyes, and narrated within more than one story. It is increasingly recognised that no individual, group or institution has the right – or, indeed, any longer the power – to define the culture and stories of others. But this democratising approach to heritage and the arts has so far stopped short of addressing the issue of racism, of confronting Britain's selective amnesia about its former empire, and of reflecting the diverse composition of its present population. (Parekh, 2000: 163)

In fact the main thrust of Hall's treatise on 'the multi-cultural question' (Hall, 2000) informs chapters 2 and 3 of the *Parekh Report*. Hall speaks of 'multicultural drift' rather than 'conscious policy' (Parekh, 2000: 14), and advocates intervention on the part of agencies and government to ratify and legitimate Britain's culture as one steeped in difference. Hall identifies seven recent trends including globalisation, the end of empire and social pluralism, which have 'unsettled' Britain's sense of itself as a homogenous nation-state. Falling back on a mythical history is no longer viable, let alone desirable:

> First, Britain is not and never has been the unified, conflict-free land of popular imagination. There is no single white majority. Second, the 'minority' communities do not live in separate, self-sufficient enclaves, and they do display substantial internal differences. They too must be reimagined. (Parekh, 2000: 26)

The *Parekh Report* is important because it grasps the nettle firmly, and does not make assumptions about Britain's multicultural status. While it recognises good practice in many areas of public life, it does not hide behind liberal intentions, but rather, engages directly with what needs to be done. Hall's involvement with the Commission in the areas of race, ethnicity and culture is substantial, despite the collective nature of the Report's findings and recommendations. What is particularly notable is the extent to which the Report gives concrete practical suggestions for activists and policy makers. There is clearly a major role to be played by government departments as well as independent organisations.

Hall's signature to the report therefore endorses a very practical engagement that is designed to impact at all levels. Some would argue that this is at odds with Hall's approach, for if there is one aspect of Hall's work more criticised than any other, it is that he does not offer concrete solutions to the problems he identifies. But Hall has never considered himself to be a major theorist, nor modelled himself as a guru or politician. He has been primarily a teacher and a cultural critic. A Jamaican intellectual (un)settled in Britain who has 'lived all my adult life in England, in the shadow of the black diaspora – "in the belly of the beast"' (Hall, cited in Baker, Diawara and Lindeborg, 1996: 211). Persuading government to take seriously the issue of culture and representation has surely been one of Hall's greatest achievements to date.

further reading

Gilroy, P. (1987) *There ain't no Black in the Union Jack: The Cultural Politics of Race and Nation.* Hutchinson: London.

Gilroy, P. (1993) *The Black Atlantic: Modernity and Double Consciousness.* Verso: London.

Hall, S. (1999) 'Unsettling the heritage: re-imagining the post-nation', in Department for Culture, Media and Sport (1999) *Whose Heritage?* HMSO: London.

Hesse, B. (2000) *Un/settled multiculturalisms.* Zed Books: London.

Jameson, F. (1991) *Postmodernism or the Cultural Logic of Late Capitalism.* Verso: London.

Laclau, E. and Mouffe, C. (1985) *Hegemony and Socialist Strategy.* Verso: London.

8

'fragmented and concrete', in conversation with stuart hall

In the winter of 1998, Marxism Today *was resurrected for one last special issue. The subject was New Labour and the cover bore an image of Tony Blair with the word 'wrong' in large red letters: Geoff Mulgan, a former contributor to* Marxism Today *now an advisor to the new government, launched an attack on Hall and Hobsbawm for their failure to make specific their objections to New Labour policy: 'It would have been interesting if instead of tilting at windmills, Hall and Hobsbawm had attempted a more serious analysis of New Labour's political strategy' (Mulgan, 1998: 16). How does Hall react to the criticism that he never offered up a political programme himself?*

I have a very realistic sense of who I am and what I can do. The fact that I didn't, has to do with the sort of person I am. I don't have those skills. I'm not an economist, I'm not a policy person, you know, I'm interested in them, but I can't think creatively as a policy person. I can't make myself into something I'm not. That has no implications for what *you* should do, if *you're* an economist you should be thinking about it and helping me! We can't all do everything! And I have a very real sense of what I can do. What I can do, you know – I'm an intellectual – and I can fight the intellectual struggle. I can't pretend to be a horny-handed son of toil – it's ridiculous, it's absurd. It's inauthentic, so I never thought that everybody must follow me. 'Everybody must be in an independent position' – no not at all! If you can join the Labour party, then get in there! Because how do we transmit our ideas into it, unless people take it inside? So, none of it is a recommendation.

If you are a civil servant I don't expect you to learn how to teach! I expect you to advance the cause in what you are doing. Everybody can advance the cause in what they are doing. What will make a difference is all of us added together! So I don't think I've confused myself by thinking 'because you do this, it is an implicit model and let us all do it in this way.' This is how I live with what I can do in what I think is the most effective way. If we can find a basis in which our differences re-inforce one another, we can achieve a lot. That's a model for a more differentiated notion of solidarity. Not because we're all the same, and can do the same things, but because we are all different, we can find common ground.

Given this question of difference, to what extent had Hall been aware of his own difference, specifically his own ethnicity during his undergraduate days at Oxford? Had class to some extent obscured questions of ethnic or national identity?

That's the point where I am least conscious of my own ethnicity. This is when I decide not to go home. This is when I decide that I'm not going, my life is not going to be participating in Jamaica, in politics of the Caribbean, in regional politics, it's going to be here. I'm thinking I'm going to live in this country for the rest of my life. How am I going to do it? So the socialist movement subsumes all those questions, it's the moment of my least identification. It's not until after the New Left, when I'm aware that the West Indians I have seen trickling into London in the 1950s, are going to be a substantial number, and that they're going to be staying here, that they are a new diaspora, and that the questions of cultural identity and all of that which I think I've now left behind, and I can't stand them, are here!

So rather than play out the middle-class role assigned to him by parents and peers, Hall chose to stay. He thought he had escaped the ethnic and class strictures of his home-nation, only to find that these issues were about to re-surface in Britain.

Of course, that's what I realised, that's why I didn't go back to it! That's why I left it! And didn't go back to it. But I never tried to play that role. I had friends and I did intervene in a very marginal way but after that, my entire constituency for that kind of area of thinking is here. I'm interested in the Caribbean in terms of what is the culture they are bringing into this situation and I'm also interested in what is going to happen to them when they have to make another diaspora negotiating along with the European host culture. All my writing is directed towards this constituency not that constituency. I am constantly referring to the Caribbean because my line of thinking is that they are going to have some of the same kinds of problem of cultural negotiation as I had, because they come from a society which is already culturally complex, especially in relation to 'origins', okay? So I have to argue about that because there is the definition that they are all African, and these are very nativist definitions – so I have a constant argument with that, and recently I wrote a lot about diaspora and about the Caribbean and so on, but I am writing about the Caribbean in relation to the problem which is here, not over there. So I want to clarify all the questions about Africanness because I want to understand what happens when Rastafarianism arises in Isleworth, and when Babylon is not Norman Manley but Roy Hattersley! My focal point is this, although it is partly an argument about the past – I'm writing about Creolisation right at the very moment – but this is always in relation to 'was Jamaican society really Creolised, and therefore is the problem now, that an already Creolised diaspora is being Creolised a second time in the context of globalisation?' These people have a particular problem of multiple positioning because they bring multiple positioning into the situation. They bring Creolised Africanness to England and that's where they have to re-Creolise or re-hybridise it all, and those are the arguments for that.'

How did Hall see the move from the 1970s to the 1980s?

There's a more direct confrontation in the 70s. There's more of a politics of confrontation going on in all these proliferating areas – race, gender – the kind of basic case for women's equality has been made, but now you get organised femininsm. You get a s sharpening of contradictions in the 70s. But I don't hanker for a return to the 1970s and in relation to what we were talking about before, I think this is the last gasp of the old politics, with lots of new elements mixed in, but the new elements are in suspension. Not until Thatcherism, because I think

195

the dividing line is globalisation, the onset of the new kind of globalisation which happens in 1975 – the oil price, the IMF – the Labour government has to go to the IMF – that is the end of social democracy, the comprehensive schools, full employment, you know the Wilson white heat, – it's the end of that post-war kind of consensus. That's what's collapsing there, and that's what we tried to define in what we write about that period in *Policing the Crisis*, but we're not yet at something to which we could return, because the full implications of the onset of the new kind of globalisation doesn't arise until it's politically embodied in Thatcher and Reagan. Then they begin the politics of post-globalisation and that's the new era. That changes a lot.

By the way another thing that is going on in the 70s is the possibility, theoretically is the possibility, of a return to Marx which is not reductionist. So there's Gramsci and Althusser, you know make possible a kind of Marxism. It's the last time a kind of Marxism, that's not, that is trying to think its way out of economic reductionism. So that's all about, all part of that maelstrom which generates feminism, and it s new politics, and politics around race, it's the climax of the social movements as new social forces and they are harbingers of things to come, but they co-exist with the Labour party, labour, socialism, Marxism, with some of the conventional traditions. It's not until we get into the 80s and you see a quite new configuration beginning to emerge under neo-liberalism, under marketisation, under privatisation, it tries to pick out of the 70s and encapsulated certain trends, individualism, consumerism, and valorate those and separate those out from more radical challenge to the system. So the terms seem to me to change between the 70s and the 80s. And we couldn't answer the problems now posed by going back to the 70s, despite the energy, confrontation, the sense that you were almost coming to some kind of crisis. We used the word crisis, and all this stuff about the miners' strike in the 70s. The miners' strike in the 70s was successful as opposed to what happened later. There are the riots in Brixton, and all that in 81 – it's sort of climaxing – the problems of the old society are really beginning to climax, and it feels like an exciting political time, but how it disaggregates itself into the 80s, is another kind of question. You have to put another kind of screen in – the projection before you get the problems we have post-Thatcher, post neo-liberalism and living with that.

And so our political solutions are unlikely to come via a simple return. And that's where I get into trouble because that's really what I

196

say in the pieces on Thatcherism, the *Marxism Today* pieces. We can talk about *MT* in another context because I have a lot of things today about that but what I tried to say is this is really a new historical situation. So we can't go back, just return to the past. I was critical of a sort of traditional labourism, traditional leftism, as I am critical of new liberalism. And I did share a platform more than once with Tony Benn, but I shared a platform after the 82 election with Tony Benn and I am his opponent. It's the point at which the left confuses itself. Gives itself hope on an unrealistic basis.

It seems that this was the point at which many on the left felt betrayed by Hall's position and were unwilling to look at the real historical configurations that were enabling the rise of Thatcherism. How does Hall square the idea of reform with the old Labour agenda of welfare provision?

The principle of the National Health Service which is not what Tony Blair says – which is free at the point of delivery – it is the de-commodification of illness and death. It is not a commodity. Well I would like to see that now. We could have real continuity with those things but that does not mean I need to preserve the full National Health Service until the end of time. I can't say that there's nothing that needs to change, on the other hand what does need to happen is that it is de-commodified! So we need to find some combination of change and continuity with the principles of the past which generate new forms. And that is a harder argument to sell. Lots of people were being converted to Thatcherism and to New Labour. Lots of people were willing to stand in the way, class forces resist – but the hard graft of really looking at what new globalisation meant – the ability of modern corporations to make profits in the West and exploit cheap labour, men and women in the East, in the South – that is the lynchpin. And that must do something to where the class struggle is located. The class struggle is now located between women working for one dollar a day in GAP out there, and Brent Cross. That's where the class struggle lies. You cannot think that world in exactly the same point as if the class struggle is represented by the Labour party, or the trade unions. We were in an argument with British entrepreneurs who own GAP – it's not true, they don't own GAP, America owns GAP and their products are being produced in Taiwan. What does that do to the class struggle here? Of course there's a connection but it's not a connection you can think in terms of the era in which socialism in one country was developing, which is the period when real welfare gains could be made. Once that national framework was strong, you could bargain within it, but to bargain globally you need different institutions, a different picture of the world, a better understanding of how the global interacts on the local, etc. and that needs thinking and these are ideas that I don't know how to think about because I'm not an economist. And I know it needs to be thought about, and that is a very hard message to sell. Of course, we also weren't terribly sure-footed about it so occasionally we exaggerated things. My *New Times* piece which is what is often quoted is the one where I am closest to a postmodernist position – I don't think I would defend everything that is in it or how it is formulated. I'm throwing out provocative possibilities to start a new programme. It's certainly not what Giddens is saying, which is 'we have passed this transition – this is the new world – we've got to live with it and that means we must have New Labour, and markets and the public finance initiative'.

One of the dangers of Giddens' position seems to be that it runs the risk of identifying global economic trends as if they are a naturally occurring phenomenon, which you just have to accept and cannot really challenge.

Exactly, so people say well we didn't quite get it right on every occasion, but we were thinking in outer space. We were just coming to terms with the fact that this had happened and that this was really what Thatcherism represented. It didn't just represent the old baddies back. They weren't the old baddies back in power at all. These were new baddies! Under a new philosophy, in new conditions. So a lot of that was just guess-work. And I wouldn't defend everything I wrote in that period. But I think it is consistent enough, by the time the book is put together – *The Hard Road to Renewal* – it's clear it's more about the difficulties, what the Left needs to do to measure up to this, than about Thatcherism itself. It's Thatcherism mark I, not New Labour which is another thing we need to think about. But Thatcherism mark I we knew enough about and really the question was basically a very simple question – 'would Labour really sign up to this new world and adapt to it or was it capable of generating a new analysis and pulling the old principles into new forms of a comprehensive scale – comprehensive enough to match the comprehensiveness of new liberalism?'. And the answer is no. And that's why the Left is floundering around now. It doesn't like what's going on, feels it's being betrayed, doesn't feel it can quite defend Spanish practices, so if you are in favour of modernisation, does that mean you are in favour of less hours for firemen etc.? That's what I think needs to be thought about. There isn't a *Marxism Today* around to try it out on. I'm massively frustrated about it because I see what is needed and I don't see anybody really offering it. So that's why I talk to the television all the time!

Was there ever a time when it was easier to make such arguments?

This again takes us back to the 70s and after. Because of the crisis, things were more clear-cut. You could have a debate about bias in the media and access and all of that, but that was just part of a more confrontational politics. Now what you have is a sort of liberal miasma. Plus what Hugo Young calls one-party politics. Everyone is somewhere inside the Blair New Labour box. They don't like a lot of things, they don't like him very much and they are willing to be critical. The *Guardian* could be critical from now till the cows come home but it will never break with the underlying assumption – it just won't.

We don't have a clear division between left and right any longer, the market must be powerful, we must get foreign investment, equality is an out of date notion, redistribution can only go so far because people want their money and the corporate sector – certain basic parameters define what I would call broadly the New Labour position has been swallowed wholesale and you couldn't conduct today a discussion debate-programme without it's being framed by those assumptions. Within the framework the liberal well-meaning presenters are not self-conscious about how much they're carrying the baggage of contemporary neo-liberalism, 'that everything has changed, we're now in an entrepreneurial society'.

This idea of liberal positioning on the part of the media would seem to indicate a general fear around extreme positions. Liberalism is of course a very 'civilised' idea and it may be that evidence from the global situation is taken to explain away extremists as dangerous and terrifying.

Yes it is that, you see it comes back to not making the debates I think we need to be having as part of the mainstream. If we were able to make them part of the mainstream, the media would be obliged by the very nature of their neutrality to recognise that, well you are not a screaming weirdie, so perhaps you have something to say – 'would you like to come on and say it?' See what I mean? So it is a fear of the extreme and it is a kind of clustering around the dominant consensus – which is really what I used to argue. I always thought the media worked from an implicit unstated consensus which matches the unstated political consensus of the wider society. And you have to break that in order to become visible, and this framework, and any-thing outside that is deemed 'extreme'. So then 'the BNP's extreme' and 'terrorists are extreme'. So the media cannot deal with the question of whether terrorists, suicide bombers bombing in Palestine are the same as Al Queda. It cannot confront that. It is too complicated. It requires making distinctions between legitimate violence and illegiti-mate violence. Not that I am in favour of suicide bombers, but Palestinians have a right to defend the armed occupation of their land. It's absolutely basic – that's what Britain did in the second world war. And that is not the same thing as planning to drive into the twin tow-ers. It is not the same thing. But all of that is lumped together, old labour, terrorism, the extreme left, Scargillism, and on the other side, racists, BNP. Inside that is a sort of argument with and around govern-ment and the new ideological configuration. Another thing the media do, they narrow politics to the parliamentary, and to the parties and it's less and less true that either political parties or parliament represent the width of politic debate and feeling, political sentiment of the country.

We wrote a lot about modernisation, but only in recent times have I understood what a tricky word it is. We were in favour of moderni-sation. We thought it was rubbish that we are still not citizens. That it's complete rubbish that we have a hereditary monarchy, it's just so out of date. There are all sorts of things about England that are just so out of date. Things that don't match a twenty-first century modern forward-looking society. And included with modernisation there is a degree of what is called 'individualism'. Modern people have a better idea of what they want, provided they have a guarantee of the economic basis for it. They don't want to be poor but if they are reasonably well-off they want the choice of a different lifestyle – modern in that sense.

Modern in the sense that patriarchal relations are not just not right, but that they are completely out of date. They don't reflect the actual real position of women in the society. So I don't apologise for being modern in that sense. It is true that the Labour Party has taken over the term 'modernisation' but what they mean by it is marketisation, individualism, going to the private market, getting everything to model entrepreneurship, falling in love with the corporate agenda and worshipping at the shrine of businessmen. Modernisation in that sense has been superimposed on the other definition and it is true that we were responsible – we didn't see that one could be confused with the other, and they ought to have been much more clearly distinguished. And retrospectively – that's another of the articles I would sometime like to write – 'Their modernisation and ours' – just as I would argue 'Their globalisation and ours'. I don't believe that you can go back to everyone planting their own food etc. I think that we are in a much more global environment, just not a global environment run by capital! So these are shady distinctions. How do you distinguish between an anti-globalisation movement that is in favour of the 'right kind' of globalisation? How do you distinguish between the right kind of modernisation and modernisation which is nothing but the neo-liberal agenda writ large? These are fine distinctions and I do think that some elements of *Marxism Today* did make that tip over, which is why some of them floated off into New Labour. Geoff Mulgan was one of our 'decentralisers' who then made it through the Chancellor's office to Blair's right-hand man and castigated me roundly for being a whinging intellectual. Others allied themselves with the modernising agenda of *Marxism Today*, but were also in the other kind of modernisation and so followed out of *Marxism Today* into New Labour, into Giddens, into Blair etc. So a lot of people went that route. Demos itself went that route. In the moment when Martin [Jacques] founded Demos I did not take part in anything in Demos. I did lend my name to the idea that it should be founded, but I never attended Demos meetings. I never wrote for Demos. By then I was already separating off from that trend that I could see was leaning towards that point – that was extrapolating another meaning. People can say, you can say 'well he was confused and he didn't make it clear'. It's quite true. My excuse is, they were confusing times and we were trying to say something new even if you couldn't say anything. But if you say something new, you have to take the consequences of the risk. We confused a lot of people. I don't think we ever subscribed to New Labour. Once New Labour sufficiently articulated itself as a new formation, certainly Martin and I were opposed to it.

There was a time when I though *Marxism Today* was going too far in the kind of modernising of consumerism, and that is one of the things that hangs over *Marxism Today* – the idea of 'designer socialism' and all of that. I think it is liable to that – it's open to that accusation. And in so far as I didn't do anything about it, it's open to me too. I don't ever think it was my position and I think that *Marxism Today* quickly backed off from that position. Martin and I did write the 'Thatcherism with a human face' piece the Sunday before the 1997 election and in the *Marxism Today* special issue, we were fiercely anti-Blair. If it was true in that hazy period when nobody quite knew what Blairism was, a lot of people didn't see what it was, at first, we were open to the charge that we sort of dismantled some of the traditional defences of the left, in the attempt to think new things and somehow we didn't gauge that correctly. And that may have opened the possibility for it's being taken in another direction, but most people who wanted to take it in another direction had to leave the *Marxism Today* project. By the end of *Marxism Today* it was perfectly clear that this had happened and that these were two strands rather than one. I would like sometime to write this. It's another retrospective clarification I'd like to write. These are misunderstandings which I think I could clarify without sounding defensive.

Once Marxism Today *folded, there was a gap in political publishing, which has never been quite filled. The journal* Soundings[1] *carries Hall's name on the editorial board. However, Hall's role has been more enabling than editorial.*

I think it's a great space to open up debate, but it's not me. I have great differences with *Soundings* because I think in this period, it should have continued what *Marxism Today* was doing in polemicising against New Labour, against new liberalism, and opening the critique of globalisation and it steadfastly avoided that. It didn't want to become entrammelled in intra-party politics debate so it's gone to the other end, finding other sources, which is a useful thing, looking at what's happening in psychotherapy, social work and these are all good things. But it doesn't get to the crunch point. It's not sufficiently politically engaged for me. So though it sees itself as sort of picking up the tradition of *Marxism Today*, it also has some differences of emphasis. It sort of replaces the space of a discussion journal, but it's not into the same questions.

More recently Hall has been in a position to focus on another aspect of cultural production that brings him into direct contact with artists and audiences. One of these projects resulted in Difference, *a co-authored text with Mark Sealy (2001) that brought together the work of many Black and Asian photographers living and working in Britain.*

I have always been interested in film, in photography. I have always been interested in the image more than I have been interested in media studies as such. Although I think you must be interested in media studies to be interested in modern culture, because the media are the carriers of the culture, so you can't not be interested, but my own work has been less and less on the media more generally, on media policy, – I used to be involved but I have sort of given up. Public service broadcasting and commercialism – I have thoughts about it but I don't write about it. But I have been interested in the image and I was interested in discovering that there was this wave of Afro-Caribbean and Asian artists from the 80s onwards, many of them born in Britain, using the image as a way to write about identity and politics, gender and sexuality and all of that. So I spoke at the founding of the organisation Autograph[2] – the association of Black photographers and I agreed to become the chair of that board and then I was involved in discussions on how to set up a Black Arts visual arts centre which InIVA[3] inherited and I was invited to chair the Board. They started to think about making a joint lottery bid for a building and a project centre and a media centre. We received £5 million from the lottery so I have been involved with the team trying to buy a place in London in order to build the centre.

I decided to spend more time in this area rather than continuing teaching. I never wanted to be an administrator, I didn't want to be a Dean of anything, or a vice-Chancellor. I wanted to teach. That means you become head of your Department and you make another course. I didn't want to make another course. I've written units and courses until my eyes popped out and taught summer school year after year. I've done it and the last two years when I really wasn't well were a strain. I got to 65 and I decided that was it. I didn't want to think 'well now what am I to do?' so partly because I have also been spending more time writing about race and cultural diversity, and cultural identity and post-colonialism, so it made sense with the focus on visuals and art; it seemed more of a piece with what I was writing about and lots of things that I had written turned out to be influential for artists and critics and curators in that area. They were actually reading this stuff and there were debates about identity in which my work was actually playing a part, so it made sense as a sort of post-retirement place to spend my energies. When I say that I mean in terms of how I spend my formal time, not to sit on other committees, not to continue going to the Open University where I am an Emeritus Professor. In so far as I have formal commitments, they are to *Autograph* and then the project (InIVA) and now to getting the project going. The other things are more occasional[4]. I want to bring together all the writings on race and cultural identity in a single volume with a long introduction as to why my focus on it has changed and what is consistent. The only problem is I keep writing new pieces! Instead of doing the volume, I keep adding to it. So I don't have a big writing project, but I am working.

Over the years Hall has made clear his intellectual debt to Gramsci, among others and I wondered whether there were other aspects of Gramsci's method which appealed to him in particular.

I think there are certain commonalities. I think there is some parallelism between the Caribbean and Sardinia in relation to Italy, in quite a colonial setting. He's essentially a colonial boy. His preoccupation with the agrarian Southern problem is a preoccupation with trying to think the specificities of the agrarian South in relation to the modernisation of the rest of Italy; the formation of the rest of Italy, its modernisation and its place in Europe. Much as the way in which again, I think there is a kind of parallelism in thinking the specificity of the Caribbean in relation to the role that the slave played in capitalist expansion and globalisation and industrialisation, and thinking in terms of its peripheries, of its constituent elements, African, Indian, European, Spanish, French, Dutch – so there are commonalities like that. There is another commonality – there is no book that looks like Gramsci's theory of the world – you have to piece Gramsci together from his various writings, a lot of which are about specific things: 'this is about Italy', 'this is about' etc. So his general theorising of concrete historical examples is much closer to my own kind of conjunctural thinking, so I think he's a sort of model for me like that. I think of him in that context, and I think of Walter Benjamin in that context, because although Walter Benjamin wrote massive tomes, there's no one text which is Benjamin's 'theory'. So I like thinkers that are fragmented in that way.

Fragmented and concrete?

Yeah. Fragmented and concrete.

London, November 2002.

endnotes

chapter 1

encountering the mother country

1 'Raphael was its engine, its political motor, its moving spirit. His political will, determination and energy were limitless'. Hall writing on the occasion of Samuel's death, *New Left Review* January/February 1997 no. 221 p. 121.

2 The editors of *Universities and New Left Review (UNLR)* organised a public debate in Oxford between Hoggart and Williams. See *UNLR* vol. no. 5.

3 Stuart Hall in conversation with the author, November 2002.

4 Like most of his Caribbean peers at Oxford, Hall would have been expected to return home in order to take up a bureaucratic post within the colonial administration.

5 Antony Crosland MP was a leading intellectual in the Labour Party, intent on revising the party's socialist agenda.

6 Labour Party Leader from 1955–63

7 Society for Education in Film and Television.

8 The Crowther Report was published in 1959.

9 Ultimately the new Labour Government under Harold Wilson rejected the recommendations of the Pilkington Report but the public debate had already been fuelled by the release of the Report.

chapter 2

a deadly serious matter

1 *Women Take Issue* is an important collection of essays that ploughs a new furrow across the terrain of cultural studies. The importance of this intervention is discussed further in Chapter 5.

2 The study of election results and their trends.

chapter 3

the media in question

1 Structuralism, as the term suggests, is concerned with the analysis of deep underlying structures in texts and the relationships between different elements that govern meaning. See Hawkes (1992), which is a useful text with a very good bibliography. Stam et al. (1994) give excellent summaries plus a very useful bibliography.

2 Anne Showstack Sassoon (1980) and Roger Simon (1982) give excellent accounts of Gramsci's ideas and his political formation in Sardinia.

3 UNESCO stands for the United Nations Educational, Social and Cultural Organisation.

4 Marshall McLuhan, a Canadian critic wrote a popular treatise entitled *The Medium is the Message*.

5 Walter Benjamin wrote a seminal essay entitled "The Work of Art in the Age of Mechanical Reproduction" in which he discussed the "aura" associated with works of art. Benjamin argued that the mass reproduction of art diluted and diminished the original. According to Benjamin, as an image becomes increasingly commonplace, so the power of the original work of art is diminished.

6 InIVA stands for the Institute for International Visual Arts. Stuart Hall was appointed as Director in 1996. InIVA can be found at www.iniva.org.uk

7 London School of Economics.

8 The Irish Republican Army is a major paramilitary republican organisation in Ireland.

9 On the morning of 30 January 1972, a civil rights demonstration in Derry, Northern Ireland, ended in the massacre of thirteen civilians and the injury of another twenty two when members of the Parachute regiment of the British Army opened fire on the demonstrators. The subsequent government enquiry was deemed to be a 'whitewash' and no members of the army were ever

brought to trial for murder. The army maintained that it had only returned fire when fired upon. Many civilian witness accounts disputed that testimony. A second public enquiry is currently underway.

chapter 4

wrestling with the angels

1 Egypt and Syria attacked Israel in 1973. The 'seven day war', as it became known, led to the oil-producing Arab nations cutting their supply to the West in order to prevent them giving support to Israel. This pushed up the price of oil and led to national shortages, a reduction in the number of days that industry could function and power cuts.

2 This is often referred to as the 'rivers of blood' speech.

3 Stuart Hall in conversation with the author, November 2002.

4. The 'Enlightenment' refers to the period roughly corresponding from the French Revolution through the nineteenth century, when enormous 'advances' were made in science, medicine, law and philosophy.

5 Reification refers to the process whereby a person is discussed or treated as if s/he were an object. Capitalism reifies individuals by using labour as a commodity that is valued according to its exchange value.

chapter 5

the politics of representation

1 References in this chapter refer to the full text of this public talk, which was published by the BBC/CRE in *Five Views of Multiracial Britain* in August 1978. The talk was broadcast on Radio 3 in July of the same year. Extracts from the broadcast were reprinted in *The Listener* magazine on 20th July 1978.

2 A detailed discussion of this work is contained later in this chapter.

3 One of a series of noon-time lectures organised by Thomas Blair and subsequently published in a collection entitled *The Inner Cities. A Condition of England Question* (1978b).

4 *Race Today* was a highly influential journal based in Brixton that led the campaign against police harassment of blacks during the 1970s. The journal was the production of a group of black activists known as the *Race Today* collective. The journal's editorial espoused the rights of blacks to 'refuse to work' under the present climate of racist capitalist labour relations.

5 Darcus Howe, editor of the journal *Race Today* was a key figure in the debate around black youth and crime, which was pursued in the pages of *Race Today* and the *Black Liberator*.
6 Stuart Hall in conversation with the author, November 2002.
7 Stuart Hall in conversation with the author, November 2002.
8 Stuart Hall in conversation with the author, November 2002.
9 Stuart Hall in conversation with the author, November 2002.
10 Stuart Hall in conversation with the author, November 2002.
11 Stuart Hall in conversation with the author, November 2002.
12 Stuart Hall in conversation with the author, November 2002.
13 Stuart Hall in conversation with the author, November 2002.
14 Stuart Hall in conversation with the author, November 2002.

chapter 6

1 In conversation with Stuart Hall.
2 This article and many others published by Hall in *Marxism Today* were reprinted in a single volume called *The Hard Road to Renewal* in 1988. I will reference this collection throughout this chapter.
3 'The problem of ideology; Marxism without guarantees' in Matthews (ed) (1983) *Marx: 100 Years On*. Lawrence and Wishart: London.
4 Stuart Hall in Conversation with the author, November 2002.

chapter 7

In the belly of the beast

1 Stuart Hall in conversation with the author, November 2002
2 'Manichean' refers to the dualistic philosophy underpinning religions which recognise the co-existence of good and evil.
3 Stephen Lawrence, a black teenager, was murdered on the evening of 22 April 1993 in Eltham, South London, by a gang of six white men. Despite the eye witness testimony of his friend Duwayne Brooks and others at the scene, the police were unable to build an effective case for prosecution although the suspects were well known to the police for racist violence, and quickly identified. Despite a criminal case, a private prosecution brought by the family, an inquest and a public inquiry, no-one has ever been convicted of the murder.
4 Perry Anderson criticised what he regarded as an over-emphasis on Gramsci on the basis that it had little relevance for the investigation of

developing world or non-European economies. When Perry Anderson took over the editorialship of *New Left Review*, the journal underwent a profound shift towards a focus on international Marxism and its relationship to global economics.

5 Benedict Anderson's *Imaginary Communities* is premised on the idea that our relationship to questions of society and nationalism are profoundly influenced and shaped by determining ideological and symbolic structures and beliefs.

6 The BNP, British National Party is an extremely rightwing political organisation which espouses racist views. It has recently tried to shake off its Neo-nazi image.

7 'Dirty Washing.' *Time Out* (London) 14–20 November 1985.

8 See Mulvey, L. (1975) 'Visual pleasure and narrative cinema' in *Screen* 16/3 pp 6–18.

9 See Bakhtin's theory of dialogic voices within novelistic discourse in Morris, P. (ed) (1994) *The Bakhtin Reader*. Edward Arnold: London.

10 See Bakhtin's theory of the carnivalesque, Morris (1994).

11 This was the ship that brought West Indian families to Britain in 1956, an historic staging point in the history of British post-war multi-culturalism.

12 The Commission on the Future of Multi-ethnic Britain was set up by the Runnymede Trust, an independent organisation which is committed to analysing and monitoring racial justice in the UK.

chapter 8

1 *Soundings* is edited by Martin Rustin and Doreen Massey, published by Lawrence and Wishart.

2 Autograph can be found at http://www.autograph-abp.co.uk

3 InIVA stands for the Institute for International Visual Arts. Their website is at http://www.iniva.org.uk

4 Hall recently gave an opening address entitled 'Democracy unrealised', a critique of the 'third way' in Vienna for Documenta, which is available to download at http://www.documenta.de/data/english/platform1/index. html and is currently revising a talk recently given to the Prince Claus Foundation. Please see and http://www.princeclausfund.nl

bibliography

Adorno, T. (1992) *The Culture Industry.* Routledge: London.

Althusser, L. (1970) *For Marx.* Vintage: New York.

Althusser, L. (1971) *Lenin and Philosophy.* New Left Books: London.

Alvarado, M. and Thompson, J.O. (1990) *The Media Reader.* BFI: London.

Anderson, B. (1991) *Imagined Communities.* Verso: London.

Arts Council of England/DCMS (2000) *Whose Heritage? The Impact of Cultural Diversity on Britain's Living Heritage.* Sage: London.

Bahktin, M. (1981) *The Dialogic Imagination.* Translated and edited by Holquist, M. University of Texas Press: Austin.

Baker, H., Diawara M., and Lindeborg, R. (1996) *Black British Cultural Studies.* Chicago University Press: Chicago.

Barker, F. et al. (1977) (eds) *Literature Society and the Sociology of Literature.* University of Essex: Colchester.

Barker, M. and Beezer, A. (1992) *Reading into Cultural Studies.* Routledge: London.

Barthes, R. (1999) *The Pleasure of the Text.* Hill and Wang: New York.

Beck, U. (1992) *Risk Society.* Sage: London.

Benyon, J. and Solomos, I. (1987) (eds) *The Roots of Urban Unrest.* Pergamon Press: Oxford.

Berker, T. (1974) (ed.) *The Long March of Everyman.* Andre Deutch: London.

Bhabha, H. (1994) *The Location of Culture.* Routledge: London.

Bloomfield, J. (1977) *Class, Hegemony and Party.* Lawrence and Wishart: London.

Brennan, T. (1999) 'Poetry and polemic', in *Race and Class* vol. 41 no. 1/2 July–Dec pp. 23–34.

Brown, P. and Sparks, R. (1994) *Beyond Thatcherism.* Oxford University Press: Buckingham.

Brunsdon, C. (1990) 'Television, aesthetics and audiences', in P. Mellenkamp (ed.) *Logics of Television.* BFI: London.

Brunsdon, C., D'Acci, J. and Spigel, L. (1997) *Feminist Television Criticism: A Reader.* Oxford University Press: Oxford.

Buckingham, D. (1987) *Public Secrets: Eastenders and its Audiences.* British Film Institute: London.

Buckingham, D. and Sefton-Green, J. (1994) 'Intervening in culture: media studies, English and the response to "mass" culture', in Buckingham, D. and Sefton-Green, J. *Cultural Studies Goes to School.* Taylor & Francis: London. pp. 123–144.

Butterworth, E. and Weir, D. (eds) (1972) *Social Problems of Modern Britain.* Fontana: London.

Calhoun, C. (1997) *Nationalism.* Oxford University Press: Buckingham.

Cannadine, D. (2000) *Class.* Penguin: London.

Carr, E.H. (1990) *What is History?* Peguin: London.

Cathcart, B. (2000) *The Case of Stephen Lawrence.* Penguin: London.

Caughie, J. (2000) *British Television Drama.* Blackwells: Oxford.

CCCS (1982) *The Empire Strikes Back, Race and Racism in 70s Britain.* Routledge: London.

Chen K. (1996) 'The formation of a diasporic intellectual', an interview with Stuart Hall in Kuan-Hsing in Morley, D. and Hsing, K. (eds) *Stuart Hall, Critical Dialogues in Cultural Studies.* Routledge: London. pp. 484–502.

Cohen, S. and Young, J. (1973) *The Manufacture of News.* Constable: London.

Commission on Racial Equality (1978) *Five Views of Multi-racial Britain.* Commission for Racial Equality: London.

Cruz, J. and Lewis, J. (1994) *Viewing, Reading, Listening, Audiences and Cultural Reception.* Westview Press: Oxford.

Curran, J., Gurevitch, M. and Wollacott J. (1977) (eds) *Mass Communication and Society* Edward Arnold: London.

Danaher, G., Schirato, T. and Webb, J. (2000) *Understanding Foucault.* Sage: London.

Department for Culture, Media and Sport (1999) *Whose Heritage?* Her Majesty's Stationers Office: London.

Derrida, J. (1978) *Writing and Difference.* University of Chicago Press: Chicago.

Donald, J. and Rattansi, A. (eds) (1992) *Race, Culture and Difference.* Sage: London.

Dyer, R. (1988) *'White' Screen* vol. 29, no. 4, pp. 44–65.

Eagleton, T. (1991) *Ideology, an Introduction.* Verso: London.

Essed, P. and Goldberg, D. (2002) *Race Critical Theories.* Blackwell: Oxford.

Evans, J. and Hall, S. (1999) *Visual Culture: A Reader.* Sage: London.

Ferguson, B. (1998) *Representing Race.* Edward Arnold: London.

Fiske, J. (1995) *Reading the Popular.* Unwin Hyman: Boston.

Foucault, M. (1972) *The Archeology of knowledge.* Partheon Books: New York.

Foucault, M. (1980) *Power/Knowledge: Selected Interviews and the Writings.* (ed.) Gordon, C. Partheon Books: New York.

Geraghty, C. (1991) *Women and Soap Opera.* Polity: London.

Giddens, A. (1998) *The Third Way, the Renewal of Social Democracy.* Polity: London.

Gilroy, P. (1987) *There ain't no Black in the Union Jack: The Cultural Politics of Race and Nation.* Hutchinson: London.

Gilroy, P. (1993) *The Black Atlantic: Modernity and Double Consciousness.* Verso: London.

Gilroy, P., Grossberg, L. and McRobbie, A. (2000) *Without Guarantees, in Honour of Stuart Hall.* Verso: London.

Gramsci, A. (1971) *Selections from the Prison Notebooks.* Lawrence and Wishart: London.

Grossberg, L., Nelson C. and Treichler P. (eds) (1992) *Cultural Studies.* Routledge: New York.

Hall, S. (1958) *A Sense of Classlessness.* Universities and Left Review Vol. 5, pp. 26–32.

Hall, S. (1960a) 'The supply of demand', in Thompson, E. (ed.) *Out of Apathy.* New Left Books: London.

Hall, S. (1960b) 'Crosland territory', in *New Left Review* 2 (24) pp. 2–3.

Hall, S. and Whannel, P. (1964) *The Popular Arts.* Hutchinson: London.

Hall, S. (1966) 'The formation of political consciousness', in Clements, S. and Bright, L. (eds) *The Committed Church.* Darton, Longman and Todd: London.

Hall, S. (1967a) 'The world of the gossip column', in Hoggart, R. (ed.) *Your Sunday Paper.* London University Press: London.

Hall, S. (1967b) 'Class and the media', in R. Maby (ed.) *Class.* Anthony Blond Ltd: London. pp. 93–114.

Hall, S. (1967c) 'Cultural Analysis' *Cambridge Review.* Cambridge University Press: Cambridge. vol. 89, pp. 154–7.

Hall, S. (1967d) *Young Englanders.* National Committee of Commonwealth Immigrants: London.

Hall, S. (1969) 'The Hippies: an American "moment"', in J. Nagel (ed.) *Student Power.* Merlin Press: London. pp. 170–202.

Hall, S. (1970a) 'A world at one with itself', *New Society* no. 403.

Hall, S. (1970b) 'Black Britons', *Community* vol. 1, pp. 3–5.

Hall, S. (1971a) 'Deviancy, politics and the media', CCCS Stencilled paper no. 11.

Hall, S. (1971b) 'Innovation and decline in the treatment of culture on British television', UNESCO: Paris.

Hall, S. (1972a) 'The limitations of broadcasting', *The Listener.* pp. 328–329 16 March. vol. 87.

Hall, S. (1972b) 'The determination of news photographs', *Working Papers in Cultural Studies* 3. CCCS: University of Birmingham.

Hall, S. (1973a) 'The determination of news photographs', republished in S. Cohen and J. Young (1973) *The Manufacture of News.* Constable: London.

Hall, S. (1973b) 'Encoding and decoding in the media discourse', CCCS stencilled paper: University of Birmingham.

Hall, S. and Walton, P. (eds) (1973) *Situating Marx.* Human Context Books: London.

Hall, S. (1974) 'Marx's notes on method: a "reading" of the "1857 introduction to the *Grundrisse*"', *Working Papers in Cultural Studies.* no. 6. University of Birmingham: Birmingham.

Hall, S. (1974) 'Media power: the double bind', *Journal of Communication.* 24 (4) pp.19–26.

Hall, S., and Jefferson, T. (1975) *Mugging and Law n' Order.* Stencilled papers no 36: University of Birmingham.

Hall, S., and Jefferson, T. (eds) (1976) *Resistance Through Rituals: Youth Subcultures in Postwar Britain.* Hutchinson: London.

Hall, S., Connell, I., and Curtis, L. (1976) 'The unity of current affairs television', *Working Papers in Cultural Studies* 9 CCCS: University of Birmingham.

Hall, S. (1977a) 'Culture, the media and the ideological effect', in Curran, J. Gurevitch, M. and Wollacott, J. (eds) (1977) *Mass Communication and Society.* Edward Arnold: London. pp. 315–348.

Hall, S. (1977b) 'Rethinking the base and superstructure metaphor', in Bloomfield, J. et al. *Class, Hegemony and Party.* Lawrence and Wishart: London.

Hall, S., Connell, I., Curtis, L., Chambers, I. and Jefferson, T. (1977) 'Marxism and culture: a reply to Ros Coward', *Screen* vol. 18, no. 4, pp. 109–111.

Hall, S. (1978a) 'Pluralism, race and class in Caribbean society', in *Race and Class in Post-colonial Society.* Unesco: Paris.

Hall, S. (1978b) 'Race and poverty', in Blair, T. (ed) *The Inner Cities.* Central London polytechnic papers on the environment: London.

Hall, S. (1978c) 'The racist within' *The Listener,* pp. 66–68.

Hall, S., Crichter, C., Jefferson, T., Clarke, J., and Roberts, B. (1978a) *Policing the Crisis.* Macmillan Press Ltd: London.

Hall, S., Lumley, B. and McLennan, G. (1978b) *On Ideology.* Hutchinson: London.

Hall, S. (1980a) 'Race, articulation and societies structured in dominance', in Baker, M., Diawara, M. and Lindeborg, R. (eds) (1996) *Black British Cultural Studies.* Chicago University Press: Chicago. pp. 16–60.

Hall, S. (1980b) 'Encoding and decoding' in Hall, S., Hobson, D., Lowe, A. and Willis, P. (eds) *Culture, Media, Language.* Hutchinson: London.

Hall, S. (1981) 'The whites of their eyes: racist ideologies and the media', in Bridges, G. and Brunt, R. (eds) *Silver Linings.* Lawrence and Wishart: London. pp. 28–52.

Hall, S. (1985b) 'Realignment for what?' *Marxism Today.* December pp. 12–17.

Hall, S. (1987a) 'Minimal selves' in Appignanesi, L. *Identity.* ICA: London.

Hall, S. (1987b) 'New ethnicities', in Baker, H., Diawara, M. and Lindeborg, R. (1996) *Black British Cultural Studies.* Chicago University Press: Chicago.

Hall, S. (1987c) 'Gramsci and us' *Marxism Today.* June pp. 16–21.

Hall, S., and Jacques, M. (1987) (eds) *The Politics of Thatcherism.* Lawrence and Wishart: London.

Hall, S. (1988a) *The Hard Road to Renewal.* Verso: London.

Hall, S. (1988b) 'The toad in the garden. Thatcherism amongst the theorists', in Nelson, C. and Grossberg, L. (eds) *Marxism and the Interpretation of Culture.* University of Illinois Press: Urbana. pp. 35–73.

Hall, S., and Jacques, M. (eds) (1989) *New Times.* Lawrence and Wishart: London.

Hall, S. (1991) 'Reading Gramsci', in Simon, R. *Gramsci's Political Thought.* Lawrence and Wishart: London. pp. 7–10.

Hall, S. (1992) 'Cultural studies and its theoretical legacies', reprinted in Morley, D. and Chen, K. (eds) (1996) *Stuart Hall, Critical Dialogues.* Routledge: London.

Hall, S. (1994) 'Whose English' in Bazalgette, C. (ed.) *Report of the Commission into English.* BFI: London.

Hall, S. (1995a) 'Authoritarian populism: a reply to Jessop et al.', *New Left Review* no. 151, pp. 115–24.

Hall, S. (1995b) 'Negotiating Caribbean Identities', *New Left Review* no. 209, pp. 3–14.

Hall, S. (1996a) 'What is this black in black popular culture?', in Morley, D. and Chen, K. (eds) *Stuart Hall: Critical Dialogues.* Routledge: London.

Hall, S. (1996b) 'Who needs identity?' in Hall, S. and Du Gay, P. (eds) *Questions of Cultural Identity.* Sage: London.

Hall, S. (1997) 'Tribute to Raphael Samuel', *New Left Review* no. 221, pp. 119–127.

Hall, S. (1998) 'The great moving nowhere show', *Marxism Today* Nov/Dec

Hall, S. (1999) 'Unsettling the heritage: re-imagining the post-nation', in Department for Culture, Media and Sport (1999) *Whose Heritage?* HMSO: London.

Hall, S. (2000) 'The multicultural question', in Hesse, B. (2000) *Un/settled Multiculturalisms.* Zed Books: London. pp. 209–241.

Hartley, J. (1992) *The Politics of Pictures: The Creation of the Public in the Age of Popular media.* Routledge: London.

Hawkes, T (1992) *Structuralism and Semiotics.* Routledge: London.

Heath, E. (1998) *The Course of My Life.* Hodder & Stoughton: London.

Hebdige, D. (1979) *Subculture, the Meaning of Style.* Routledge: London.

Hennessey, R. (2000) *Profit and Pleasure: Sexual Identiting in Late Capitalism.* Routledge: London & New York.

Hesse, B. (ed.) (2000) *Un/settled Multiculturalisms, Diasporas, Entanglements, Transruptions.* Zed Books: London.

Hobsbawm, E. (2002) *Interesting Times.* Allen Lane/Penguin: London.

Hoggart, R. (1959) *The Uses of Literacy.* Penguin: London.

Horkheimer M. and Adorno, T. (1997) *The Dialectic of Enlightenment (1944)* Verso: London.

Hunt, A. (1978) *Class and Class Structure.* Lawrence and Wishart: London.

Hunt, A. (1980) *Marxism and Democracy.* Lawrence and Wishart: London.

Ingham, R. (1978) (ed.) *Football Hooliganism: The Wider Context.* Interaction: London.

Jacques, M. (1997) 'The great moving centre show' *New Statesman* 21 November pp. 26–28.

Jacques, M. and Hall, S. (1997) *'Les enfants du* Marx and CocaCola' *New Statesman,* 28 November vol. 126 pp. 34–6.

Jacques, M. and Hall, S. (1997) 'Cultural revolutions' *New Statesman* Dec 5th vol. 126, pp. 24–6.

Jameson, F. (1991) *Postmodernism or the Cultural Logic of Late Capitalism.* Verso: London.

Jessop, B., Bonnet, K., Bromley S. and Ling, T. (1988) *Thatcherism.* Polity: London.

Kavanagh, D. and Morris, P. (1989) *Consensus Politics from Atlee to Thatcher.* Blackwell: Oxford.

Kenny, M. (1995) *The First New Left.* Lawrence and Wishart: London.

Laclau, E. and Mouffe, C. (1985) *Hegemony and Socialist Strategy.* Verso: London.

Larrain, J. (1996) 'Stuart Hall and the Marxist concept of ideology', reprinted in Morley, D. and Chen, K. (eds) *Stuart Hall, Critical Dialogues in Cultural Studies.* Routledge: London. Originally published in the journal *Theory, Culture & Society* (1991) no. 8 Sage: London. pp. 1–28.

Lusted, D. (1991) *The Media Studies Book, a Guide for Teachers.* Routledge: London.

Mabey, R. (1967) *Class: A Symposium.* Anthony Blond: London.

Masterman, L. (1991) *Teaching About Television.* Macmillan: London.

Masterman, L. (1992) *Teaching the Media.* Routledge: London.

McGuigan, J. (1992) *Cultural Populism.* Routledge: London.

McRobbie, A. (1981) 'Settling accounts with subcultures: a feminist critique', in Bennett, T., Martin, G., Mercer, C. and Woollacott, J. (eds) *Culture, Ideology and Social Process: A Reader.* Open University Press: London.

McRobbie, A. (1996) 'Looking back at *New Times* and its critics', in Morley, D. and Chen, K. (eds) *Stuart Hall, Critical Dialogues in Cultural Studies.* Routledge: London.

Morley, D. and Chen, K. (1996) *Stuart Hall: Critical Dialogues.* Routledge: London.

Morley, D. (1980) *The Nationwide Audience.* British Film Institute: London.

Morley, D. (2002) *Television, Audiences and Cultural Studies.* Routledge: London.

Morris, P. (1994) (ed.) *The Bakhtin Reader.* Edward Arnold: London.

Mulvey, L. (1975) 'Visual pleasure and narrative cinema', in *Screen* 16/3 pp. 6–18.

Nagel, J. (1969) (ed.) *Student Power.* Merlin Press: London.

'Parekh Report of the Commission on the future of multi-ethnic Britain' (2000) The Runnymede Trust/Profile Books: London.

Poulantzas, N. (1979) *State, Power, Socialism.* New Left Books: London.

Radway, J. (1987) *Reading the Romance.* Verso: London.

Raphael, S. (1981) *People's History and Socialist Theory.* Routledge, Kegan and Paul: London.

216

Rock, P. and Mcintosh, M. (1973) *Deviance and Social Control*. Tavistock: London.

Rustin, M. (1999) 'Editorial: A third way with teeth' *Soundings*. Lawrence and Wishart, Issue 11, Spring 1999 pp. 7–21.

San Juan Junior, E. (2002) *Racism and Cultural Studies, Critiques of Multiculturalist Ideology and the Politics of Difference*. Duke University Press: Durham and London.

Showstack Sassoon, A. (1980) *Gramsci's Politics*. Minnesota University Press: Mineapolis.

Shuttleworth, A., Heck, C., Hall, S. and Lloyd, A. (1974) *Television Violence: Crime, Drama and the Analysis of Content*. CCCS stencilled paper: University of Birmingham.

Simon, R. (1982) *Gramsci's Political Thought*. Lawrence & Wishart: London.

Sparks, C. (1996) 'Stuart Hall, cultural studies and marxism', in Morley, D. and Chen, K. (eds) *Stuart Hall, Critical Dialogues in Cultural Studies*. Routledge: London. p. 71–101.

Stam, R., Burgoyne, R., and Flitterman-Lewis, S. (1994) *New Vocabularies in Film Semiotics*. Routledge: London.

Storey, J (2001) *Cultural Theory and Popular Culture*. Prentice Hall: London.

Thatcher, M. (1995) *The Downing Street Years*. Harper Collins: London.

Thompson, E.P. (1963) *The Making of the English Working Classes*. Penguin: Harmondsworth.

Turner, G. (2000) *British Cultural Studies*. Routledge: London.

Twitchin, J. (1993) (ed.) *The Black and White Media Book*. Trentham Books: Stoke on Trent.

Williams, R. (1958) *Culture and Society*. Chatto & Windus: London.

Williams, R. (1969) (ed.) *May Day Manifesto*. Penguin: London.

Williams, R. (1974) *Television, Technology and Cultural Form*. Routledge: London.

Winship, J. (1980) 'Advertising in women's magazines: 1956–74', CCCS Stencilled paper no. 59.

Wood, B. (1998) 'Stuart Hall's cultural studies and the problem of hegemony', *The British Journal of Sociology*. Vol. 49, no. 3, pp. 399–414.

index

n indicates endnotes

Adorno, T. 43
advertising 21–2, 35, 44–5
aesthetics, television 51–2
African/Caribbean identity 185–6
Althusser, L. 15, 31, 47–8, 54, 56, 72, 84–5,
    89, 90, 152–3, 166, 169
  and Marxism 69, 74–5, 76, 77, 78
America 108, 124
Anderson, B. 180, 210*n*
Anderson, P. 11, 148–9, 176, 209–10*n*
articulation
  and identity 161, 163, 169, 186
  and multiculturalism 184
  politics of 180–1
Asians *see* race; racism; *entries beginning black*
audience
  encoding/decoding model 42, 60–7
  research 59–60
'authoritarian populism' 139, 142–6, 149, 150
  see also Thatcherism

Baker, H. et al. 2, 182, 184, 185, 191
Barthes, R. 21, 22, 45, 64, 83
Benjamin, W. 52–3, 207*n*
Benn, Tony 151, 197
Black Audio Film Collective 168
black British youth 99–100, 117–18
black immigrant identity 179–82
Black Panthers 124–5
black resistance 123–5
'black underclass' 102–3
black working class 121–6
black/Asian film makers/artists 168, 182,
    183, 184, 185, 203

Blair, Tony 157, 158
'Bloody Sunday' 58–9, 207–8*n*
British culture and television 49–51
British Film Institute (BFI) 18, 168
British National Party (BNP) 182–3, 210*n*
'Britishness'
  and multiculturalism 2, 188
  see also 'Englishness'; race; racism

Campaign Against Racism in the Media
    (CARM) 103–4
capitalism
  and class 80–1
  and race 116–18
  and trade union movement 84, 111
  see also consumerism/consumption;
    Marxism
Caribbean/African identity 185–6
Cathcart, B. 167
Centre for Contemporary Cultural
    Studies, Birmingham 23–4, 26–8
  break from orthodoxy 59–60
  'complex Marxism' 72, 73
  impact of feminism 126–30
  Policing the Crisis 104–5
  sense of purpose 29–31
Centre for Racial Equality (CRE) 100, 102
class
  and capitalism 80–1
  and consumerism 12–13, 16–17, 32–3
  and globalisation 197–8
  and identity 177–8
  and the mass media 34–7
  and the political climate 31–4
  postmodern *vs* Marxist approaches
    161–2, 166

class *cont.*
  and race 125–6, 166–7
  and skin colour 6–8, 182–3
  see also hegemony; working class
classlessness, sense of 11–18
code(s) 64
  dominant and oppositional 65–6
  encoding/decoding model 42, 60–7
Cohen, S. and Young, J. 42
colonialism
  and black working class 121–4
  Enlightenment project 2–3, 74, 208*n*
  Jamaica 2, 5–6, 10, 176, 180, 206*n*
common sense
  definition of 81
  'discourse' 165
  function of 81–2, 83
  and Thatcherism 138, 140–1, 146
Communists/Communist Party 7, 8
'complex Marxism' 72, 73–4
consensus/consent
  and conflict 43–4, 48, 54–7, 71–2
  and hegemony 46–7, 111–12
  'legitimate' 86
  news media manufacture of 42–4, 48, 89, 91–2
Conservative(s)
  false consciousness of working class
    134–5, 136
  governments 32–3, 70–1, 95, 135
  racism 34
  see also Far Right; Thatcherism; *named*
    politicians
consumerism/consumption
  and class 12–13, 16–17, 32–3
  and Labour Party 17–18
  and production 75, 80–1
counter-culture 37–9, 84
crime
  Marxist theory of 118–21
  see also 'mugging'
Crosland, Anthony 16–17, 206*n*
Crowther Report 19, 206*n*
Cruz, J. and Lewis, J. 41, 66, 162
cultural function of television 52–4
cultural studies 3, 161–2
  see also Centre for Contemporary
    Cultural Studies, Birmingham
'cultural turn' 163–6

decade of discontent (1960s-70s) 70–3
decoding televisual text 63–6
Derrida, J. 162
deviancy
  'black underclass' 102–3
  and mass media 55–9, 67

dialogical nature of popular culture 187, 210*n*
diasporic experience 6, 185–6, 194–5
'discourse' 164–6, 167–8
dominance 64–6
  see also hegemony; ideology; state
Dyer, R. 183

economic base and superstructure 78
editorial roles 10–11, 16–17
encoding/decoding model 42, 60–7
Engels, F. 13–14, 15
'Englishness'
  and the 'Tebbit test' 171–3
  and Thatcherism 183
  see also 'Britishness'; race; racism
Enlightenment project 2–3, 74, 208*n*
Essed, P. and Goldberg, D. 162, 164, 165–6
ethnicity(ies) 2, 156–7, 179–82
  new 182–4
  see also identity; race
Evans, J. and Hall, S. 98

failure of labourism 135–6, 138
failure of liberalism 102–4, 189–90
false consciousness 33, 37
  and ideology 83, 154–5
  and Thatcherism 149–52, 154, 159
  of working class Conservatives 134–5, 136
Fanon, F. 124, 125, 185
Far Right 133–5
  see also Thatcherism
fashion magazines 36
feminism 28, 163, 164, 181, 207*n*
  impact of 126–30
  reclaiming the personal 167–8
  and women's work 71, 120
Ferguson, B. 48
film makers/artists, black/Asian 168, 182,
  183, 184, 185, 203
football hooliganism
  news media 72, 90–5
  official responses 95–6
Foucault, M. 162, 164, 167–8, 185
friendships and influences, Oxford 6–7, 10
frustration, sense of 31–2, 73, 199

Gaitskell, Hugh 17, 206*n*
Giddens, A. 198
Gilroy, P. 168
globalisation 80–1, 197–9
Gramsci, A. 15, 29, 30, 31, 46–7, 65, 82,
  84, 85, 90, 113, 138–9, 142, 157, 166,
  169, 178, 184
  and Marxism 46, 78–9, 173–5
  relevance for Hall 175–7, 204–5

Hall, S. and Whannel, P. 19, 20–2, 23, 44–5
Heath, Edward 70, 71, 135, 141
hegemony
    concept of 46–7, 65, 166, 169, 181
    and race 105–7, 169–71, 173, 177–8
    and resistance 177–9
    and 'ruling ideas' 152
    Thatcherism 145–7
    see also ideology; state
Hennessy, R. 161, 164
Hesse, B. 187, 188
Hippie movement 37–9, 84
'historic bloc' thesis 138–9
historical interpretation 74–6, 78, 82
Hoggart, R. 7, 9, 18, 20, 23–4, 27, 206n
Holbrook, D. 22
Howe, D. 120–1, 123, 209n
Hungary, invasion of 7, 8
'hustling' 120–1, 124–5

identity
    African/Caribbean 185–6
    articulation 161, 163, 169, 186
    and class 177–8
    'Englishness' and the 'Tebbit test' 171–3
    policing black 186–8
    postmodern approach 161–3, 180, 181
    production of 184–5
    subjective experience/subjectivity 27–8,
        32, 177–8
    theoretical approaches 167–70
    see also ethnicity(ies); race
ideological state apparatuses (ISAs) 47–8,
    85, 89–90, 109
ideology
    and common sense 81–2
    definitions/theories 47–8, 151–5
    and language 162
    and mass media 85–90
    practice of 82–4
    and social relations 79–80
'imaginary community' 180, 210n
immigration 34, 70–1, 99–100
    see also racism
inequality 125–6
Institute for International Visual Arts
    (InIVA) 54, 207n
internet 49–50
interpellation 47, 48
    problems of 152–3
Irish Republican Army (IRA) 57–9, 207n

Jacques, M. 1, 155–6, 157, 158
Jamaica 2, 5–6, 10, 176, 180, 206n
James, S. and Della Costa, M. 120

Jameson, F. 163
Jessop, B. et al. 142–5, 146–9, 151–2
Journal of Communication Inquiry 170
Julien, I. 168

Kenny, M. 11–12, 148–9
knowledge, nature of 29–30
Kureshi, Hanif 183

Labour Party/governments 10, 17
    and consumerism 17–18
    critique of 33–4
    influence of New Left movement 11–12
    New Labour 157–8
    and state 137–8, 140
    and 'swing to the right' 134–5, 137, 138, 139
labourism, failure of 135–6, 138
language 82–4, 116
    and ideology 162
Larrain, J. 153, 154–5
'law and order' society 140, 142
    see also policing
Lawrence, Stephen 167, 188, 209n
Leavis, F.R. 20, 21, 28
Left see Labour Party/governments; labourism,
    failure of; entries beginning New
liberalism 2–3
    failure of 102–4, 189–90
    of news media 199–200
London School of Economics (LSE) 57
lumpenprolatariat 118–19
    and wagelessness 118–23

McCluhan, M. 50, 207n
MacPhearson Report 167
McRobbie, A. 155, 159, 168
Marxism 12, 13–14, 15, 16
    and Althusser 69, 74–5, 76, 77, 78
    'complex Marxism' 72, 73–4
    and Gramsci 46, 78–9, 173–5
    ideology theory and Thatcherism 153, 154–5
    and New Left movement 28, 31, 69
    theory of crime 118–21
    vs postmodernism/structuralism
        161–4, 166, 169–70
    see also false consciousness
Marxism Today 133–4, 148, 157–8, 193,
    201, 202–3
mass media 15–16, 17–19, 21
    audience research 59–60
    and class 34–7
    and deviancy 55–9, 67
    encoding/decoding model 42, 60–7
    functions of 87–90
    and ideology 85–90

mass media *cont.*
  see also news media; popular culture/arts;
    television
Masterman, L. 18, 22, 23
Merton College, Oxford 6
minority/majority paradigm 57–8
modernisation 200–1
moral panics 107–10
Morley, D. and Chen, K.-H. 6, 7, 28, 29,
    30, 31, 156, 159, 169, 170–1, 173, 175,
    177, 186, 187
'mugging' 103, 123
  Policing the Crisis 104–18
Muligan, G. 193, 201
multiculturalism 2, 184, 187–8
  Parekh Report 188–91, 210*n*

National Committee for Commonwealth
    Immigrants (NCCI) 99
National Health Service 32–3, 197
National Union of Teachers (NUT), 1960
    Conference 18, 20–1
nationalism 182–3
Nelson and Grossberg 76, 77, 78
New Labour 157–8, 193–4, 198–9, 201–2
New Left movement 6–11, 16
  influence on Labour politics 11–12
  and Marxism 28, 31, 69
  see also Centre for Contemporary
    Cultural Studies, Birmingham
New Left Review 8–9, 10–11, 16–17, 148–9
New Reasoner 9, 10
New Times 155–6
  and Thatcherism 156–7, 159
news media
  black/inner city crime 102–3, 108–9
  Campaign Against Racism in the Media
    (CARM) 103–4
  determination of photographs 44–5
  football hooliganism 72, 90–5
  liberalism 199–200
  manufacture of consent/consensus
    42–4, 48, 89, 91–2
  news *vs* soap operas 62–3, 64
newspapers 35–6
Notting Hill riots 99, 100

oil crisis (1973) 70, 208*n*
Open University 130, 132, 168
'organic intellectual' role 29–30,
    31, 46
Oxford University 6–7, 10

Parekh Report 188–91, 210*n*
photographs, news media 44–5

Pilkington Report 19, 206*n*
policing
  black identity 186–8
  Policing the Crisis 104–18
political climate
  1960s 31–4, 42, 55, 57
  1960s-70s 70–3
  1970s-80s 195–7, 199
political violence 44
  IRA 57–9, 207*n*
politics of articulation 180–1
politics of difference 2
popular culture/arts 15–16, 18–21
  critique of 21–4
  dialogical nature of 187, 210*n*
  see also mass media
postmodernism/structuralism
  identity 161–3, 180, 181
  vs Marxism 161–4, 166, 169–70
Powell, Enoch (Powellism) 70–1, 99, 100,
    102, 116, 172, 208*n*
power *see* hegemony
psephology 32, 207*n*
purpose, sense of 29–31

race
  and capitalism 116–18
  and class 125–6, 166–7
  and hegemony 105–7, 169–71, 173, 177–8
  and integration 100
  signification spiral 112–13
  see also ethnicity(ies); identity; 'mugging';
    racism; *entries beginning black*
Race Today 120–1, 123, 208*n*, 209*n*
racism 34, 99–102, 170–1
  'discourse' 165
  enemy within 115–16
  failure of liberalism 102–4, 189–90
  'institutional racism' 167
  Parekh Report 188–91, 210*n*
recognition 42
reification of labour 75, 208*n*
resistance
  black 123–5
  consensus and conflict 43–4, 48, 54–7, 71–2
  and hegemony 177–9
  riots 44, 99, 100
Russia/Soviet Union 7, 8

Samuel, R. 7, 8, 9, 10, 11, 16, 206*n*
Sankofa Workshop 168
scholarships 6, 7
self-education 27
signification 57, 58, 59
  spiral 112–13

Simon, R. 78–9
soap opera 61–3, 64
social relations and ideology 79–80
socialism 13–14, 16
  see also New Left movement
Society for Education in Film and
    Television (SEFT) 18
Soviet Union/Russia 7, 8
Sparks, C. 15–16
sport
  and news media 92, 93
  see also football hooliganism
state
  function of 84–7
  ideological state apparatuses (ISAs)
    47–8, 85, 89–90, 109
  and Labour 137–8, 140
  see also policing
strikes (1970s) 71, 110–11, 113
structuralism 45, 76, 77, 78, 207n
subjective experience/subjectivity 27–8, 32, 177–8
Suez crisis 7–8
Summer of Love *see* Hippie movement
superstructure and economic base 78
'swing to the right' 134–5, 137, 138, 139

Taylor, Charles 7, 8
teaching roles 7, 9, 11, 18, 203–4
'Tebbit test' 171–3
television 19–20, 36, 168
  aesthetics 51–2
  and British culture 49–51
  cultural function of 52–4
  decoding text 63–6
  encoding discourse 63
  limits of broadcasting 54–5
  soap opera 61–3, 64
  UNESCO report 48–9, 53, 54, 67, 207n
Thatcherism 2, 103, 133–4, 136, 137, 138–9
  appeal to working class 138, 140–2, 174
  'authoritarian populism' 139, 142–6, 149, 150
  and 'Englishness' 183
  false consciousness 149–52, 154, 159
  and ideology theories 152–5
  Jessop *vs* Hall on 146–9, 151–2
  and *New Times* 156–7, 159
  see also Far Right

theory, role of 77–9
Thompson, E.P. 9, 10, 11, 15, 16
Tory governments 32–3, 70–1, 95, 135
  see also Thatcherism; *named politicians*
trade union movement 84, 111
Trinidad riots 44
Turner, G. 21

unemployment 71, 151
  see also wagelessness
UNESCO 48–9, 53, 54, 67, 169, 170, 207n
Universities and Left Review (ULR) 8–10
University of Birmingham
  student militancy 57
  see also Centre for Contemporary
    Cultural Studies, Birmingham

values
  consumerism and class 12–13, 16–17, 32–3
  counter-culture 38
  and cultural judgement 27–8
vigilance, sense of 59
violence *see* football hooliganism;
    'mugging'; political violence; riots

wagelessness 118–23
  see also unemployment
'war of position' 157, 184
Watney, Simon 164
Weber, M. 28
Whannel, P. 42–3
  Hall, S. and 19, 20–2, 23, 44–5
Williams, R. 7, 9, 11, 15, 18, 20, 206n
women *see* feminism
working class
  appeal of Thatcherism 138, 140–2, 174
  black 121–3
  and capitalism in crisis 110–11
  false consciousness 134–5, 136
  and Labour governments 135–6
  studies/theories 9, 12–13, 15, 16–17

youth
  black British 99–100, 117–18
  culture 23, 72